MEMOIRS

OF THE

COMTE DE RAMBUTEAU

The Comte de Rambuteau. 1843.

MEMOIRS

OF THE

COMTE DE RAMBUTEAU

EDITED BY HIS GRANDSON

TRANSLATED FROM THE FRENCH

BY J. C. BROGAN

LONDON: J. M. DENT & CO.
NEW YORK: G. P. PUTNAM'S SONS
MCMVIII

Printed by BALLANTYNE, HANSON & Co.
At the Ballantyne Press, Edinburgh

PREFACE

THESE pages, which I offer with some diffidence to
the public, and especially to my own friends and
those of my family, were bequeathed to me by my
grandfather. Guided by a marvellous memory, he dictated
them to his secretary during his long retirement, leaving
me to dispose of them in whatever manner I deemed best.

The present moment seems the fitting one for their
publication. For have not the political agitations of last
century been reduced to mere reminiscences, thanks to
that overwhelming wave of democratic influence which has
transformed the combatants of yesterday into the conquered
of to-day?

And yet that struggle was a noble one!

Men's minds were fired with patriotism: their ambition
was to achieve a well-regulated liberty, and well would it
be for ourselves if we could revive the echoes of those
utterances at sound of which the hearts of our gallant
opponents were wont to kindle.

History loves the "Green Room," with its cunning
devices and all its "behind-scenes" mechanism, whereby
those stage effects are produced which so successfully de-
lude contemporary onlookers.

Mémoires give us the *entrée* to the actual stage, where
we can glide amongst the actors, great and small, each of
whom has his own allotted part to play.

And when, as in this case, mémoires are written for no
malicious purpose and without any rancour (being, in fact,
the outcome of a benevolent mind, enlightened by the
experiences of a long life), they possess the perfume of a

generous old wine of native growth. If I mistake not, the reader will be struck by the distinctly "other-century" atmosphere pervading these pages and conveying such a vivid impression of the way people lived under the three successive reigns.

Moreover, these annals are blemished by none of that bitterness which sometimes survives the grave, nor with the least indiscretion with regard to the private lives of individuals.

I can only trust that if they contribute to the reader's happiness, they will inspire him with a feeling of sympathy for my grandfather, who was, above all things, an honest man and a Frenchman of his time and country.

In his later years he was very prescient of the rising wind which was to freshen into such a succession of storms, and he would often exclaim, " I have seen too many revolutions : God preserve me from any more ! "

His prayer was heard, for he died in the spring of 1869.

Very few of those who knew him are alive now, but the ideas he cherished are very far from becoming obsolete in France.

True ! Time modifies everything, but it has not yet sapped the foundations of patriotism, nor eradicated all love of their country from the breasts of Frenchmen.

It was of that sacred love that my grandfather was one of the most indefatigable champions.

Lastly, a stroke of good fortune has befallen these time-faded pages !

They have been collated with rare skill by a remarkably talented author (a Burgundian, attached to the Lycée Lamartine), who has at the same time supplied a faithful picture of the writer of the manuscript.

Herewith I tender my sincere thanks to him.

RAMBUTEAU.

CONTENTS

LIST OF PHOTOGRAVURES

INTRODUCTION

"HE who has nothing to boast of but his ancestors," says Swift, "is like a potato: the only good belonging to him is underground." No one would have relished this witticism better than Comte de Rambuteau, for no one has ever borne a title with more modesty, or has had a keener sense of duty. He was much more indebted for his success in life to his own merits than to those of his forefathers, and we shall see how faithfully he adhered to the path which he traced out for himself, in the first lines of his Memoirs: "The remembrance of the deeds of our ancestors should incite us to courage and self-sacrifice." These deeds he outstripped, leaving his name more illustrious than when he received it; but in any case he would have created a place in history for himself, for was not the whole of his long life devoted to his country's service?

Claude Philibert de Rambuteau sprang from a noble family, originally belonging to the south of France, but which settled in Burgundy in the middle of the sixteenth century. As captains or soldiers they fought on every battlefield of the period—a period singularly prolific in fighting —notably in Italy, where they remained long enough to forfeit their right to certain properties in France. These, however, were restored to them by Henry II. No doubt it was from Italy that they brought back with them the lovely Nativity of Cimabue which adorns the chapel of Rambuteau. Gradually their relations extended, and they formed alliances with many other noble families; in the seventeenth and eighteenth centuries they intermarried with the Saint-Agnans, the Roche-Aymons, the d'Achons, and the Damas-d'Audours; one of them even won the regard of the Princesse de Conti; they were distinguished in the army, were colonels, brigadier-generals, made no account of their blood and money in the service of the King, and, by ruining themselves, gained a good many Crosses of St. Louis.

Nevertheless, the last of this gallant race was no warrior. He was eight years old when the Revolution broke out. It did away with the cornet's commission which every infant nobleman at that time of day found in his cradle. But if he were no soldier, he was none the less a supporter of the honour of his house. In his various capacities as Chamberlain of the Emperor, Prefect of several Departments in peculiarly difficult circumstances, Member of the Chamber of Representatives, Peer of France, Councillor of State, Prefect of Paris, he displayed, always and everywhere, the activity, decision, and rectitude of his race—all the fruits of a long and sound heredity.

We shall see how he brought back the remnants of the French army which had occupied Switzerland; how he organised the defence of the Loire, distributing arms, improvising battalions, creating National Guards, making a stout resistance even when Paris and Lyons had fallen—we shall see too, how, as an administrator of the first rank, he evinced genuine strategic qualities, such as must have delighted the paternal shade of the brilliant soldier of Coni.

He was born in 1781, in the Château of Champgrenon, on one of those sunny hills that are the glory of Le Mâconnais. His infancy was passed under the shade of the great trees of a fine park, which commanded an extensive view of wide pastures, watered by the Saône, and the green woodlands of La Bruse, with Mount Jura rising beyond them, and the snow-clad crests of the Alps and the peak of Mont Blanc still farther in the background. It is a superb panorama, distinguished by a beauty at once calm and cheerful, having a well-balanced and sustained harmony that rests the mind as well as the eyes; and if, as Taine asserts, the individual is the inevitable outcome of his native soil, it is but reasonable to suppose that so smiling and peaceful an environment, with its gently undulating slopes and temperate climate, must necessarily beget a certain degree of equanimity to the character, resulting in well-regulated mental powers.

Among our provinces, all of which have their own characteristic charms, Burgundy has one exceptional feature. Whilst lacking grand landscapes, it is rich in beautiful views in miniature landscape. Lending itself as it does to all kinds of culture, it breaks its plains into irregular forms, it hollows its mountains into gentle valleys, and moderates the course of its waters; whilst its sunshine gilds the harvests without scorching them, its cicadas enliven without deafening the listener, its joyous wine makes the heart merry but does not intoxicate, and the clear light of its skies is as far removed from the fogs of the north as from the dazzling splendour of the south. A happy land of oaks and vines, it inspires its sons with the mirth and vigour of a well-balanced mind, endowing them with that moral rectitude which induces a remarkable subordination of genius to reason, whilst it regulates their powers of discernment, and curbs all undue flights of the imagination.

Grand types of that fine race (each in their own way presenting a different aspect of their racial characteristics) are to be found in Bossuet, the sturdy Burgundian, whose genial personality and well-balanced temperament made him detest all that was mean and underhand; in Madame de Sevigné, the charming Marquise, whose wisdom was so subtle and so circumspect; in Buffon, that grand, indefatigable worker; and finally in President de Brosses, who was to teach Voltaire that wit was no less common at Dijon than at Paris. These all drank alike from the same spring, which the Count claimed as his natal source also.

Reared, like Lamartine, under the eyes of his mother, free to roam at will over hill and dale, his first care was given to the trees in his ancestral park, with whose green life the child apparently identified his own in a curiously realistic degree. To him, they represented real friends, in whose every murmur he heard a message, especially his own, and the close friendship thus formed in early days became lifelong.

And when an insane Revolution drove the Count into the "unemployed" before his time, it was beneath the grateful shade of those dear trees, which had cradled his infancy, soothed his later labours, and softened many a disappointment, that he settled himself down to compile his Mémoires.

This feeling for nature is one of the distinctive traits of his character; not for that nature of which we get glimpses in the *Gardens* of Delille, the *Seasons* of Saint-Lambert, or the *Months* of Roucher, but for that nature " pure and indefiled " which is loved for itself in all its rustic simplicity. With Rambuteau the sentiment was entirely spontaneous; he had never studied the writers of the day, unknown, for that matter, to Champgrenon; for the muse of Ronsard was the only muse that was ever likely to wander anew through the windings of the flower-bordered alleys, where of yore the poet gathered the roses of his friend Rymon, in company with Ponthus de Thiard.

He "discoursed no sweet music" upon the classic pan-pipes of mythology, nor did he gambol with shepherdesses in silk attire, keeping their be-ribboned white sheep. But he whistled his tunes shrilly through the sap-swollen bark of the April willow-twigs, awakened to the sound of the grasshoppers' chirruping, played with other boys on the hillsides, and amongst the meadows and vineyards, and climbed trees like Lamartine the future poet, who was shortly to be born amongst the "shepherd folks" near by.[1]

All this seems to us quite natural; but then it was a great novelty. The eighteenth century had inherited the preceding century's ignorance or dislike of all that was rural, and, even after Rousseau had made country life fashionable, it was not really understood. In vain did the

---

[1] Comte de Rambuteau signed, on October 22, 1790, in a rather childish hand, the register at the baptism of Lamartine, at which he was present with his parents; he also held the large wax taper, in accordance with an old local custom.

grand drawing-room of the château open its windows on
woods and meadows—no one looked out of them; every
one, intensely bored, was only waiting for the arrival of the
Mercure de France, and eager to learn the last good thing
said by Sophie Arnould. Voltaire was settled at *Les Délices*,
on the banks of an enchanting lake and in front of the
glorious Alps; yet he never alludes to either. "The
people of the city," Jean Jacques tells us, "do not like
the country, for the very good reason that, even when they
are there, they hardly know what they are about; they
despise its labours and its pleasures, being equally ignorant
of both, and, feeling themselves in a foreign land, no wonder
they are so bored. Those Parisians who imagine themselves
in the country are not practically there at all, for wherever
they go they carry Paris with them."

Are we to believe that the men of sentiment in the
Revolution, those sorry pupils of Rousseau, who were for
ever prating about Nature, had really any deep feeling for
it? How preposterous! Think of Larévellière-Lépeaux,
Member of the Institut (a botanist, if you please!), who,
when describing his little estate in Anjou, bursts into a
lyrical apostrophe: "Dear Clémentine, thou wert then our
only child. It was thou who didst lay the first stone of
that edifice which the fury of civil warfare was to make
so transitory. The first vegetable (it was a carrot) which
we reared in our garden was pulled up in thine and thy
mother's presence; it was thou who carried it indoors, it
was she who prepared it for the table. How we enjoyed
that first product of our property!"

This is not the language employed by Comte de Rambuteau, when, "betrayed by politics," he returns to seek
peace and quiet in the play-place of his childhood, finding
in the midst of his pines, his larches, his oaks and elms,
growing beside the still waters, the most satisfactory solace.
"Gardening," he said, in a discourse delivered before the
Agricultural Society of Mâcon, "has always offered the
sweetest consolations to fallen greatness, from the time of
Diocletian, who preferred his lettuces at Salona to the empire

of the world, to that of Josephine, who found compensation for the loss of a throne in the flowers of Malmaison. . . . I have always held that, at any rate, we ought to cultivate the soil of our country, when we cannot serve it otherwise, and so I have joyfully resumed my spade and pruning-knife." The inborn simplicity of his nature, wholly untainted by the artificial sentiment of that time, was his only teacher ; the fresh, healthy impressions of his youth were always with him—a youth as free as that of Chateaubriand, but spent in a pleasanter, kindlier country, where he never tasted the perils of melancholy, "that siren of souls, for ever singing and calling,"[1] but who never suffers those to return who have been lured by her voice.

To this influence of soil and environment must be added yet another, and that an unusual one—namely, the tenderness of a mother. We all know how extraordinarily circumscribed the family life of a child was in the seventeenth century. The age was too didactic, just as the eighteenth century was too frivolous, to appreciate the dainty graces of childhood. They found no representation either in literature or in works of art, unless we except the introduction of sundry chubby cherubs, who disported themselves in groups and garlands on wainscots and ceilings. Ought we to infer from this, that the children of that day were uncared for? Not necessarily, but the manner of love meted out to them then was widely different from ours. It lacked all outward demonstration in the form of smiles or caresses.

They were confided to the hands of strangers, and these hands were frequently rough ; they were seldom spoken to, and often whipped. The journal of Dubois, the *valet de chambre*, on the education of Louis XIV., is one long record of punishments and canings.

As soon as they had learnt to curtsey gracefully, they were permitted to salute their parents every day, and were henceforward expected to comply with every rule of etiquette, no matter what their age might be. There is a

[1] Flaubert.

story told of an old gentleman, who, having seen his daughter and her husband kissing each other as they came into the drawing-room in the morning (they had only been married a week), promptly and publicly rebuked them :

"Monsieur, mon gendre, et Madame ma fille," he inquired, "would it not be possible for you to manage to come downstairs ready-kissed ?"

Perhaps the century was growing milder toward its close ; or perhaps the atmosphere of Burgundy had more of a domestic savour—any way, the Comte de Rambuteau, like Lamartine, was fortunate in having an admirable mother, whose whole pride was centred in his training. The tenderness of her love for him was boundless ; and from her he, in his turn, learnt the art of loving. All that he advised in later life in the cause of childhood, the almost maternal solicitude which led the Prefect of Paris into the public nurseries and foundling asylums, that pity for "the poor little waifs brought thither in the morning, their rags wet with the rain of the night before," was all the work of his mother, the touching evidence of his recollection of her past care for him. From her he learnt wisdom, gentleness, and forbearance, to serve God and to help the needy. His noblest feelings were implanted and developed by her. And when, later on, we meet with the warm tribute he offers to her memory, it is hard to say to whom it does the greatest credit—to his mother or himself? He makes equally affectionate mention of his kind and good father, the gallant soldier. This latter was one of the finest types of those liberal aristocrats who were far more inclined— than any one expected at the time—to change the old order and bring about the revolution which was so shortly to attack all classes of the nobility.

It was from his father's precepts and practice that, from his earliest years, de Rambuteau learnt the duty of patriotism. He refused to emigrate ; he preferred to face the storm and "eat French bread." Then, when a new régime had replaced the old, his wise and straightforward nature led him to realise that it was all over with a superannuated past ;

b

that for new institutions, new men were needed, that France was superior to all forms of government, and that the duty of his son was to serve her in his turn.

Thus it would seem that his heredity, his native soil, his family, all combine to endow Count de Rambuteau with what Montaigne calls *une tête bien faite;* in other words, a sound mind and a sound body, an even temper, keen and vigorous reasoning powers, and a moral equilibrium. Add to these a simple and kindly disposition, a tendency to good-natured forbearance, an inflexible conscience, a rare capacity for work, and an intense love for his country, and we have the portrait of this fine-looking youth in his twentieth year, of whom Madame Lamartine wrote in 1801 : "Everything about him indicates nobility and loftiness of character and absolute integrity."

Of this forecast, he proved himself more than worthy. Owing to the disturbed state of the times, his education was perforce neglected. All the same he learnt enough to pass his examination at the École Polytechnique, whilst the knowledge acquired by his private studies received many valuable additions from his contact with the world in general and his father-in-law in particular. He had taken to wife the daughter of Count Louis de Narbonne, one of the former Ministers of Louis XVI.

"I do not believe," says Villemain, in the book which he dedicates to the Count's memory, "that either during the close of the last century or the beginning of this—a period replete with extraordinary vicissitudes and crowded with notable politicians—I do not believe, I say, that it held a choicer spirit than Count Louis de Narbonne, who was the impersonation of all that was noble, chivalrous, and cultured. He was a man remarkable alike for his fearlessness and courtesy, combining sound judgment with undoubted capacity for accomplishing great undertakings." [1]

The ranks of the French nobility at that time afforded a sorry spectacle of disorder. Some of the aristocracy had

---

[1] Villemain : *Souvenirs Contemporains d'Histoire et de Littérature : M. de Narbonne.*

emigrated under the impression that their exile would entail but a short excursion into foreign parts, and would be speedily rewarded with royal favours. When they realised their mistake, a faithful few remained with the exiled Princes, having abandoned all hope of a possible return, but still preserving their dignity; but a far larger number went back to France to solicit service under Bonaparte. These had an eye to the loaves and fishes which might reasonably be expected from a newly-made sovereign on the look-out for courtiers. Others who had remained in France, or who had only fled quite temporarily to save their heads, asked for nothing better than to be allowed to transfer their help and support to a régime that was both strong and national. To the latter class belonged the Comte de Narbonne. By his advice, his son-in-law accepted the post of Chamberlain to the Emperor, not from ambition—for he was not "one of those tools of heroism the handle of which can be grasped by vanity"—but prompted by the reflection that the Empire had saved France from anarchy and had restored order to society.

Napoleon, who was an excellent judge of men, very soon detected the qualities of the new-comer, whose manners had been formed in the salons of the Choiseuls, Luynes, Lavals, and Coignys; whose good-breeding emphasised his merits, and who supplied a striking contrast to his associates, whose petty humours and jealous rivalries lacked the varnish of the old Court manners. Napoleon observed the Count narrowly, and, noting his solid qualities, his sound judgment and his loyalty, attached him specially to his own person.

On his side de Rambuteau was fascinated by the prestige of this remarkable man, whose genius held something of the supernatural. He started by simply admiring him, but the admiration soon deepened into genuine love, which was the outcome of no blind fanaticism, but real and heartfelt; and it was this affection which made him cling to Bonaparte to the very end, long after he had lost faith in him, having fully realised his many faults and mistakes;

because, when the crisis came, Rambuteau was well aware that, *vis-à-vis* to the enemy, Napoleon represented France.

He was never one of Bonaparte's satellites (to use a term much in vogue at that date), nor of any one else, for that matter ; neither did he identify himself with any party, except, perhaps, with that of the "Optimates" of ancient Rome, who advocated patriotism in its most impersonal and enlightened aspect. "Never," he declares, "have I betrayed any confidence, never have I sold myself to any cause, and though it is true that I have served my country under three different Governments, I have done so in all rectitude and probity. No one can convict me of ever having cringed!"

And he might honestly have added, "Neither was I ever guilty of consulting my own advantage!"

The policy summed up in this declaration was, as we shall see, the one rule of action which he adopted both as Prefect and Minister, and which may be condensed into the three words of an old motto, "*Fide, non astu.*" As Prefect, he seemed born for the position (I am speaking of the functions of a Prefect in former times), so marked was the spirit of initiative and conciliatory firmness that he displayed. According to his own account, he owed his success less to his natural gifts than to what he had learned during his constant attendance on the Emperor. It is undoubtedly true that, while other Chamberlains sought only such advantages and pleasures as their connection with the Court brought in their way, he only sought to gain instruction. Being present at every State Council, he learned from Cambacérès to place small reliance on mere words, whilst he listened eagerly to those unrivalled organisers who endowed France with such excellent administrative institutions that succeeding régimes have scarcely changed anything in them.

In administering the three Departments to which he was successively appointed, he evinced a rare capacity for fulfilling his duty and at the same time winning the affection of the people, and this in the teeth of the strong political animus which was universally rife.

In the case of le Valais, whose soil still reeked with such recent bloodshed that its population might well have taken advantage of the Invasion to revenge themselves on the Count, what really happened? Did not the simple folk instantly rally round him, offering him the protection of their impregnable hillsides along with the willing service of their sturdy arms?

Again, in the Department of la Loire, which he defended against the Allies more like a soldier than a prefect, he left such pleasant memories of his administration, both under the Emperor and under the King, that the Council General sent him the expression of its respectful gratitude, even after his retirement to Champgrenon.

Finally, at Montauban, where the angry strife between Royalists and Liberals was mingled with the bitter animosity between Catholics and Protestants — an animosity which actually culminated in assassinations—he managed to restore peace and order without resorting to any measures of coercion, and was, consequently, entreated to remain in office by all the leading inhabitants.

In what lay the secret of his authority? In the self-control and independence which to him were second nature. Being the slave of neither Bourbons nor Bonaparte, he was fettered by none of those political obligations which so often involve the sacrifice of conscience to party interests. Incapable of betraying any cause which he had embraced, or of being only lukewarm in its support, de Rambuteau always recognised the authority of the rulers of the hour, though he never allowed himself to become their tool. Within his own jurisdiction, he suffered the existence of neither oppressor nor oppressed, but misfortune always claimed his respect, and he steadily opposed all form of retaliation. When this was demanded of him, he retorted by tendering his resignation.

The first Restoration, with the Charter and the constitutional guarantees that succeeded the absolutism of the

Empire, appeared to him to be the only régime compatible
with the circumstances. It mattered little to him how or
from whom France gained her liberty, provided that she
might enjoy it. Nevertheless, it was dearly purchased!
The sight of foreign soldiers lining the road to Paris, the
mortifying condescension of an overbearing conqueror,
broke his heart. He submitted, partly from necessity and
partly because the Emperor had absolved him from his
oath. But the Restoration fell far short of redemption.
The Emperor returned, the King fled, and days of anguish
ensued for upright and patriotic men; for it is sometimes
harder to know one's duty than to fulfil it. To which
side did the rightful authority belong? To the runaway
King, who had abandoned both his crown and his loyal
supporters? or to the idol of the people whom all the
nation eulogised? Was the King or the Emperor to reign,
and what was to be the national cry? And what did
de Rambuteau answer? "*Vive la France!* Let that be
our one and only cry," he said, "for that belongs to all
times and seasons." And when he saw that the enemy had
crossed the frontier, he believed that France was siding
with the true defender.

Such men command esteem. The Government of Louis
XVIII. knew his worth too well not to wish to attach him
to their side. The Abbé de Montesquiou, his relative,
Minister of the Interior and dispenser of the royal favours,
offered him a prefectship or a military command, whichever
of the two he preferred. He refused these offers, as later
he refused a seat in the Senate during the Second Empire.
He preferred living on his estate, like an honest country
gentleman, and this retirement contributed both to his
dignity and his interests. The Revolution, and the five
subsequent years which he had spent in an office that
brought him no wealth, had lessened the value of his
patrimony to a very considerable degree. He restored it
by wise management; he drained, planted, gardened; he
created Rambuteau.

At that time of day it was a green and somewhat

uncultured valley, overgrown with broom and heather, and occupying one of the most picturesque regions of the Charollais. Lovers of nature in her wildest and most rugged aspects, who delight in steep precipices and the sullen roar of mountain torrents, would find little to please them in the calm beauty of the Champgrenon scenery, with its gently undulating mountains, whose grassy folds hold many pleasant surprises for the tourist. For from beneath those low mountain brows many a charming view may be enjoyed. For more than a hundred miles, the eye may roam unhindered over an extent of green country stretching from the Loire to the Saône, and embracing lakes and forests, wide corn lands and cultured fields, some of the latter gleaming with crops of the golden-flowered colza, others aglow with purple clover. Here the rising sun sheds light and life, just as at sunset his parting beams invest every bell-tower with ruby tints.

Here at the foot of Montmelard, between the old Gallic hills of Dun and Suin, Rambuteau sought a well-earned rest. The paternal mansion, which was much out of repair, he rebuilt entirely, except the little chapel which his great-grandfather, Philibert Barthelot d'Ozenay had built in 1640. After that he proceeded to surround it with wide plantations. As was to be expected from such a refined lover of real nature, he did not take as models the artificial parks, which, after the fashion of the preceding century, were still studded with romantic ruins—rocks of plaster, stucco grottoes, and scantily-clad nymphs pouring water from cracked urns into basins of cement. He had a remarkable knowledge of the soil, and was consequently successful in introducing a number of the coniferæ he had admired in the Valais among the trees which were indigenous to the locality. Thus he happily mingled slim pines with massive beeches, sturdy oaks with slender larches, sombre firs with silvery birches. And so whilst the breezes played amongst their branches, and the sunbeams filtered through their foliage, these "sons of the forest" grew apace, intermingling their scents and their whispers. For the

grandson has respected the trees of the grandfather; never
has sound of axe echoed through the woods of Rambuteau.
They are all there, their feet sunk in the fern, their heads
swaying to and fro in continuous murmurs, so that at
every step one expects to surprise groups of mist-enshrouded
nymphs, such as Corot would have painted, gliding between
the tree-trunks.

But no one ever thinks of planting during the snow
season. And so every winter Comte de Rambuteau returned to Paris to enjoy the society of the friends he had
made during the Empire—Drouot, Caulaincourt, Sebastiani.
Through them he quickly formed the acquaintance of the
entire Liberal Opposition, of General Foy, the two Périers,
Dupont de l'Eure, and, soon afterwards of the Doctrinaires,
Broglie, Guizot, Royer-Collard. The latter did not influence him; he was too practical to follow them into their
"ivory tower"; he was a man of action, not of formulas.
Consequently, he promptly ranged himself on the side of
Casimir Périer. Elected in 1827, he sat in the Left Centre
among the defenders of the Charter, all of whom were
faithful to the King, but also to liberty; and, if the Throne
had trusted to their loyalty, it might, perhaps, be standing
still. Charles X. did not understand them. The address
of the 221 was their answer. Comte de Rambuteau signed
this address; he could not do otherwise, considering his
principles and his past, than identify himself with this firm
protest made by anxious but not careless subjects; for, having
condemned the policy of 1815, he could not possibly sanction
that of 1830.

Absent from Paris during the days of July, he rallied
to the House of Orléans, because none other could fulfil
the obligations of royalty to the nation or prevent France
from relapsing into anarchy. At this period he was not
acquainted with Louis-Philippe; for, although he had seldom
visited the Tuileries, he was still less known at the Palais-
Royal, which he had refused to enter from a scruple of
loyalty. He never yielded to that contagious impulse which
precipitates men into revolutions; formed his resolutions

coolly and with that deliberation which influenced all his acts throughout life; and he accepted the Orléans as he had accepted the Bourbons in 1814, "not willingly but of necessity" (for personally they were indifferent to him); all he cared for was his country's good.

Then he resumed his place in the Chamber, where he had already made himself conspicuous. His colleagues were quick to appreciate his genial disposition, his wide knowledge of affairs, his moderation, his power of assimilation, and all the qualities which had been brought to light by his steadfast, dogged devotion to work. He was known among them as *le piocheur*—the hard worker—was placed on all committees, and enjoyed general esteem; Casimir Périer, Broglie, Thiers, Molé, Guizot, the Chancellor, Pasquier, honoured him with their friendship, and the Court attached great value to his experience, although he was but a poor courtier.

To what office was he likely to aspire? That of Minister? He was certainly not afraid of the tribune, but he took his place in it as a man of business, not as an orator. Besides, he was not fond of politics, and by no means cut out for a party leader. That of a Secretary of State? He deserved something better than that. He had proved himself an incomparable administrator, as much by his knowledge of facts as by his knowledge of men. Thus, when Louis-Philippe appointed him Prefect of Paris, he put the right man in the right place, and only acted in accordance with public opinion, which had already selected him for the post. The words of Thiers were prophetic in this respect: "Your career will be a long and splendid one, you will witness the fall of more than one Ministry; and, as regards yourself, the memory you will leave behind you will be noble and lasting."

The day following his installation at the Hôtel de Ville, the new Prefect visited the hospitals: he wished, he said, his first visit to be to the poor, and he also announced his intention with regard to them; for he was endowed with an inexhaustible fund of benevolence, being of the fibre of Malesherbes and Turgots, with the addition of a more deeply-seated kindliness and tenderness. He identified himself witH the people, took the humblest by the hand, entered into their material and moral needs, spoke to them in their own language, and was as much at home among a group of artisans as in his own drawing-rooms.

And, being convinced that, to influence the man, you must begin with the child, it was on the child that he first lavished his cares. All that has since been effected by a zeal for progress, which has perhaps, on the whole, achieved more noise than success; asylums, lectures for adults, technical drawing-schools, workshops, choral societies, public school deposit books for savings-banks, &c., all these he originated, as he tells us in his usual simple style. No one can fail to be struck by the *extent* of his philanthropy—too vast to particularise—which found expression in all kinds of institutions, which was as remarkable for its foresight as for its strongly emphasised Christian spirit.

Comte de Rambuteau was not a *dévot*, but he was a believer. Taught by the Gospel to love his neighbour, he did not consider that our obligations to the poor were limited to allowing them to glean in the harvest-fields of the rich, and pick up the crumbs of their pleasures; he wished to enable them by labour and economy, to reap their own harvests in their own fields. He impressed on the workman that "it costs more to feed one vice than two children." He taught him economy, he demonstrated that a sound education is a safe tool for earning a remunerative wage, he warned him against those demoralising theories that flatter the worst instincts, and, like Proud'hon, he repudiated " that impotent, immoral Socialism, fit only to make dupes and swindlers." He found his reward in a healthy popularity; he experienced the joy of being loved, of hearing himself called *the workmen's father*, and of knowing that when the mob sacked the Hôtel de Ville in '48, they paused respectfully before his portrait. This incident must have reminded him of how, during the Terror, the municipality of his village had protected his infirm old father by spreading the municipal scarves across his bed.

Neither the improvements of all kinds, in matters of hygiene, sewerage, and embellishments, which he introduced during his fifteen years' administration, can we describe in detail; they transformed the Paris of 1830, and were the beginning of modern Paris. But although their enumeration might prove tedious to us now—for they possess at best but a retrospective interest—no one can help admiring the power and capability of this untiring worker, who accomplished so much with such scrupulous economy, husbanding the public funds far more carefully than he would have spared his own. In fact, he left the Hôtel de Ville poorer than when he entered it. He had mortgaged his private fortune in order that the first magistrate of Paris might do honour to the capital; his fêtes and receptions were long the talk of the city, and were always thronged by the most famous personages of the time; and he was profuse in all the expenses which his rank demanded.

We may find an explanation of this in the fact that the indefatigable Count, who rose at daylight, examined the minutest details of his administration, and insisted on seeing everything with his own eyes, was also a polished man of the world, married to a charming woman, who inherited the graces of the old Court. Among his guests were the most illustrious members of the European aristocracy, men famous in politics, diplomacy, literature, and art. Of the correspondence which he exchanged with them, there remain more than two thousand specimens—letters of all sorts, petitions amiable or urgent, invitations, thanks, notes such as used to be written before the telegraph was substituted for the pen, a collection of autographs so vast as to rouse the envy of any collector.[1]

---

[1] This note we quote at random from two correspondents :—

"MY DEAR COUNT,—It is said that all the pretty women have little favours to ask of you. Of course I cannot be included among them, yet as I am

He had many faithful friends besides, in whose companionship he found relaxation from his labours, and who, after his retirement, often cheered the enforced idleness of an inactive life, which at times weighed heavily on the vigour of his seventy years. He had noted the on-coming of the storm ; the Revolution did not take him by surprise ; he resigned without bitterness the honours which he had exercised without ambition, and, when he returned to private life, he declared that : " All I now desire on earth is henceforth to lead a peaceful existence beneath the shade of the trees I planted, and to enjoy at the same time the good-will and esteem of my fellow-citizens."

He had a longer and calmer existence than he would have ventured to expect, dividing his time between Paris, Rambuteau, and Champgrenon, according to the season. He lived twenty years after his retirement, to the joy of his grandchildren, his friends, and of his beloved trees, whose green branches waved gladly above his head. He diffused around him the subtle charm of old age, rich in memories, relating what he had seen, dictating what he had done, evoking the past, without any chagrin or rancour for the present, discussing men and matters with his customary good-nature. " We have taken our leave of public life," Victor Cousin wrote to him. " Having left it with honour and acquitted ourselves none too badly, we feel no grudge against those who occupy the stage to-day. We are too wise to embitter the close of our career with vain regrets

---

a *woman*, I hope this mere title, unadorned with any epithet, will dispose you to receive my petition. There is a post vacant in the Hôtel de Ville . . . &c.
"Lady Holland."

On the same day, and probably with reference to the same post, we find a long and serious letter from Victor Hugo, in favour of the father of a family :—

" . . . A small post in your great administration, it is a trifling matter, so far as you are concerned, but it will be everything for him. Prove once again, M. le Préfet, that your paternal functions are in paternal hands. Every day, you are the originator of good works in general ; this will be a good work in particular, &c., &c.   Victor Hugo."

One might fill a volume with such quotations.

or ill-humour. It was for us that the phrase was written, *Otium cum dignitate*."

In this fashion he completed his eightieth year in the peace of a pure conscience, in that expectant hopefulness which Pindar calls *the kindly nurse of the aged*. He was in the full possession of all his faculties to the end. Owing to cararact his sight failed him, so that he could no longer look on the surrroundings he loved so well. But he scarcely needed his eyes, so well able was he to find his own way about his winding hot-houses. He knew exactly where to find his rarest plants, and led his visitors to them unerringly. He took long walks in the woods, even going so far as the Calvary of Rambuteau. erected at his own expense, and where, to-day, the bees, having penetrated some orifice visible only to themselves, into the interior of the hollow metal figure of the Christ, secrete their honey in this hiding-place, which trickles from the wounds of the Divine Victim. Never was the aged Count known to miss his way. It almost seemed as if the trees knew his footsteps and drew aside their branches before him, whilst their good old friend would touch them with his hand, stroke the bark, putting his arms around them to see if they had grown thicker.

He died in the spring of 1869, on the eve of our reverses. God spared him the spectacle of the misfortunes which he had foreseen, for he was not duped by the homage paid to France by Europe. He felt that this splendour had no firm basis, and that our wealth was too surely exciting the envy and greed of our neighbours. Death was merciful and took him in time. He did not see the horrors of our disasters—the defeat, the capitulation, the enemy defiling through the capital, the helmeted King at the tomb of Napoleon, the Empire of Germany bearing date from Versailles, and, worst of all, while France was gasping out her life, Paris, *his* Paris, *his* city (which fifteen years of love had indeed made his own), *his* Hôtel de Ville, *his house*, wrapt in the sacrilegious flames which had been kindled by the French themselves!

His death was painless and gentle. He was going to meet the dear companion who, thirteen years before, had preceded him to the tomb; and I cannot help saying of him, with Cicero, "As for myself, Crassus, when I consider the glory of thy life and the happy seasonableness of thy death, it seems to me that the goodness of God has traced out thy birth and the close of thy life. Thy firmness and virtue might, perhaps, have brought thy destruction by the sword of civil war, or, if Fortune had preserved thee from the rage of the assassin, she would not have saved thee from witnessing the obsequies of thy country, or from bewailing, not only the tyranny of the wicked, but also the victory of the good, stained with the blood of so many citizens."

Such is the man, and such is the book.

The latter does not consist of secret memoirs, spiced with anecdotes calculated to gratify an unwholesome curiosity. History has nothing to gain from that sort of indiscretions, which only come naturally from the lips of gossiping valets. Doubtless, Comte de Rambuteau was in a position to say and to hear many things, and he was acquainted with a large number of illustrious personages, beginning with Napoleon. But he was not one to keep a register of petty human weaknesses, least of all of those of the Prince whom he served. He tells everything about the Emperor which we have any right to know. He admired him, but not fanatically. Still his admiration for him reaches a pitch that may lead us to form too favourable an estimate of the mighty conqueror; for in depicting any hero, is not each one of us prone to invest him with every virtue, just as on the other hand one is wont to attribute every imaginable vice to certain notorious monsters?

In one respect, at any rate, the Count has done well. He has refrained from giving any of those thrilling revelations which tend to upset old-established traditions. On the contrary, these latter are confirmed by his straightforward and well-authenticated statements.

The reader will be impressed by his frank ingenuous-

ness and by that modesty which saves him from the shoal
upon which the authors of so many memoirs are wrecked
—egotism. The Chamberlain never obtrudes himself.
In fact, he keeps so much in the background, occupying
such a subordinate position relatively to M. de Narbonne,
that we sometimes feel as if we were perusing the memoirs
of the aide-de-camp and not those of M. de Rambuteau.
We never find the deputy quoting from his own reports
and speeches; the Prefect simply relates, point by point,
the drama of '48. It is only when we come to the close of
the work that we find any personal references, and they are
of such a noble, generous nature that no one could object
to them.

Perhaps, too, the form of this narrative will dissipate a
certain legend which has received some credit in the press.
Men in power have always been fair game for journalists
whose object is to afford amusement to their readers.
First, they are treated to an insinuation, then follows a
harmless jest, next a poisoned shaft is let fly, and the witticism becomes calumnious: an impression is created, and the
caricature spreads rapidly among the public. It was in this
fashion that the umbrella of Louis-Philippe, the puns of
Dupin, and Comte de Rambuteau's errors of style found a
place in history.

Doctor P. Ménière has already protested in his *Journal*
against this imputation. Prévost-Paradol, surely a good
judge in such a matter, says: "He was a delightful conver-
sationalist, thanks to the abundance and accuracy of his
recollections. He had seen much and retained much; he
could relate the events of the past charmingly and instruc-
tively." Villemain, who had these *Mémoires* in his hands
and made use of everything in them relating to M. de
Narbonne, wrote as follows to the courteous lender:
"Pray do not accuse yourself of negligence. Nothing
can be better or more instructive than the homely tone you
adopt; it is so familiar and so true. With a few words
you make us feel what you have felt; you bring before our
eyes what you have seen and what is garnered in your heart."

And this, we believe, will be the opinion of the world at large. And since we have appealed to the testimony of his contemporaries, we shall conclude by borrowing from one of them this delicately sketched portrait : [1]

" Connected with the old régime by his birth and by his wife, who was one of the most charming women of his time, yet a firm supporter of a constitutional form of government by his ideas; as thoroughly acquainted with his budget of revenue and expenditure as an accountant; knowing more about architecture than an architect; thrifty in small things in order to be generous in great; a wise adviser, fruitful in suggestions and happy in his methods of utilising them; amiable (shall I say gallant?) in his salon, which attracted every one who was worth knowing in Europe; courteous, with all the well-bred politeness which is the secret of the patrician world; conversant with literature and proficient in every branch of general knowledge; skilfully availing himself of three things in making the most of wealth—time, credit, and experience; finally, everywhere on the spot, accessible to all, and ever ready with an answer for every question, M. de Rambuteau was pre-eminently the Prefect of the age, of the society, and of the great city which he represented."

GEORGES LEQUIN.

MÂCON, *July* 15, 1904.

---

[1] Barrière, *Journal des Débats.*

MEMOIRS OF
COMTE DE RAMBUTEAU

CHAPTER I

EARLY RECOLLECTIONS

"WE are not grand aristocrats," my father used often to say to me in my boyhood, "but honest gentlemen of a good old house, neither more nor less. And what more do we want? Without undue pride, our position is surely good enough to dispense us from all need either of petty self-assertion on the one hand, or servility on the other? For *noblesse oblige*. The remembrance of our ancestors' exploits should incite us to courage, fidelity, and devotion, and with this object in view it is surely permissible to speak of them." In order to elucidate certain points in this narrative, I must mention a few genealogical particulars with regard to my family. These were verified by the *Chambre de la Noblesse* of Burgundy in 1724. This authentication could not go further back than the sixteenth century, owing to the burning of the Château de Mersault and the consequent loss of all the early title-deeds of the family, as recorded in the official report of the Lieutenant-General of Mâcon, dated October 10, 1652.

The Barthelots, originally from the neighbourhood of Montauban, owned the lands of Meursault, Ozenay, and Crary, in the middle of the sixteenth century. Rambuteau was acquired by them in 1545. A little later (1552), Henry II. granted letters patent to "Messires Claude and

Henri de Barthelot, captains of a hundred men-at-arms, lords of Meursault and Crary," for the renewal of their rights as landholders, which they had allowed to lapse during their service in Italy under François I. During the wars of religion, the abbey of St. Philibert de Tournus was repeatedly defended against the Huguenots by the Sire Claude de Barthelot, Lord of Ozenay. Hence the custom in our family of transmitting from father to son the baptismal names of *Claude* and *Philibert*. In 1574 he married Mlle. de Rymon, daughter of Aimé de Rymon, the King's Attorney at Mâcon, who, aided by the Lieutenant-General of the bailiwick, Philibert de Laguiche, had preserved the Protestants from a repetition of the massacre of the Vespers of St. Bartholomew.

I owe a few words to Rymon, who was a good citizen, always zealous in the service of his prince and country. On the death of Henry III. he persuaded Mâcon to submit to the authority of Henry IV. When the city was besieged by the Leaguers of Lyons, he happened to be visiting one of his sons-in-law at Royer, near Tournus. With the latter, and two of his own sons, he jumped into a little boat, and, in spite of the besiegers' fire, made his way into the city, inspired the inhabitants with renewed courage, and repulsed the enemy. In 1580 he built the Château of Champgrenon. He was the friend of Ponthus de Thiard, Bishop of Châlons, one of the poetic Pleiades, and delighted to receive this son of the Muses in his new residence, together with Ronsard, du Bellay, and du Bartas. By way of expressing this feeling, he had the following verse engraved over the door:

Campus Grynæus, Musis et Apollini sacer.

The Hospice de la Charité at Mâcon was partly endowed by him. Henri IV. ennobled him in 1594 by letters royal, in which his services are enumerated; and added to this favour the grant of the toll over the bridge at Mâcon.

Philibert de Barthelot, son of Claude, married Mlle. de Bullion, daughter of Bullion de Fervaques (Superintendent of the Finances under Louis XIII.; and of this marriage was born Henry de Barthelot, who married Marguerite Chapuis de Lafay. With the two sons of the latter, the family split into two branches : that of Ozenay and that of Rambuteau.

Philibert de Rambuteau, Lieutenant of the King in Mâconnais, married, in 1677, Marie de Rymon, the last descendant of Aimé de Rymon, whose line—so to speak—died out in ours. He did not live long after his marriage. He was very jealous of his hunting rights, and had several quarrels on the subject with one of his neighbours, the Lord of Montrouen, which ended one day in a duel with hunting knives on the Bridge of Barrin. Montrouen was slain, and Rambuteau, grievously wounded, survived only a few years, after receiving the royal pardon ; duelling at that period being heavily punishable. He left three sons, all soldiers : the eldest, François, was killed at the battle of Luzzara ; the second, Claude, was my grandfather ; the third, Philibert, never married.

Claude de Rambuteau entered the army at a very early age. His courage, handsome appearance, and remarkable height (he stood six feet) made him very conspicuous amongst other officers. At twenty-seven he was lieutenant-colonel of the Villeroy Regiment, the titular colonel of which was just five years old. During the War of the Spanish Succession he victualled his men almost entirely at his own expense during two consecutive campaigns. To achieve this he was obliged to sell his estates of Villars and Crary, and cut down all his forests. Money was then so rare that a cartload of wood was sold for fifteen sous ! In return for these sacrifices, the King appointed him brigadier of his armies, and presented him with three tattered standards belonging to his regiment. These are still at Rambuteau, my father having had them placed in front of the altar.[1] He had been already invested with the Cross

[1] They are guidons of white silk, framed in rich silver embroidery· Two bear a golden sun darting its rays over green mountains, an eagle with wings outspread, and this motto : *Et Solem et Praelia.* The third has the dazzling sun of Louis XIV., *Nec pluribus impar.* At Rambuteau likewise may be seen the breastplates of these military leaders, indented here and there by bullets, and, among the family portraits, a very fine one of the poet Rotrou.

of Saint Louis, and with the most brilliant career opening
before him (thanks to his valour and to the friendship
of Marshal Villeroy), at forty-five he was attacked by
paralysis of the optic nerve, and thus compelled to quit
the service.   He had married, somewhat late in life, Mlle.
de Rotrou, granddaughter of the poet, a love match to
which he sacrificed his engagement with Mlle. de la
Roche-Aymon, a rich heiress.   He left two sons, each of
whom, as soon as they attained the age of fifteen, were
provided with a company of cavalry in the Conti Regiment.

The elder brother, Claude[1] (he was my father), had
the good luck to distinguish himself at the battle of Coni
by his plucky rescue of some military waggons, and thus
contributed his share to the Prince de Conti's victory.
My father was then twenty-four.   The Prince attached
him to his service, and obtained for him the Cross of
Saint Louis, which was not generally bestowed upon less
than thirty years' service.   As an old man, he loved to
describe how he accompanied the Prince to Versailles in
his velvet coat, richly braided *à la Bourgogne* on every
seam, his own youthfulness and the Cross of Saint Louis
serving as "sesame" to all doors, and, if I mistake not,
all hearts as well.

He received much notice from the Princess de Conti
(*née* d'Orléans), whose portrait is at Champgrenon, and to
the day of her death she showed him unfailing kindness.

She was very anxious to marry him to Mlle. de
Lambert, the daughter of her lady-in-waiting, and it was
to please his fiancée that the Count planted the long avenue
of alternate peach and cherry trees at Champgrenon.
Alas! the trees were longer lived than the love which
their planting should have represented.   For, after having
undergone a terrible illness, the young lady retired to a
convent on her recovery.

---

[1] Born in the Rue Sainte-Avoye, Paris, in the house in which his father
had died. So, when the name *Rue de Rambuteau* was given to the great
street opened up from the Rue Paradis to Sainte-Eustache, it was a mark of
respect paid not only to the Prefect of Paris, but to his family.

The Princesse de Conti was very witty. "My friend," she would say to him, "never marry a girl from the moneyed classes, for she will devour all her own property, and then yours, leaving only the dregs for you. If you take a girl of good family you will get less money with her, but she will live at home quietly in your château when you are with your regiment, and, *though wealth may not rain in showers, it will fall in drops.*" He followed this advice, and married Mlle. de Laviefville-Vignacourt, who came of a very old family in Picardy that had supplied two Grand Masters to the Order of Malta. He might have married another woman with ten times her dowry, but soon afterwards, owing to the death of her father and brother, she became a great heiress. Her properties, large even after the losses incurred during the Revolution, were still further increased in 1825 by a part of the estates of the Duchesse de Saint-Aignan, so that, if fortune did not rain in showers, it most certainly did in drops. How vain, for that matter, are all pecuniary calculations, and how brittle are matrimonial expectations! M. Laviefville, my grandfather, had been married by his guardian and cousin, Marshal de Noailles, to Mlle. Chopin d'Arnouville. His only brother was very rich, but such a sickly hunchback, that his life was considered almost a question of days. Consequently it was a foregone conclusion that his sister would be a great heiress. As it turned out, however, this diminutive man (he was only four and a half feet high) lived to be eighty. His hump did not hinder him from becoming a very distinguished man. He was Counsellor to the Parliament of Paris, First President of the Cour des Aides, and left eight children at his death.

As to my uncle Philibert, also a Chevalier of Saint Louis, his military career was cut short by an unfortunate love affair. It is a sad story, somewhat like that of M. de Rancé. On going to keep his tryst with the woman he loved, he found her dead. This tragedy changed his life, and he became extremely devout; so that whenever Comte (afterward Marshal) de Mun invited him to dinner, he used to say to his officers : " Gentlemen, no frivolous conversation ; the Chevalier de Rambuteau dines with us to-day." After the peace of 1763, he left the army and entered the Abbey of Sept-Fonts, of which he built the part that bears his name. Although he never took the vows, he spent the rest of his life as a severe ascetic. He bequeathed his library to La Trappe,, and also an income sufficient to provide the monastery with rice and oil, on condition that the Order should pray for members of his family when sick and after their death, when requested to do so. Consequently, when my mother was attacked by smallpox in 1791, my father's first care was to despatch his valet to Sept-Fonts, with a request for the prayers of the community, to which he was convinced that we owed her subsequent recovery. The Chevalier died in 1780 at Mâcon, during a visit to my father. My mother, a wife of four years' standing, but with no children, nursed him with the most devoted affection. On the evening before his death, he said to her : " Sister, I know what you long for, and if God is merciful to me, you will have a son within the year."[1] I was born eleven months later, and my parents always believed my birth was due to their brother's intercession.

The year 1791, which nearly deprived me of a mother, came near to being fatal to myself and my sister. The smallpox was raging at the time. My mother was in such terror of it that, directly she heard of its appearance in the neighbourhood of wherever she might happen to be, she at once ordered her carriage and fled. My sister and myself were the first to be attacked. Then she was struck down while nursing us. She did endeavour, when the disease first appeared, to obey the doctor's orders, and to content herself with looking at us through one of our

[1] The Calvary of Rambuteau, erected by the Chevalier in 1769, and carved by an unknown artist, was broken and mutilated during the Revolution. The new Calvary, blessed in 1860, reproduces the Christ of Bouchardon and the statues of Pradier. The original pedestals have been taken up, and along with the mutilated statues have been placed in the enclosure.

windows opening on a balcony. But after a little she could not restrain her loving anxiety, and at length, in despite of all prohibition, she devoted herself entirely to us. She never left us for a single minute. Poor mother, how tender she was, and how proud she was of her son! She was never tired of telling me the story of how, at a religious festival in the Cathedral of Sens, when I was standing on a chair during the procession, headed by Cardinal de La Roche-Aymon, the latter stopped before us, and, tapping me on the cheek, said: "What a fine child!" It was one of her sweetest memories. The disease had more terrible consequences for her than for us, for, whereas we escaped all scars, she lost her beauty and bore the marks of her devotion until her dying day. My father was at Champgrenon, in a state of great apprehension, anxiously awaiting the arrival of the couriers despatched at short intervals to report our condition.

Directly all danger of infection was over, I was sent to him, but it was many months before my mother could bring herself to rejoin him, so acutely did she realise what the extent of his distress would be on seeing her terribly disfigured features. At first she always wore a veil in his presence, but his rapidly-increasing blindness—due to on-coming cataract—soon made this precaution unnecessary.

The malady which we both shared at the same time drew the bond of affection still closer between my sister and me. We were born the same day, the 9th of November—I in 1781, she in 1783. We had the same nurse, the same cradle (later it was also my eldest daughter's), the same masters, and the same education. During the whole of our youth, we were only once parted; even during the worst days of the Terror we were not separated. My father, in fact, had refused to emigrate. "If I were young," he said, "with no infirmities, I should take my stand beside the King; but to seek the aid of foreign arms is simply to compromise his cause and insult the country. By staying in France, I defend the interests of my children, and I remain true to my political and religious creed. Perhaps we may suffer for it; but at any rate, we shall eat French bread." Besides, what cause had he for fear! During the long years he had resided on his estates, he had been unsparing in good deeds, and had every reason to believe himself beloved. A practical proof of the affection with which he was regarded was given in 1792, when the volunteers, on their way to join the army, invaded Champgrenon and threatened to sack the château. The municipality rallied round the bed upon which he lay, blind and infirm, covering him with their tricolour scarfs for protection. He received the volunteers with dignified calmness. He told them he was an old soldier, who had seen active service from the age of fifteen, and had always, even in the enemy's country, shown respect to old age. They retired in silence, without doing any damage.

But the Terror came, and my parents were arrested and taken to Mâcon. There my mother was imprisoned in the Hospice de la Charité, and afterwards in the Hôpital, institutions which owed their existence to the generosity of our family. Thence she was transferred to Autun, where she remained a prisoner for ten months. On the day of her departure, my sister and I, with the other children belonging to those who had been arrested, were taken before the Société Populaire to entreat the release of our parents. We were promptly repulsed. Thereupon we flew to the quay in order to embrace our mother before she entered the boat. Here my sister, nimbler than myself, slipped under a gendarme's horse, and, throwing her arms about her, she wept so bitterly that the commissaries were touched and did not insist on their separation. As for my poor blind father, his release was demanded by the neighbouring communes, which consented to be responsible for him. Although he was allowed to return to his house, the seals which had been affixed on the doors were not removed, for, in spite of his infirmity, he had been placed on the list of emigrants, and his goods were under sequestration. In vain, Mademoiselle Rochefort, my mother's maid, and the only servant who had stayed with us, did her best to procure a replevin with which to redeem my father's possessions, but though she was reinforced with numerous medical certificates, her efforts were fruitless. The President of the District tore them from her hands and threw them into the fire, saying, "This is what you should do yourself, if you were a good Republican."

At length the 9th Thermidor came to my parents' rescue, just as they were on the point of being brought before the Revolutionary Tribunal, which would probably have condemned them to death, notwithstanding the affection which was universally felt for them. A few years later, when I was still quite a youth, I happened one day to lose my way in a forest near Charolles. Meeting some sabot-makers, I asked the road to Rambuteau. " Might I ask if you are the son of M. le Marquis ? " inquired one of them. " Ah, what a good man he was ! He was always so kind to the poor. We are all glad to have a chance of obliging his son." And they insisted on accompanying me to the house, refusing to accept anything from me. The impression I received then has never been effaced from my memory.

But, though my parents had weathered the storm safely, how many dear heads among our relatives had fallen ! Eight were executed in one day, and we saw the whole family of Mme. de Rézy,[1] my mother's sister, mount the steps of the scaffold. By a refinement of cruelty, Mme. de Rézy was made to remain at the foot of the guillotine until the others were beheaded. This was such a terrible blow to my father that he could never be persuaded to set foot in Paris again ; he could not endure to revisit a city that had been the theatre of such horrors.

Among the victims were Comte d'Achon, late governor of the Duc de Bourbon, and the Marquis and Marquise d'Achon. We were united with them by a kinship that

---

[1] Descendants of the Échevin Langlois de Rézy, who opened the gates of Paris to Henri IV. on the night of the 22nd of March 1694, and was named by the King Prévôt des Marchands.

went back to the beginning of the seventeenth century, and by ties of friendship so close that a double alliance had been planned between our two families : Mlle. d'Achon and her brother had been betrothed almost in their cradles to me and my sister. The Revolution shattered all these contracts. Young d'Achon died soon after its close, and Mlle. d'Achon became so great an heiress as to be presumably too grand a match for myself. However, after a long separation, and being aware of the plans which our respective parents had originally made for her, she expressed a wish to make my acquaintance. In consequence, we met frequently, for eighteen months. But she had a governess who ruled the roost, and who was accessible only to bribery. My mother was not the woman to descend to such methods. I personally was too young to attach much value to money, and all I wanted was to secure my cousin's affection, as she, apparently, had some liking for me. One fine day, however, we learned that an alliance had been arranged between her and M. de Riancourt at the price of great sacrifices on the part of the bride. It did not insure her happiness : the poor woman died very young.

To return, however, to the Revolution, with which my remotest memories are connected. In 1796 I accompanied my mother on horseback from Paris to Rambuteau. There were four of us altogether, and, as we had but two horses, we were forced to walk half the way. Near Vigousset, the night grew so dark that I and my steed tumbled into a bog, which to this day is known as Amable's Pond.[1] It was a matter of considerable difficulty to rescue horse and rider from their unpleasant predicament. Luckily, we were near home. Later we went to Lyons to visit M. Petit, a famous oculist, whom my father wished to consult. We were present every day at the hospital, watching intently the operations, and noting M. Petit's success in dealing with a score of consecutive cases. On learning this, my father decided to have an operation performed, and, some months later, the oculist was summoned to Champgrenon.

[1] Amable was the name of Comte de Rambuteau's youngest daughter.

It was done very quickly. I held his hand while the incision was being made. His first look when he saw the light was for me ; but the operation was not entirely successful. He recovered the sight of only one eye, the other was lost. Still, he could see with that one until his death, and for the next fifteen years was able to write letters of four pages in a delicate, close hand. Lyons at this period offered a singular spectacle : it was the time of the great reaction. Quite a number of young men belonging to the army of Condé had returned, and, finding their families decimated, their houses destroyed, their properties sold, and the laws powerless, these *émigrés* avenged themselves on their executioners. A vendetta was promptly organised. A search was made for informers, called *Mativons*, from the name of their ringleader. Every moment a *Mativon* was to be seen going through the street, accompanied by an escort who forced him to walk by prodding him with a dagger. "Oh! it's only a *Mativon*, whom they're taking to the river," was the careless reply to any inquiry. Arrived at the bank, he was forced down on his knees, stabbed repeatedly, and then flung into the stream ; after which every one returned unconcernedly to his business. I witnessed these executions on two or three occasions.

The elegant youth of the day adopted a sort of distinctive uniform : they wore a short-skirted body-coat with black collar ; and had two long locks of hair falling down each side of the face, called *oreilles de chien*. They carried a cane, leaded at both ends, and pistols ; whilst after dark a lamp, suspended from a button-hole, completed the costume. I was very young at the time, scarcely fourteen, and it was in this dress, to which I clung during my several visits to Lyons, that I made my début in society. The fact was I was very tall for my age—five feet eight, and I looked much older than I was. My mentor was a near relative of my mother, M. de Brévannes, and he introduced me to a select circle, the leading lights of which were Mesdames Fleurieu, de Jessé, Champlieu, Cuzieu, de

Montpensier, and de la Salle. The latter was the hostess of all the returning *émigrés*, and at her house I became acquainted with MM. de Ligondès, Desrives, La Rochette, Pujol, and others whom I was to meet later on in Paris.

When the 18th Fructidor broke out, my mother, who had only too good cause to dread imprisonment, decided on leaving France. Not daring to pass through Mâcon, she selected the route by Cluny and Cormatin, and reached Tournus and Bourg. There hearing reassuring tidings, she returned to Rambuteau, afterwards taking my sister and me to Paris, whither our interests as well as our education called us. The roads were then in such ill condition that it took seven days for our big berline and six horses to achieve the journey. We lodged with my aunt, de Boisgelin, at the Hôtel Brévannes, Rue d'Orléans, in the Marais. Ah! many a time, when as Prefect of Paris I took my morning walk, did I pause to gaze at the windows of that little house where my youth was spent.

One of our masters was M. Despréaux, author of the poem on Dancing, the husband of Mlle. Guimard,[1] and one of the cleverest men of the time. We were indebted for his consent to teach us to my mother's first cousin, M. de Vindé. It was in Mme. Despréaux's salon, Rue de la Chaussé d'Antin, that M. de la Harpe gave his course on literature. We also had lessons from the Abbé Guyon, afterwards bishop, and always my faithful friend till death.

The next year I prepared for the École Polytechnique, which was the only course I could take to enter the service, except as a common soldier. I worked hard, and, thanks to my professor of mathematics, M. Lefort, I passed the examinations successfully. But as, after the 18th Brumaire, families began to feel more secure, my mother was less anxious about my future, and she did not like me to remain away from her at school for two years more. I have always

[1] The famous dancer of the Opéra, but celebrated especially for her mad extravagance, the luxury of her hôtel in the Chaussée d'Antin, and the plays given in her private theatre, where all the *prémières* of Collé were represented.

The Comte de Rambuteau,
as a Young Man.

regretted that I did not finish the course I had begun so happily. From that moment I mixed in society.

Bonaparte's *coup d'état*, by restoring order, had to a certain extent restored social conditions. The salons were opening in all directions ; my mother " received " once a week, and had a dance at her receptions. She was very anxious to develop my taste for good society. Thanks to her liberality, I was able to give some nice breakfasts to my friends Brévannes, Montholon, Scipion Nicolaï, d'Orsay, the two d'Estournels, the two Chopins, Dupaty, and Sainte-Aulaire, whose acquaintance I made either at the balls of our dancing-master, Gaillet, or at the studio of M. Lemire, professor of drawing to the École Polytechnique, or at the Pellier riding-school, Rue de Florence. My mother gave me three francs a day to spend on going to and fro my lessons, but these I generally economised in order to spend them on entertaining my friends. What a happy time it was ! We lived in a magnificent *rez-de-chaussée* in the Rue d'Anjou, with coach-house, seven horses, and a cook. My sister, in the flower of her eighteen years, was very much sought after. Her hand was asked in marriage four times during the year 1801 by MM. de Brévannes, Lepelletier d'Aunay, d'Arbaud de Jouques, and de Vallin. The latter and I were great friends, although he was twelve years my senior. In fact, he was the best friend I had. I shall never forget a visit we paid together to the Grande Chartreuse with Mme. de Krudener, whom he had known in Germany. She wrote a description of it to Chateaubriand on the spot on the backs of envelopes, and I have kept a copy.[1]

On the 8th of December 1802, my sister married M. de Mesgrigny. Not wishing that any pecuniary consideration should stand in the way of her happiness, I begged my parents to allow me to bestow such property on her as I deemed right. I was amply rewarded on reading my father's answer to the first overtures of MM. de Mesgrigny : " Gentlemen, it is my son who gives his sister in marriage.

---

[1] Unfortunately we have been unable to find this curious letter.

We will sign whatever he proposes without looking at it."
This was to be my mother's last happiness in this world.
She had been ill for several months, and could hardly get
down to the chapel. We did not make any show of rejoicing, for we felt that death was already seated at our hearth.
She died, indeed, on the 8th of January following. I was
in despair. I lost not only the tenderest of mothers, from
whom I had never been separated, but the unfailing guide
of my youth, a guide whose sagacity was never at fault.
She had been the providence of her husband and children ;
and, knowing the support she had always been to us, she
realised the void she would leave behind her. Her great
sorrow lay not in having to die, but in having to leave us.
She rebelled at the thought, crying aloud in her distress :
" O God, Thou canst not require such a sacrifice ! See these
children who still need me ! See this old man to whose
declining years my care is necessary ! " Nothing but the
consolations of religion could reconcile her to so cruel a
separation. The Abbé Repey, her confessor, an able and
kind-hearted priest, succeeded in inspiring her with a supreme
resignation by assuring her that God would replace her in
caring for her dear ones, and that her sacrifice would most
surely be turned into a blessing for them.

It was reserved for me, fifty years later, to witness the
same heartrending anguish in similar circumstances in the
case of my daughter. In these horrible trials I realised how
religion alone can bring consolation when all human efforts
are impotent. Then I understood its value, its sanctity,
the obligation to respect it in others, as well as that of cultivating it in oneself, as the sole refuge for despairing souls.
All my life I have honoured religion. It was from religion
that my father derived the courage and strength needed to
endure so irreparable a calamity, the bitterness of which all
the tenderness of my own affection for him would have been
powerless to soothe.

The death of my mother deprived me of her advice at
the very moment when I was about to want it most. For

I had reached that time of life when it behoved me to think of my future.   In what direction was I to steer my course ? Toward the past, which had been swept away by the whirl-wind of the Revolution ?   Toward the present, so new and so precarious ?   My own tastes, the prestige of victory and the earnest advice of my friends, drew me towards the Empire. In 1806, M. de Beausset, Prefect of the Palace, mentioned my name to Josephine, who was on intimate terms with my brother-in-law, M. de Mesgrigny.[1]   He also recommended me to M. de Caulaincourt, a distant relative of the Lavief-villes, and it was settled that I should apply for a presenta-tion to the Emperor.

   This took place in July at Saint Cloud.   First I was ushered into the ante-chamber, where I saw the Prince of Baden and the Prince of Schwarzenberg, the eldest brother of the Duke of Krumau.[2]   Here I waited for nearly three hours.   The Emperor received me very warmly ; he spoke of Burgundy, inquired about my family, and asked why I was not in the army, seeing that I belonged to a house which had always been attached to the service.   I told him that I had been admitted to the École Polytechnique and had wished, after the news of Marengo and the appeal addressed to the youth of Paris, to follow the example of my comrades, Flahaut, Lagrange, and Menou d'Astorg, but that my mother was opposed to this, and, after her death, I could not leave my old father.   I added that I ardently desired to devote myself to his government and to his person, and this with the consent of my father, who had written to me that, while at his time of life one was inclined to cling to old traditions, at my age I might enjoy the privilege of choice, and that I ought to belong to my time and country. His letter was intended to be a guide for my future conduct, and was a complete treatise on delicate questions of political

---

[1] She had made his acquaintance during the Terror in the Luxembourg prison.
[2] The Duke of Krumau, an Austrian general, was ambassador at Paris after the treaty of Vienna.   He will be often mentioned in this narrative, but under the name of Prince de Schwarzenberg, which he bore as well as his brother.

loyalty. The Emperor smiled and promised that he would not forget me. Henceforward I was included in the Court invitations, and was present at the Saint Napoleon Fête. I well remember wearing a costume embroidered with white silk and *strass* (floss silk) and covered with spangles, which was so much admired that I at once secured a place among the exquisites of the Court. This did not help me much, however. I had still three years to wait for the coveted key of a Chamberlain.

During this interval I continued to appear at Saint Cloud, but not with particular assiduity. Truth to tell I was now beginning to think of settling down, and, as several matches were proposed for me, I thought it as well to await results ; so that I might accommodate my politics to those of my new family. Mme. de Jaucourt did her best to bring about a marriage between me and Mlle. Marescalchi, the daughter of the Italian minister at Paris. But I was only moderately attracted to this young person, and the great splendour and luxury of her surroundings led me to fear that a girl brought up in such opulence was scarcely likely to be satisfied with our modest life in the country. I loved my father too well to neglect him, and it was entirely owing to his liberality that I was able to live in much better style than most of my contemporaries. I kept five or six horses in Paris, a cook, &c. In the country he allowed me to receive my friends during the several months I spent with him, and, when my sister was there, we lived in grand style, with retinues of attendants, &c. I shrank in consequence from doing anything that might run counter to his tastes, and so I rejected an alliance that would at the onset have brought me nearer to the Emperor. After this, M. de Vallin wished me to marry Mlle. de Savaron, while my grandmother de Laviefville and her brother Chopin d'Arnouville, President of the Cour des Aides, intended me for Mlle. de Narbonne. The latter project found favour with every one ; the matter was settled in December, and my contract was signed early in January 1809.

The Comte de Narbonne, my father-in-law, ex-Minister

of War to Louis XVI.—his last War Minister in fact [1]—
had married Mlle. de Montholon,[2] by whom he had two
daughters : the first, Louise de Riom (the town of Riom
had been her godmother), who, in 1806, married M. de
Sobral,[3] the Portuguese Minister ; the second, Marie
Adélaïde, who became my wife. No more dramatic existence can be imagined than that which my fiancée led for a
time. Born at Bellevue,[4] in 1790, and confided, with her
nurse, to the care of the concierges of the château on the
day when Mesdames and her mother started for a foreign
land, she remained on their hands, her father (forced to fly
in his turn) having been unable to make any arrangements
with respect to her. During the Terror, the concierges
became alarmed at having this child of proscribed parents
with them, and deposited it in the porch of the church. She
was picked up by a former servant of Mesdames, named
Ardon, who for several years reared and treated her as his
own daughter. She went to the school at the Sèvres manufactory with the village children, and, later on, the Emperor
enjoyed showing Marie Louise the meadow, on the road
to Meudon, where Mlle. de Narbonne used to keep her
foster-father's cow. This worthy man grew so fond of the
child that it was only when he was threatened with legal
proceedings, that he would consent to give her up, when her
two grandfathers, MM. de Narbonne and de Montholon
came to claim her. Needless to say that their gratitude to
her guardian took a very substantial form. Marie Adélaïde

---

[1] The Comte de Narbonne, born 1755, in the palace of Elizabeth de
Bourbon, Duchess of Parma, in whose Court his parents held high office,
was descended from the ancient family of the Laras of Castile. His father,
Duke of Narbonne-Lara, was Grandee of Spain. After the death of the
Infanta, his mother was lady of honour to Mesdames of France. (See
Villemain, *Souvenirs contemporains*, 1re. partie ; *Le Comte de Narbonne*.)

[2] Daughter of M. Montholon, ex-First President of the Parliament of
Rouen.

[3] Count de Braamcamp de Sobral, President of the Cortes, &c., one of
the most distinguished men that lived during this agitated period of Portuguese history.

[4] Residence of Mme. de Pompadour, given by Marie Antoinette to her
aunts, Mesdames Victoire and Adélaïde, who resided there before their
emigration.

was placed in a Paris boarding-school, and, on her mother's return from the Emigration in 1805, was brought by her father to Agen, where the Comtesse de Narbonne was residing. And thus, after a separation of fifteen years, husband and wife met again for the marriage of a daughter who was unknown to both of them.

My marriage was delayed for family reasons. Ruined by the Revolution, M. de Montholon[1] saw himself forced to sell his hôtel on the Boulevard Poissonnière for 340,000 francs, after having expended one million on it. With a yearly income reduced by two-thirds, he had to face those continuous debts which are the ordinary accessories of a great fortune for those to whom reverses have taught neither discretion nor foresight. In short, he had been living from hand to mouth for several years, when he obtained the post of member of the Administrative Commission of Hospitals which brought him 9000 francs a year. He claimed it on the ground that he had been a member of the Conseil Général of the said hospitals. True, it was somewhat of a come down in his case, to descend from a superintendent to be one of the superintended ; but it made life easier for him.

Two months were spent in negotiations, during which my position was rather anomalous, for, though my contract was duly signed, I had not yet made acquaintance with my intended. Everybody in the social world was astonished at these delays. On the other hand, I saw M. de Narbonne frequently, and the more I saw of him the more I loved him. I was particularly impressed by his integrity. "Certain people," he said, "look out for a son-in-law ; I want to find a son. I have heard nothing but good of you. And although every one hinted at some trifling little drawback, every one added : 'But he's such a good fellow !' Well, I have given my daughter to this *good young fellow*." Indeed he always treated me as his son, a fact which I shall never weary of repeating. His affection for me

---

[1] Mme. de Montholon had also lost her whole fortune, which brought her an income of 300,000 livres, in the revolution of Santo Domingo.

Marie-Adélaide de Montholon.

Hélio§. Dujardin. Paris

was an open secret. The Emperor was especially aware of it, for, when he promised him on his departure as Ambassador to Vienna in 1813 the title of duke, with an endowment large enough to correspond adequately to the position, he further bestowed on him the right to adopt me.

M. de Narbonne at that time lived with Mme. de Laval[1] in a small pavilion in the Rue Roquépine, where she held a reception every evening for the celebrities of the period : MM. de Talleyrand, de Choiseul-Gouffier, de Jaucourt, Comte de La Marck, the friend of Mirabeau, Comte de Clary, son-in-law of Prince de Ligne, Prince Poniatowski, the Duc de Laval, Adrien de Montmorency, and Mmes. de Choiseul, de Jaucourt, de La Tour du Pin, de Vicence,[2] de Baufremont, de Coigny,[3] de Balbi,[4] de Souza,[5] &c. It was a select and limited circle in which scarcely any one of my age appeared. The honour of sharing it, therefore, was most gratifying to me, for it was the school of grand manners and of great traditions and memories. Not that much reference was made to the past. A large proportion of the guests had rallied round Napoleon, without family ties or old friendships being affected by the change. On the contrary, the lively and interesting discussions which took place lost nothing of their animation, whatever differences of opinion might exist, because they were conducted with courtesy and regard for one another's feelings. For nearly a whole year I met the Duchess de Fitz-James there. She

---

[1] They had become acquainted during the Emigration in Switzerland. The result was one of these *liaisons* so frequent in the eighteenth century that custom rendered them, to some extent, regular. This one lasted for life.

[2] The Marquise de Caulaincourt.

[3] The Marquise de Coigny, of whom Marie Antoinette said : "I am Queen only of Versailles, Mme. de Coigny is Queen of Paris."

[4] Ex-mistress of the Comte de Provence (later Louis XVIII.), whom she followed to Coblentz. After her return to France under the Consulate, she was exiled to Montauban, where Comte de Rambuteau will find her in 1815.

[5] One of the most charming women during the Imperial epoch for her grace and wit. A widow at thirty—the Comte de Flahault, her husband, was guillotined in 1793—she married, in 1803, the Baron de Souza, a Portuguese author and diplomatist.

was the victim of an incurable malady, and the genuine
kindliness and loving zeal with which those I have mentioned tried to alleviate her sufferings were marked by all
the grace and courtesy of a vanished epoch—a light and
frivolous epoch, may be ; but also an epoch which held
many true and faithful friendships. I never missed a day
from 1808 to 1813 : sometimes, I brought my little contingent of news to the party ; at others, I slipped behind an
armchair and listened to stories of the ancient Court, to
the anecdotes of M. de Choiseul, the repartees of M. de
Narbonne, the sallies of M. de Talleyrand, by which Mme.
de Laval was so much impressed that I once said to M. de
Narbonne, " *Pardieu,* in this proverb of yours, he plays
the lover and you the husband."

I was also a frequent visitor to the Hôtel de Luynes,
where I was on a footing of intimacy, for my father-in-law
had brought about a marriage between Mlle. de Narbonne-
Pelet and the heir of the Duke.[1]   Mme. de Chevreuse, at
that time noted for her fortune, and a mirror of fashion as
well, was the queen of the salon.   I had made the acquaintance of her brothers, three or four years previously, at a
little society theatre behind the Madeleine, where the Nar-
bonnes, Étienne de Choiseul, Louis de Périgord, Bons,
Castellane, Marguery, Ganay, and some others used to act.
They met at my rooms, to which fact I owed my title of
" manager of the company."   Dazincourt and Chenard[2]
coached us on the rehearsals. This sort of thing was all the
fashion in 1805. I believe Castellane and I are the only
survivors.

Mme. de Luynes' circle of acquaintances was the same
as that of Mme. de Laval.   She was very fond of cards,
and, almost every evening, there was a bank in her salon.
She played for small stakes, but her friends did not imitate
her.   For that matter, gambling was the rage.   On one

---

[1] D'Albert, Duc de Chevreuse. The Duchesse de Chevreuse, Lady of
the Palace to the Empress, was soon exiled forty leagues from Paris, for
some remarks that were thought seditious.

[2] The one belonged to the Comédie-Française, the other to the Comédie-
Italienne.   Dazincourt had given lessons to Marie Antoinette.

occasion I remember seeing M. de Lavaubalière lose 70,000 francs there. The misadventure and exile of Mme. de Chevreuse closed the Hôtel de Luynes. The Duchesse devoted herself entirely to her daughter-in-law, and her husband remained at Dampierre. One day, during a hunt, the Emperor stopped at the château : " Monsieur le Duc," said he, on leaving and thanking him for his hospitality, " have you nothing to ask of me ? " " Sire, I thank you for the honour you have done me, and I now ask permission to retire." So Mme. de Chevreuse remained in exile !

I cannot help recalling the charm of these salons, which, as it were, marked a return to life. After the revolutionary whirlwind, every one hastened to enjoy the first hours of security under a government that had substituted order for anarchy. It was the compensation of the French aristocracy for denunciation, exile, and the guillotine ; it spelt oblivion of the past with all its terrors, and emphasised the sense of joy at re-finding the hearth, and discovering that a spark was all that was needed to rekindle a genial flame under its ruins.

Certainly, a great simplicity marked these receptions. Brilliancy, wit, conversation, were the only contributions that they levied. Simple dances, modest suppers, varied the entertainment, and those who wished to see the luxury of sumptuous festivals sought it in the mansions of the contractors who had been enriched by the Republic. How many illustrious personages have either found the glory of their first triumphs in those salons, or the consolations of their old age ! Chateaubriand in those of Mmes. de Beaumont and Récamier, Pasquier in that of Mme. de Vintimille ! For thirty years Mmes. de la Briche and de Rumfort reigned without a rival over the Faubourg Saint-Honoré ; the one, who was the mother-in-law of M. Molé, rallying round her the survivors of the eighteenth century, Saint-Lambert and Mme. d'Houdetot, along with literary men like Fontanes and Suard ; the other, Lavoisier's widow, and the friend of Cuvier and d'Arago, preferring to receive notable scientists.

What a volume might be written of hospitable houses (whose influence was far greater than was generally supposed), such as those of Mme. de Vaudémont and Mme. de Montesson,[1] Grand Mistress of the Lodge of St. Caroline, whose Warden was the Arch-Chancellor [2]—as well as those of Mmes. de Rémusat, de Nansouty, de Morfontaine, all associated alike with the events of 1814.

But as I am talking of receptions, I must mention one of quite a different character, to which I was introduced by M. de Narbonne. It was on the occasion of a course of lectures delivered by Gall (he had not begun to propound his system) for Mmes. de Talleyrand, de Choiseul-Gouffier, de Berenger, de Laborde, the celebrated Cuvier, the Duchesse de Levis, &c. I have retained a vivid recollection of these lessons, as much for the novelty of the theories as for the lecturer's anatomical knowledge. Gall found it hard to defend himself in the face of certain grave consequences resulting from his system ; such as the predisposition and arbitrary instincts which neutralise all exercise of free will. But the clearness of his diction, his lucid arguments, and his genuine enthusiasm for his convictions inspired both esteem and confidence. He claimed that a primary knowledge of the natural instincts was an excellent guide for the education of children, because thereby we should be enabled to prepare them for the future by fostering those tendencies that were beneficial and suppressing those that were harmful. I have always retained his lecture on the medulla oblongata, which, developing in the cerebellum, becomes the source of thought and of intelligence—of that intelligence at all times ready to be warped as soon as the safety-valve is closed. This alone explains why madness is more likely to threaten men of great genius than those of ordinary capacity ; while, on the other hand, the abuse of certain faculties, by exhausting the restorative fluid of life and circulation, either by excess, hard work, or old age, induces imbecility and idiocy.

[1] Married secretly to the father of Philippe-Égalité, the Duc d'Orléans, who died in 1785.   [2] Cambacérès.

It was also during this winter of 1808 that I made the acquaintance of M. de Metternich. He was then in the full heyday of his youth, the enjoyment of which, however, did not interfere with his capacity for business. Not content with the success he had already scored in the case of both Mme. Murat and Mme. de Junot, he strove to make a conquest of a certain young woman, who had evinced a special liking for me. This rivalry drew us together, and I received much kindness both from himself and his wife, who was then devoted to M. de Moustier.

At length, in the early days of March, I started with my brother-in-law, M. de Mesgrigny, for Agen, where I was to have my first interview with Mlle. de Narbonne. At Bordeaux he said : " You don't know your fiancée. Supposing you didn't like her ? " " I should have no hesitation," was my answer, " in seeking M. de Narbonne and saying to him : ' I will not be a party to a union which would render your daughter unhappy. Lay all the blame on my shoulders ; I will not contradict anything you say, but I leave, for her sake as well as my own.' "

Immediately after the presentation, Adrien drew me aside : " Well ? " he said. " Well," I answered, laughing, " I am not leaving." In fact, although Adélaïde was not very pretty, her eyes were bright and intelligent, she had an extremely sweet expression and a graceful figure ; whilst I soon discovered her noble character.

She was just the daughter-in-law I desired for my father, to whom I owed so much veneration and love. During the five years I lived in Paris, I always hastened to him directly he summoned me, never allowing any pleasure, however tempting, to delay my departure. I only once received a rather sharp letter from him, reprimanding me for an intimacy, which my grandmother De Laviefville had told him might lead to an imprudent marriage. An hour later, I had set out, accomplished the journey in thirty-six hours, and throwing myself into his arms, I exclaimed : " Did you believe that anything in the world could separate us ? This is my answer ! " The noble old man embraced me with

tears in his eyes, whilst I promised that the choice of my
wife should rest with him.

My marriage was celebrated in the chapel of the Bishop
of Agen. The wedding feast took place in the Hôtel de
Narbonne, which was afterwards sold and became the bishop's
palace. Two days later, I was very near losing my wife.
We were on our way, accompanied by her father, to their
château at Aubiac. Her little horse bolted with her whilst
crossing a meadow, and then, stopping dead short on the
bank of a stream, threw her. We felt sure that she must
be seriously injured, but she got up again with nothing
worse than a scratch on her breast. On our return to Paris,
we stopped first at Bordeaux with M. Lally-Tollendal, an
old friend of M. de Narbonne, and then at Les Ormes with
M. d'Argenson.

My father-in-law did everything in his power to insure
his daughter's success in society. I followed all his counsels.
One visit I paid displeased him—that to Mme. de Morny,
the sister of General de Caulaincourt, against whom, for
some reason or other, he was very much prejudiced. But
we soon resumed our usual good understanding. M. de
Talleyrand was particularly kind to us ; he promised to try
to interest the Emperor in my favour. For that matter, we
were universally well received. I remember a grand dinner
given by Mme. Junot d'Arbrantës, at which Cardinal
Maury had a rather hot discussion with M. de Narbonne,
who thought some of the Cardinal's remarks too light to be
uttered in the presence of a bride of eighteen. At the end
of a month, I believed it time to introduce my wife to my
father. We journeyed by slow stages. We travelled in
grand style, with eight horses, three carriages, and nine
servants. Later on, I paid dearly for these youthful follies,
and I can truly say that nothing but Adélaïde's good sense
saved our fortune and our future independence. At
Champgrenon, we found that the entire population had
turned out to receive us : numberless bouquets, compliments, firing of guns, be-ribboned and garlanded sheep and
calves, gala-cakes, &c., &c. But the most touching sight

of all was that of my old father standing in the porch, leaning on his tall cane, and extending his arms to my wife : "My daughter, this is the sweetest day of my life," he cried, "for now I live again in my children. Let us go and thank God." Therewith he led us to the chapel, and to the altar where I had made my first Communion with my sister, where she had been married, and where my mother had so often come to pray for us.

I stayed eighteen months in the country, without feeling either lassitude or regret, rejoicing in my father's happiness, my wife's pregnancy, happy in my domestic joys, in our peaceful life at the paternal hearth, in the labours undertaken to restore Champgrenon, and happy above all in the gardens, the improvement of which was already my favourite dream. Through one of my neighbours, M. Febvre, I formed the acquaintance of M. Morel, the creator of Ermonville, Sceaux, and La Malmaison. His lively and picturesque conversation, his way of looking at nature, regulating its beauties and enhancing its charms, quite captivated me. I became his pupil. He was not only kind enough to sketch out a plan for the gardens, but he also took the trouble to explain to me how it was to be carried out in its smallest details.

For the last forty years, I have found my happiest moments in those occupations which at starting fitted in so admirably with my life in the country. Later on, when I was in the Emperor's service, they secured me many an interval of much needed recreation, whilst twice over (in 1815 and 1848) they proved my only consolation, when, sick at heart with all the failures and disappointments in the political world, I returned to my horticultural labour. For to replace our intercourse with man by a closer walking with nature is an excellent antidote against the shocks of a Revolution, and greatly helps us to bear it. The bitterness of Fortune's vicissitudes lies in the isolation they entail, with its consequent tedium, and it is only by overcoming this, that we can hope to remain patient and impartial both towards ourselves and others.

The year 1809 opened with the birth of my daughter. My father would have preferred a son, but we had the future before us, and the example of M. de Narbonne made me quite content with the advent of my dear Adèle. As the Molitor battalion was in garrison at Mâcon, we had a very gay winter, and we had a gala baptism. In the spring, I took my wife to Rambuteau. I had not liked to propose an earlier visit to the château, because I remembered my mother's dislike for the place, where she had spent the first four years of her married life. So my satisfaction may be imagined when I discovered that Adélaïde was struck at once with the splendid capabilities of the estate. She was charmed with it, and M. Morel, whom she invited there, suggested various grand improvements. "I have been accused," he said, "of ruining those who have carried out my plans. Here I should like to have the chance of making a fortune, and, at the same time, accomplishing a great work." We spent thirty-six years in carrying out his directions, and every year were more impressed by his strict integrity.

The campaign of Wagram took place this summer. On his return to France in 1801, M. de Narbonne eagerly sought employment at the beginning of every new year. I may as well transcribe here his letter to Bonaparte, dated 2 Nivose, year 12 (December 24, 1803). It shows his disposition and his rectitude ; besides, M. de Narbonne belongs to history :—

"CITIZEN, FIRST CONSUL,—

"I have taken the liberty to request an audience ; I have had the misfortune to learn that it has been refused : a clear proof therefore that some one has prejudiced you against me.

"Otherwise, why should the First Consul refuse to see a man who has returned to France by his permission, whom he himself reinstated in his rank in the army, and who, throughout a revolution, during which it was often difficult not to swerve from certain principles, yet never shrank, for one moment from making all the sacrifices which loyalty enjoined and the love of country demanded.

"The First Consul, whose opinion is the highest of eulogies or the greatest of calamities, would surely shrink from being unjust : and will therefore not refuse—at least I hope not—to glance at the details, which it is of the utmost importance to me to lay before him. I regret that they should be so long, but it seems to me that my whole career, as set forth in them, should vouch for me.

"My name, my fortune, a duchy and grandeeship in my family, the high positions I held at Court under the old régime, might be supposed to insure my future. A very thorough education, all the studies needed for the artillery corps, in which I began my military career, a special study of history and public law, under the most celebrated professors of Strasburg, rendered me not only less dependent on these titles, but constituted personal claims as well. Successively officer in the gendarmerie, the best school of cavalry at that period, and colonel of the Piedmont regiment, which held a distinguished rank in the army, I also pursued the study of diplomacy in the Offices of Foreign Affairs, and, influenced solely by a love of knowledge, I travelled through a great part of Europe.

"The Revolution broke out. Attached to the House of Bourbon by the obligations of duty, I owed the most respectful gratitude and the most entire devotion to Mme. Adélaïde, the King's aunt, whose Chevalier d'Honneur I was, and who for fifty years honoured my mother with the most tender friendship, and conferred the greatest benefits both on her and myself.

"Being fortunate enough not to belong to the Constituent Assembly, where I should perhaps have found it difficult to fulfil all my duties, I believed that I could satisfy my obligations by doing my best to lessen the inevitable evils of such a crisis, and, as I was convinced that the interests of my King and country could not be separated, it appeared to me worse than irrational to try to serve them outside France, or even to imagine that such a

step were possible. My regiment was in garrison at
Besançon, I accepted gratefully the command of the
National Guard of the whole province, having General
d'Arçon as my second in command. To him the First
Consul has shown kindness and consideration. I appeal to
the testimony of another man, not less highly esteemed,
General Moncey, to speak to the good that I have managed
to achieve in that province.

"An apprehension, only too cruelly justified by events,
compelled Mesdames to fly from France ; as it was possible
that I might be useful to them on their journey, I did not
hesitate to follow them. But, after my arrival in Rome, I
obtained their permission to return to France.

"It was somewhat later that the King's flight to Varennes
took place. During that unhappy time, I was nominated to
the post of Field-Marshal, but I was not actually gazetted
until after the King had accepted the Constitution. When
the Legislative Assembly met, I was asked to join the
Ministry. Though knowing full well the cruelly onerous
duties it would involve, I agreed, because I felt sure it was
desirable that the King should have Ministers whose fidelity
to him was above suspicion and on whose loyalty the non-
Jacobin party could rely. The post certainly afforded me
several opportunities for doing a little good, none of which
were, I think, neglected by me.

"The greatest misfortune at that time was the disorgani-
sation of the army ; the difficulty of restoring discipline was
extreme, for distrust, real or pretended, was at its height.
I visited most of the military divisions ; I assured all the
officers, on the part of the King, that he would only regard
those as his true servants and friends who followed his example ; I asked them for their word of honour rather than
for their oath, emphasising vehemently that treason could
never find a place in the heart of a Frenchman, no matter to
what party he belonged. This tour of inspection was useful
in showing the real state of the frontiers. But the duty of
reporting on the latter devolved upon General d'Arçon,
who accompanied me, as, owing to the rapidity with which I

was compelled to accomplish these 'forced marches,' I was quite unable to cope with any additional labour myself.

"The General's name was a sufficient guarantee for the excellence of his reports, indeed their accuracy has been proved by all the best authorities on such matters, as well as by subsequent military events.

"Another means of restoring the old discipline appeared to me to be the nomination of a commander capable of inspiring the army with confidence and respect, without giving rise to any jealousy. French names were lacking. The Duke of Brunswick stood high in military annals. I suggested him to the King, who, after he was assured that this measure would not be rejected by the popular party, ordered me to write to this Prince in his name. I think he would have accepted, if the jealousy of Prussia had not led him to abandon this idea. In spite of the favour I enjoyed in the Assembly, I was attacked in the most trivial details. To insure the execution of my plans, I formed a committee of men, most of whom were subsequently honoured by the friendship of the First Consul, General d'Arçon, General Berthier, Maison, and some others ; and my signature was always placed below theirs. It was I who had the good fortune to organise the horse artillery.

"Intrigues, the inevitable consequences, perhaps, of the moderation of my principles, as well as of my outspokenness, brought about my dismissal at the end of four months. I immediately joined the army of General de La Fayette. I had only been three days in Paris, intent on warning the King of his danger, when the 10th of August had arrived. A warrant was out for my arrest just before the 2nd of September, and I owed my escape, and consequently my life, to Mme. de Staël. Deeply as she fell into disfavour with the First Consul, he would, I feel sure, be the last to forgive me if I were false to the obligations of gratitude and friendship.

"For a time I took refuge in England. The King's trial began. I at first proposed to all his Ministers, who were there, that they should meet in some French port and protest against the responsibility which they were so unjustly trying to lay on the shoulders of the King. They made all sorts of difficulties. Then, in my own name, I solicited from the Assembly a safe-conduct to Paris. I did not obtain it, and had to content myself with drawing up a memorial which (so M. de Malesherbes sent word) might be of service when an appeal was made to the people. War was declared, and I left England to live in a neutral country.

"The line I had adopted led my inclination to coincide with my duty in avoiding all the gatherings of the émigres. During my exile I stayed, first in Switzerland, then in Suabia, then in Saxony. After the peace of Campo-Formio, I obtained permission from the Emperor[1] to join Mme. Adélaïde, to whom he granted a grudging shelter.

"Finally, the 18th Brumaire happily changed and settled for ever the destinies of France. To the First Consul I owe my reinstatement as a Frenchman, and my first care would have been to prove to him my gratitude and devotion. With this object in view, I longed to enjoy the honour and the trifling credit of setting an example to those in the same plight as myself of doing good service, by lending their active support to the Government to which we owe everything and on which alone we can found our hopes. Not one of those requests which M. de Talleyrand (my intimate friend for the last thirty years) ventured to make to the First Consul to place me in the army, or on the government, or in some diplomatic position, was favourably received.

"In the primary Assemblies which followed the 18th Brumaire, I was elected at Versailles, by a very large majority, to be member of the National List.

"Since the changes wrought by the new organic laws, I cannot advance for any nomination the most reasonable and doubtless the justest rights, that of property ; my personal fortune has been entirely confiscated, and that of my wife was in Santo Domingo. Such a situation, while appealing

[1] The Emperor of Germany.

to the benevolence of the Government, renders me to some extent diffident in demanding it. But, if I have nothing else left in the world, I have all the greater claim on the esteem of the First Consul, and I have the noble confidence that there is no Frenchman who deserves it more.[1]

"L. DE NARBONNE."

Nevertheless it was not until 1809 that the Comte de Narbonne was permitted to re-enter the service. The Emperor gave him an excellent reception, and, after Wagram, sent him to Raab as Governor of that part of Hungary, which our troops were then occupying. There, M. de Narbonne discovered that a great movement was on foot to separate Austria from Hungary, and restore the independence of the latter under a sovereign of its own choosing. He was authorised to support it. There were already three competitors for the throne—Esterhazy, Palffy, and another whose name I have forgotten. But General de Bubna, during the course of his frequent journeys to Raab, got wind of it, and as Bohemia also showed a tendency to form a distinct State, with the Archduke Charles as King, peace was hurriedly concluded. M. de Narbonne had to counsel obedience and resignation to those whom he had urged to separatism. The province had presented him with a magnificent silver service for his grand receptions ; this he returned on leaving, to the great astonishment of the donors. Pressed to accept, at least, some kind of souvenir, he would only take a Hungarian costume. He accepted some horses from General de Bubna, nearly all of which he lost from the glanders. My family requited these courtesies, as far as possible, by their care for the ex-Austrian Governor's son, then a prisoner at Mâcon.

After the peace, my father-in-law was sent to the Illyrian Provinces as second in command under the Duc

---

[1] It is surprising that M. de Villemain should not have deemed it necessary to quote this firm and dignified letter. He was acquainted with it, and surely it gives a better idea of the integrity and lofty character of M. de Narbonne than the contents of a whole volume.

de Raguse. The latter kept the generals under his orders at a great distance. M. de Narbonne was informed of this fact. Indeed, at their first interview, Marmont affected to receive him standing. After conversing for a few moments, M. de Narbonne took a chair, saying : "Come, M. le Maréchal, we had better be seated ; I have lost the habit of talking while standing, and I am afraid I might not hear your instructions distinctly." Marmont saw with whom he had to deal. Without further ceremony, my father-in-law, the ex-Minister of War and Marmont's senior, proceeded to sit down, and etiquette disappeared from their relations on this point.

Nominated shortly afterwards to be French Minister in Bavaria, at the request of King Maximilian, his old garrison comrade,[1] he spent some days in Vienna before reaching his post. His old friend, the Prince de Ligne, took advantage of his presence to invite him to a small dinner party, including Comte de la Marck and M. de Metternich. There, in the intimacy of a private conversation, the astute Austrian diplomat exercised all his ingenuity to discover his views on the recent treaty as well as on the Hungarian agitation, the separatist movement in Hungary and Bohemia, and the intrigues with which he was connected. Without denying or confirming these rumours, M. de Narbonne used them as a basis for insisting on a closer union with France, saying : "You have had a narrow escape, but you are too clear-sighted not to see that the present peace is only a suspension of arms. If there is another war, you will be crushed or divided. As matters now stand, France can only side with you or with Russia. The divorce has just been accomplished. The Emperor is bound to think of his dynasty ; he may choose either an archduchess or a grandduchess. On this choice will depend the future and the very existence of Austria."

The next day he was invited to the palace, and received

---

[1] They were both colonels at Strasburg before the Revolution. The Prince, then in the French service, became in 1799 Elector of Bavaria on the death of his uncle, Charles Theodore, and received in 1806 the title of King. His daughter married Eugène de Beauharnais.

with great kindness by the Emperor Francis, who, resuming the conversation of the evening before, told him that he favoured his views, and requested him to write to Paris stating that he was himself in favour of the alliance. M. de Narbonne addressed his letter to Fouché and not to Talleyrand, in whom he had not entire confidence. As a matter of fact, when, during the Fox[1] Ministry, Lord Lauderdale came to Paris to initiate transactions for a treaty, my father-in-law had been recommended to Napoleon by Talleyrand as the best person to take charge of the official negotiations. He had known Fox in England ; their friendly relations had continued in Switzerland and Germany, and that their intimacy had left a deep impression on him I am convinced, for more than once I heard him tell his daughter : " If I had died before you were married, I should have left you as a legacy to Fox, who, I am quite sure, would have justified my confidence by accepting the trust." But circumstances were stronger than the goodwill of the negotiator. Personal friendships, private intimacies, ties of esteem and affection, render conferences easy, but do not weigh a feather in the scales of politics. After the rupture, he incurred the Emperor's displeasure. He even spoke of exiling him. M. de Talleyrand made no protest, while, on the other hand, Fouché vouched for his conduct and loyalty, and spoke of him in the very highest terms.

Nevertheless, Napoleon's anger lasted for several years. Later on, it cooled, for he said to my father-in-law : " How is it that Talleyrand, your old-time friend, and who knew

---

[1] Fox, after a somewhat long residence in France, during which he had numerous conversations with M. de Narbonne, had returned to England, where he vigorously opposed the belligerent policy of Pitt. When he became Prime Minister on the death of the latter, it was hoped that he would promote peace. But the circumstances had altered. The camp at Boulogne and the conquests of Napoleon had widened the gap. Nevertheless, Fox owed it to himself and to his past conduct to attempt a reconciliation. It was with a negotiation for this object that Lord Lauderdale was charged—an official and confidential negotiation, which was doomed to fail, because there was no real desire for peace in England, and because Fox died at the end of a few months. With him vanished this fragile hope of reconciliation which had been entirely dependent on him.

your value, instead of helping you, has always dissuaded me from employing you ? I think that at bottom he must have feared you. He felt that your character exactly suited mine, and he was well aware that those who win their way to my confidence, assure their future at the same time." [1]

It was from this incident that the friendship of M. de Narbonne for Fouché dated.

He was also on good terms with Marshal Berthier, his former staff-officer in chief during his Ministry. I remember the family dinner given by Berthier on the occasion of my marriage. Mme. de Souza had succeeded in getting an invitation to it, and, taking advantage of the fact that my father-in-law could not ask anything for me from the Marshal, she requested him to take M. de Flahaut, her son, as his aide-de-camp. (He was then in disgrace and kept in the depths of Poland by the jealousy of Prince Murat.) "I'll take him with pleasure," said Berthier, "it will be my wedding present to Rambuteau, since not being in the service I can do nothing for him."

Such was the origin of the fortunes of Flahaut : his courage and the Princesses did all the rest for him. He became Napoleon's aide-de-camp and M. de Narbonne's colleague. As for myself, my turn was coming soon, and a better turn than I hoped for, since I was to be attached to the person of the Emperor, and that immediately.

---

[1] We know that M. de Talleyrand was never troubled with much affection for his friends, and could witness their misfortunes with great philosophy. Their disasters left him undisturbed. " Narbonne," he said, "is always chivalrous ; he has nothing, wants nothing, needs nothing. He is fond of study, books, friends—that is the fact. *We need not trouble ourselves about him.* He is too much in earnest. He is too violent, too enthusiastic, too zealous. *If he entered the Government, his devotion to affairs would be too excessive.*" We see that Napoleon hit the mark.

CHAPTER II

CHAMBERLAIN OF THE EMPEROR

ON his return from Wagram, Napoleon (pursuing the plan of action which he had begun with his divorce from Josephine) set to work to increase the prestige of the Imperial Court by making a grand promotion of Chamberlains, Equerries, Ladies of the Palace, and dignitaries of all sorts. I was included in the number as Chamberlain, and my brother-in-law, Adrien de Mesgrigny, as Master of the Horse. M. de Sémonville, our relative by marriage, and very closely associated with M. de Bassano (whose confidant he was both in public and private affairs), contributed far more to my success than M. de Talleyrand, in spite of all his promises. The good odour which M. de Narbonne was enjoying once more, as well as the recommendations of Caulaincourt and Josephine, at the time of my presentation in 1805, were likewise in my favour. There are moments when everything succeeds without effort, and others when everything fails notwithstanding the best wishes of one's friends.

This, too, was the first time I appeared at a political meeting : it was on the occasion of the Electoral Assembly of my Department, consisting of the principal land proprietors. I was very well received the first day ; on the second, however, there was some dissatisfaction. The reason was evident. My family, my antecedents, the piety of my mother, all pointed to my obligations to identify myself with the Legitimist party, although my father had not emigrated, and had always censured the Emigration. Now that I had unreservedly taken the side of the Emperor, I was reproached for it. "But what can I do?" I asked.

" My father left me a velvet coat ; it is not his fault that it is worn out, and that I have to replace it with a cloth jacket, which is now the order of the day." I was nominated by the College almost unanimously, just at the time that the Emperor appointed me Chamberlain, without the one circumstance having any influence on the other. My office obliged me to depart at once, and for a long time. I should have dearly liked to have taken my young wife with me ; but how could I leave my father alone at his age, especially after all the sacrifices he had made for me, not to speak of the embarrassed condition of the property, which required careful management ? Adélaïde devoted herself to her task with courage and affection. Thanks to her, my father's last days were spent sweetly and tranquilly. Through her my duties were amply fulfilled, and various business matters satisfactorily settled.

The beginning of my career as Chamberlain was very pleasant. The divorce was concluded. I regretted the amiable sovereign, who had been so kind to me in her prosperity, and whose son had been my *bon camarade* when we were together in Paris during our early youth. The winter was brilliant. The Emperor spent four or five evenings of the week in his sister Pauline's salon. As he was fond of amusement and gaiety, I was one of the few persons belonging to the Household selected for these reunions, with Just de Noailles, Saint-Aulaire, Lagrange, &c. This brought us often under his eye. He was at that time deeply interested in a Lady-in-waiting to the Princess, Mme. Mathis, daughter of the Senator, who was also Mayor of Alexandria. It was during this period of balls and amusements that the ballet *des échecs* (a chessboard ballet) was given at the mansion of M. de Marescalchi, the Italian Minister. The Emperor was disguised as a negro, and marched in front of the quadrille, blowing a sort of horn. The two Queens and Mmes. de Bassano and de Barral were resplendent with jewellery. I was myself the cavalier of Mme. Pellapra, for whom I had ordered the costume of a Mâconnaise peasant girl. Her dazzling beauty quickly attracted the Emperor. Bausset took charge of all the rest. His fortune started with a ball and a masquerade costume, but his devotion to Napoleon never flagged, even during the Hundred Days.[1]

Shortly afterwards the marriage of the Emperor was celebrated. I was on special duty near him, consequently I witnessed his reception under the Arc de Triomphe de l'Étoile, which was raised in canvas over a framework, much as it exists to-day. By a strange coincidence, thirty years later, I walked, as Prefect of the Seine, under this same arch which recalled so many memories, when escorting his ashes from Courbevoie to the Invalides. At the chapel I was charged to seat the Cardinals. Thirty-four chairs had been prepared, but only twenty-nine Cardinals made their appearance.[2] I ordered the empty chairs to be removed at once ; but the Emperor's first care was to count them. He sent for me on the spot to inquire if any one were missing. I was obliged to tell him how many were absent. That same evening the defaulters received orders forbidding them to appear before the Emperor or to wear their Cardinal's robes. From that day forward they were known as the Black Cardinals.

It would be impossible to imagine a more imposing spectacle than that of the long gallery of the Louvre, with its double row of men and women in their gorgeous dresses, extending from the Tuileries to the Salon Carré, which had been turned into a chapel for the religious ceremony. Stalls had been arranged in the three successive tiers, and the whole scene was dazzling with splendid decorations and beautiful dresses.

All the Queens and Princesses vied with each other in securing the loveliest women for their own retinue—

[1] M. Frédéric Masson says, in *Napoléon et les Femmes*: "At Caen Napoleon has a meeting—was it the first ?—with Mme. Pellapra, wife of the Receiver-General of Calvados, the Pellapra of the Teste Cubières lawsuit. He will find her again at Lyons in 1815, after his return from the Isle of Elba." From the above, it is clear that the first meeting took place at the ballet *des échecs*.

[2] The number of Cardinals who refused to be present at the marriage ceremony was thirteen, not five.—Tr.

Mmes. de Trivulce, de Borroméo, de Lita, de Monte-
catini, de Garlile Morio, de Papenheim, de Loewenstein,
de Bochals, de Rovigo, de Montebello, de Bassano, de
Bouillé, Duchâtel, de Périgord, d'Arenberg, de Schwartzenberg, de Reggio, de Castiglione, d'Abrantès, d'Eckmulh,
Foy, Legrand, &c. The Princesses were charming—
Pauline, Caroline, Stéphanie, Grand Duchess of Baden ;
the Queen of Westphalia, with her dazzling complexion ;
and Queen Hortense, so slim, graceful, and elegant. The
"Vice-Reine" was very beautiful. All the wealth of the world
was lavished on their ornaments, just as all the glories of
France hung on their smiles. It is easy to conceive what
the effect of such a spectacle must have been on a timid
young woman, who, though not exactly pretty, had all the
charms of youth and innocence. What wonder that she
was bewildered in all this whirl of splendour and excitement ! When Marie Louise arrived in Paris, she had a
very good figure, which, after the birth of her son, she
entirely lost. She had a fine complexion and a delicately
modelled foot. Her very timidity added a certain grace
to her : there was something so pathetically appealing about
her. She inspired her surroundings with a mixture of
respect and sympathy, and these sentiments, added to a
general conviction of her real omnipotence, won all hearts
for her. I was at every fête, and was often selected
to open the balls during the time I was waiting for my
special duties to begin, which they did after a journey
to Trianon, whither the Emperor took the Empress to
rest at the beginning of her pregnancy. This occurred
in July.

The grandest of all the balls given on the occasion of
the marriage was that of the Garde Impériale at the École
Militaire. It was the only one in which, by the Emperor's
order, we wore the correct uniform in true knightly style,
with the flat cap and scarf, but without the mantle. I was
in the first quadrille. An immense hall had been constructed for the purpose, but without proper exits, and if
a similar accident to that which happened at the fête of

the Prince of Schwartzenberg[1] had occurred, we must have nearly all perished. That fête had, indeed, very fatal consequences. Luckily it was held in a garden. It was my day of service; I was in attendance on the Emperor, and took part in the first quadrille; I danced with the Princess of Tour and Taxis, sister of the Queen of Prussia, who afterwards married Prince Esterhazy. It was very warm. Suddenly a breeze, the precursor of a storm, made the candles flare, and set fire to the light curtains and hangings. Dumanoir, one of my colleagues, ran to the windows and tried to tear down the draperies. He succeeded, but the decorations which covered the junction of the ceiling and the panels were soon ablaze, and the flames spread over the ceiling, which, varnished with spirits of turpentine, acted like a train of gunpowder. The fire quickly gained the hall.

My proper post was beside the Emperor. I pushed my way through the crowd to reach him. I did not find him on the platform reserved for the Imperial family. But, by mounting on his armchair, I was able to see his little hat in the crush. He had taken the Empress's arm, and was leading her through the garden gate. Glad to know that he was safe, I next thought how to save those around me. They were, for the most part, foreign princesses, and I succeeded in getting them through the door behind the Emperor's platform. The poor Princesse de Layen, after escaping, returned by another door in search of her daughter, and perished.[2] With the help of Colonel Jacqueminot and M. Czernicheff, I raised Prince Kourakine,[3] who was half-burned in his gold and silver uniform. It is needless to recapitulate all the rescues. I was very calm as long as I was in the midst of the danger, but once in the garden I shared the general emotion. Nevertheless, I was glad to have had a chance of testing myself when involved in such great peril, and thus make a trial of my nerve. The

[1] The Austrian Ambassador. He lived in the hôtel formerly occupied by Mme. de Montesson.

[2] She was found with a deep furrow ploughed round her head by her gold diadem which the fire had made red-hot.

[3] The Russian Ambassador.

Emperor escorted the Empress to the Place Louis XV., and then returned to the Schwartzenberg mansion, which he did not leave until he had displayed a lively interest in the efforts to subdue the fire. The next morning, at the levée, he spoke highly of my conduct, whereby he declared I had maintained the honour of my family. I have witnessed few sadder funeral ceremonies than that of the Princesse de Schwartzenberg,[1] whose maternal devotion resulted in the loss of her own life : she was in the garden, but, maddened by the thought of her daughter's danger, who was dancing in the ball-room, returned thither, and was crushed by a falling chandelier.

Some days later, I was on service at Trianon. The Emperor and I went to Saint-Cyr. I rode with the Grand Marshal [2] of the Palace and the aide-de-camp in the first carriage, which was immediately in front of his Majesty's coach. Suddenly a woman rose up before us, clad in mourning and uttering loud cries. She held out a petition which, however, she refused to surrender ; her grief, her tears, and the novelty of the incident made a stronger impression upon me than upon my comrades. When I had alighted from the carriage, the quartermaster handed me the placets. The Grand Master said I had better not bother about examining them ; I could avoid that annoyance by sending them to the Emperor's cabinet, where these sort of things were investigated. I spoke to him then of the poor woman. "Ah," he returned, smiling, "it is easy to see you are a novice. As you grow older you will not feel such pity and compassion, but I am willing to take your place at the loto party of the Empress, should you desire to go in quest of your protégée." I did so, and found her. At night, when the Emperor was about to retire, I spoke to him on the subject of the petition, although it was contrary to etiquette to trouble him with business at such a time. The husband, an ex-soldier of the army of Egypt, had insulted his officer in a drunken fit, and was to be shot the next day at nine o'clock. His Majesty listened indulgently, and answered :

---

[1] Sister-in-law of the Ambassador.   [2] Duroc.

"If you like, you may send a reprieve." At six next morning, I was awakened and informed that Marshal Moncey wanted to speak to me : I got up immediately. He said he must see the Emperor. I answered that my orders were formal, and that he would receive no one at such an hour ; "write a note," I said, "and I will hand it to him as soon as he appears." He was annoyed, even angry, and treated me somewhat cavalierly. I remained impassive. Then he told me he had come to request the pardon of a brave soldier, the man who had been just condemned. I answered that, by an act of great boldness on the previous night, I had got a reprieve and had sent it to General Hullin. He thanked me, we embraced, and he left delighted. I had reason to believe that the Emperor was much pleased with my conduct in this and other respects, especially with my politeness to everybody, which was by no means a prominent virtue amongst my colleagues.

I remember another scene in which Mme. de Kéralio was concerned. She was the widow of the Governor of Brienne when Napoleon was a student there. I mentioned her case to him. "When I have a moment to spare," he answered, "you shall go and fetch her here." One day at Saint Cloud, when I saw he was in good humour, I again spoke of her, and he consented to see her. I at once ordered a carriage and started for Auteuil, where the poor woman lived in great retirement. No one could have shown her greater kindliness and delicacy than he did ; he granted her a pension, and at the same time bestowed immediate relief on her. Unluckily for me, he added : "You have a good friend in Rambuteau. Should you need me again, address yourself to him." Now, for my sins, she had a son-in-law, who for eight months made my life a burden to me. Every day, at seven in the morning, he never failed to put in an appearance, always to ask for some post. To get rid of his importunities I had, in turn, to torment MM. de Bassano and Mollien. The latter obtained for him the Receivership of Mortain, worth 14,000 francs a year. He was satisfied, and I was left quiet.

I next became Commensal of the Tuileries, and was in attendance on his Majesty for a term of three months every year until 1813. For a time I was delighted with my position, which brought me in contact with all who approached the Emperor : ministers, princes, princesses, marshals, great officers, a whole tribe of courtiers in short, who were always on the look-out for a glance from the master, always prompt to scent the slightest symptom of favour. One of my keenest pleasures was to follow the Emperor twice a week to the Council of State. Indeed I often took the place of one of my colleagues on duty, so great was the attraction it had for me. They were always very willing to yield the post to me, for the sessions lasted sometimes till seven or eight in the evening. The Colonel-General was scarcely ever there, but the members of the Council became so accustomed to my presence that, whenever I was forced to absent myself, they took pleasure in sending me a report of the debates. It was a splendid political training to which I owe all my subsequent successes. I learned how to enter into the spirit of public affairs, to seek in every measure the relation between a principle and its consequences, and never to determine on anything without adopting the safe method which I heard one day formulated before the Council of the University by Cambacérès. A certain gentleman, who lacked neither learning nor literary culture, was anxious to make a display of his eloquence. The Emperor, who detested grandiloquence, let him go on for some time, and then made a sign to the Arch-Chancellor to answer him : "Monsieur," said Cambacérès, "we are not at the Academy. We are simply business men, and as such should not discuss matters which have no bearing upon the one object of our labours, namely, the welfare of the Government which we serve. Each of our proceedings should be a link in a great chain which is welded to the one which precedes and to the one which follows. All else is a mere waste of time."

Nor did my interest in these discussions (during which the Emperor often spoke) cease when the sessions came to and end. During the remainder of the evening, when those in waiting were generally admitted to the Emperor's presence, his conversation frequently turned upon the subjects we had been debating ; and which he would sometimes merely discuss *before* us, but just as often with us. He had plenty of discrimination with regard to our respective dispositions. In my case, for instance, he very soon convinced himself of the absolute sincerity of my devotion, and this was no doubt the reason why I was appointed to attend him on his journey to Fontainebleau. But I had now been a year away from my wife and father, with the exception of a week's leave of absence, which was granted me after the marriage festivities. I therefore asked for a *congé* of six weeks. God knows my delight in once more embracing those who were dearest to me in all the world ! On my return, I found my sister in high favour : her husband had been sent to Vienna to announce the pregnancy of the Empress, and she had herself been nominated assistant governess to Mme. de Montesquiou.[1] The Emperor had taken special notice of her, but she was as prudent as she was virtuous, and succeeded in resisting his advances without wounding his vanity. Her reward was his affectionate interest in her fortunes, an interest that never flagged.

The winter of 1811 was very brilliant. I was present at the quadrilles of Queen Hortense and Princess Pauline ; but this did not keep me away from the Emperor, whom I followed everywhere. One evening, when he was to attend a ball given by the Queen of Holland, he gave directions that the Empress should start before him, as he had some work in hand which would detain him. At eleven, he opened the door of his cabinet, and said to me : " Rambuteau, have you your carriage here ? " " Yes, Sire." " Then, you must take me with you." Fortunately, the appearance of my carriage and attendant was all that could be desired, and I was not a little proud of the fact on the present occasion.

I was on service during the night of the 20th of March,

---

[1] Governess of the future King of Rome.

when the Empress was seized with labour pains. The entire Court was assembled, seated at the little tables, where refreshments were served. I can still see Cardinal Maury, seated at one of them with the Grand Judge, the Duc de Massa,[1] both doing full honour to a *poularde au riz*, and thinking much more of the Chambertin than the clanging of the great bell of Notre Dame. At about two o'clock, the Grand Marshal appeared with such a gloomy face that we were filled with anxiety—an anxiety which he made no attempt to dissipate. It was at the very moment when the Emperor was encouraging Dubois, and saying to him : " Save the mother, it is your duty. Act as you would in the case of some grocer's wife in the Rue Saint-Denis."

Worn out with suspense and waiting, we had stretched ourselves on the carpets, when suddenly the door opened, and the Emperor rushed in shouting : *"A salute of two hundred guns!"* It was the announcement of the great event! You could have heard the beating of our hearts. A moment after, Mme. de Montesquiou appeared, holding in her arms the King of Rome, who was shown to us all. We had then some chance of getting a little rest, but only for a while, at any rate in my case, as not more than a few minutes elapsed before I was informed by the Grand Marshal that I must prepare to carry the news to the King of West-phalia. Labriffe was ordered to Naples, Nicolaï to Vienna, de France to Madrid, and Monnier to Carlsruhe.

I received the Emperor's letter at four in the morning, as well as certain instructions from M. de Bassano, together with a letter of introduction to M. Siméon, Minister of Justice at Cassel, and a friend of my father-in-law. I went like the wind, in a briska with four horses, preceded by a courier. In forty-eight hours I was at Mayence, and in seventy at Cassel. I was lodged in the palace, and treated with great distinction. Never in my life have I seen such a galaxy of pretty women as those who clustered around the Queen, and never have I witnessed greater luxury than was displayed by the members of the King's Household. There

---

[1] Régnier, Minister of Justice.

was more gold embroidery on their uniforms than there was silver on ours. I counted ninety-two carriages in the coach-houses, more than two hundred horses in the stables, and the magnificence everywhere was startling, positively incredible. At the grand festival given in honour of my mission, I happened to pay particular attention to a certain pretty young lady of the city ; the next day she was made Lady of the Palace ! I was also greatly impressed by the Gothic castle of Lowenburg, which still retains its mediæval character ; to complete the illusion, the wardens, as well as the doorkeeper and all his family, wore the costumes of the fifteenth century. I had breakfast within the walls at the invitation of the Grand Marshal, when we were waited on by the doorkeeper's daughters, just as in the time of Queen Bertha.

I was afterwards the guest of the King at a splendid breakfast, to which the whole Court was invited. He drew me into his cabinet several times, in order to discuss his personal situation and the policy of the Emperor. I was quite aware that he hankered after independence, and, one day, when he was speaking peevishly of the conduct of the French generals, I said : " Sire, no matter what crown your illustrious brother may think fit to place upon your brow, the noblest title of your Majesty, in the eyes of Europe and of posterity, will always be that of being the brother of a great man. As long as you consent to be the instrument of his designs, our marshals will bow their heads in your presence ; but should you, from motives of personal or political interest, contravene his plans, our very captains would consider themselves released from their obedience." These rather bold words of mine were taken in better part than I might have expected. On leaving, I had every reason to be satisfied with my reception by King Jérome ; he gave me his little Order in diamonds and a very beautiful casket, which necessity forced me to sell later on. Still, I was anything but edified by his surroundings. Many of the civil and military appointments were held by Westphalian gentlemen of considerable importance in their own country, and

who had rallied round the new sovereign, but amongst his
French followers, with the exception of such men as
General Eblé, M. Siméon, M. and Mme. d'Esterno, who
reflected honour upon their country, the others were entirely self-interested, and were only bent on seeking their
own advancement.

I addressed a few questions to M. Siméon on the stability
of the Government. " You can see and judge for yourself,"
was his answer. To give me a chance of doing so, he
invited me to a grand dinner, at which were present some
members of the Diplomatic Corps, all the Ministers—General
M——, Grand Equerry and Minister of War provisionally
during the absence of General Eblé in France, and various
other notabilities. The license with which every one talked
was remarkable. General M—— said to me : " You
ought to think yourself very fortunate in being able to
return to Paris. If only I could do so too ! This con-
founded country ought to be worth at least fifty thousand
francs a year to me to compensate for all the boredom I
have had to endure here. If I once had them in my pocket,
this country might go to the devil for all I cared ! " I
reported his speech afterwards to the Emperor, hence the
disgrace which overtook him when he accompanied the
King to Paris on the occasion of the baptism.

I was very glad to return and resume my service, which
was interrupted only by a week's visit to my wife and
father, with M. de Narbonne. Although my father was in
poor health, I did not anticipate any immediate danger,
otherwise nothing in the world would have persuaded me to
leave him. It took us just thirty-six hours to go and thirty-
six to return. I was on duty on the day of the christening.
When the Emperor held his son aloft to exhibit him to the
people, the enthusiasm was indescribable. Here, beneath
these very arches, nine years before, he had restored public
worship. Here, again, two years later, he had been consecrated Emperor ; so all present were ready to trust the
promises of the future. I have a vivid recollection of those
august ceremonies, at which I was present, as I was at so

many others, all equally ephemeral. The baptismal festivities were as fine as those of the marriage, particularly the fête given by Princess Pauline and the one which took place in the park of Saint Cloud. Then we started for Rambouillet, where the Court spent a few days, preparing for the journey to Cherbourg.

I was the only Chamberlain on duty near the Emperor's person, with General Comte de Lobau as aide-de-camp. It was from that period that our friendship dated. We spent three years together. He was cold and dry, but kind and good, and there never was the least misunderstanding between us. MM. de Courtemer and de Beauvau were with the Empress, as were also Mmes. de Montebello, Aldobrandini, de Périgord, de Beauvau, de Canouville, MM. de Saint-Aignan, de Mesgrigny, d'Oudenarde, as equerries, Prince de Beauharnais, Prince Aldobrandini, and General de Nansouty. In order to reach Caen, we travelled sixty leagues in one day. The question was mooted of lodging at Courtemer, a fine château, on the way ; but my poor cousin Courtemer took more trouble to escape this favour than others would have taken to obtain it, so apprehensive was he of the probable damage and dilapidation it would entail. He assured the Grand Marshal that the château of Lillers at Tubeuf would be much more suitable ; but when we reached the latter, we found that there was not accommodation for half the suite ; so we had to push on to Caen ; consequently Courtemer lost all the advantages which would certainly have accrued to him from this journey from the mere fact of his being a Norman. M. de Mathaud was far shrewder : he placed himself at the head of the Guard of Honour of Caen, and received a chamberlain's key a little afterward.

At Séez, the Emperor gave a very bad reception to the Bishop, and even went as far as to say : " Your hands are still red with the blood of civil war ! " The poor man grew so confused that he could not stammer out a word in reply. His Majesty then ordered me to summon the Grand Vicars to meet him on the next day. After I had announced them

Lobau took me aside, and said : " Monsieur, you are responsible for the safety of the Emperor and I am not, but I do not trust these black robes ; you had better be on your guard." I told him I had requested General Guyot, colonel of the Chasseurs, to keep within call, and that I should be present at the audience. The affair did not seem to me very dangerous ; still, I felt relieved when they had retired.

At Caen I met my pretty partner in the ballet *Les Échecs* again, Mme. Pellapra. I had charge of all the details of the presentations. The Prefect, M. Meschin, asked me to present to his Majesty certain notabilities of the city, among others, MM. de Tilly, Blaru, and the two Sérans, father and son. He did not conceal the fact that the son had been aide-de-camp to the Duc d'Enghien. I laid the matter before the Emperor, who answered : " I will receive these gentlemen ; but as M. de Séran is the head of the family, I shall have done my duty if I see him." He was so kind, gracious, and even fascinating, that they were all enchanted with their reception.

At Cherbourg, the Emperor inspected the works in the harbour, and then went down to the bottom of the rock-hewn basin ; I fancy I can still hear Admiral Decrès saying to him, with a smile : " Sire, you have forty fathoms above your head ! " In good truth, this roadstead is gigantic ; all the walls of the vast basin are hewn out of the granite rocks, straight down. A cutter took us to the battery on the break-water ; the sea was rather rough, and, as the Emperor had no " sea-legs," he leant on my shoulder to steady himself. It drizzled a little, and he took an umbrella from a page, which he directed me to hold over the Empress. I managed, somehow or other, to maintain my equilibrium, but I confess I was not sorry when we landed on the jetty, where we were received with a salute of twelve hundred guns. We visited several men-of-war, especially the *Orient*, from which a salvo was fired, as soon as their Majesties were between-decks. This made a deep impression on all the ladies, which was increased when the Imperial cutter passed lee-ward of the batteries and quite close to them.

The journey, for that matter, was not marked by any important incident. Between Cherbourg and Querqueville, we saw a woman in mourning, kneeling by the roadside with her two children, and holding out a petition, to which was pinned a cross of the Legion of Honour. She was the widow of a brave officer who had been known to the Emperor in Egypt. I handed her forty Napoleons ; she afterwards got a pension, and her sons received free instruction in a lyceum. I always had two or three rolls of gold for distribution ; when they were exhausted, I simply gave my note to Menneval and obtained a fresh supply. I had, in addition, a bag filled with rings, pins, and snuff-boxes, to leave behind as tokens of Imperial gratitude wherever we were hospitably entertained.

Sad tidings awaited me at Saint Cloud : the news of my father's death. This noble old man had expired in my wife's arms, displaying in his last moments the serenity that had distinguished his whole life. "It is not death," he often said, "that disturbs me ; it is the thought of the moment when I shall have to take to my bed ! " He had the sincere faith, the kindly tolerance, the genial benignity of beautiful souls, and had grown old like those generous wines that lose nothing of their strength and bouquet with the passing of time. I have spoken of his tender affection for me ; I will speak of it again, for I am too much indebted to that heartfelt love ever to forget it. How far away are those days, yet how dear and indelible are all the memories connected with them ! Once again I see myself in Paris, leading that careless, if not dissipated life, which his indulgent generosity enabled me to enjoy ; I always wrote three times a week to him. I never failed to go home directly he summoned me, or to share in the procession through our village on the festival of Corpus Christi, when he always leant on my arm ; I spent five or six months with him every year, living that restful and innocent life which recreates both head and heart, as well as health and fortune. I worked during a part of the morning ; in the afternoon, we rambled through our great

D

woods ; then we had a game of cards, and, at nine, I went
to read in the library. He did everything he could think
of to give me pleasure. Although himself a scrupulous
observer of the days of abstinence, he always insisted that I
should have a good pullet or partridge, on the pretext that
Paris had injured my health. He was equally kind and
attentive to my wife, his adopted daughter, who took my
place by his side. He had a very high opinion of her
remarkable sense, which, he believed, would surely save our
fortune, whilst her father was clearing the way for my
advancement in the Emperor's service. He died with the
conviction that she would give me a son who would be held
at the baptismal font by his Majesty, adopted by his grandfather, de Narbonne, and reared under the eyes of my
sister as the companion of the King of Rome. Dreams
that were soon to vanish—how many others have vanished
since !

There was scarcely time given me to shed a tear over
his grave, I was so soon recalled to accompany my father-in-
law on the journey to Compiègne. For the last five or six
months, the question had been mooted of attaching him
more closely to the person of the Emperor. Ever since his
conversation with the Austrian Emperor on the subject of
the marriage, the Court of Vienna had frequently expressed
an earnest desire to have him as Ambassador ; but, as
Napoleon, and especially M. de Bassano, leaned rather to
M. Otto, it was intended to indemnify him by an appointment to some high position. At first, the Emperor intended
to create him Grand Master of the Empress's Household.
Duroc was strongly in his favour ; experience, he said, had
demonstrated the incapacity of both M. de Beauharnais,
Chevalier of Honour, and of Prince Aldobrandini, First
Equerry, for their delicate functions. The same might be
said of the Duchesse de Montebello, who, while really
attached solely to her family and connections, was jealous of
any one who was likely to be a possible rival and interfere
with the influence she exercised over the Empress. The
Emperor's object in selecting these individuals was to sur-

round his wife with persons who would never dispute his will. But having assured himself of their obedience, he soon became equally convinced of their absolute incompetence. Duroc, on the other hand, could find nobody to whom he might safely transfer the direction of the Imperial Household in his absence, and especially in what concerned the control of the Empress, when the Emperor, detained by his protracted and distant campaigns, was no longer at hand to guide her, as he had done since his marriage.

There is no doubt that the influence which M. de Narbonne could not have failed to exercise over the Empress would have left its mark on the destinies of France. Providence did not however permit this, despite the desire of Napoleon, the advice of Duroc, and the approval of Prince de Schwartzenberg, the Austrian Ambassador. The coterie that surrounded Marie Louise joined forces to thrust aside the man in whom each saw, not a wise and safe guardian for her Majesty, but only a powerful and dangerous rival for themselves. Marie Louise, usually so timid and yielding, was prevailed upon to throw herself at her husband's feet and beg him to spare her this annoyance. He used every affectionate entreaty to persuade her to change her mind ; but in vain : she would not yield, and he would not coerce her. Thereupon he summoned M. de Narbonne, and said : "Since the Empress will not have you, I take you myself ; I don't think either you or I will suffer in consequence ; and so much the worse for her, if she has been unable to appreciate you." Then he proposed that he should become his aide-de-camp, and wait until some great office was vacant, adding : "Narbonne, you have no fortune, have you ?" "No, sire, but I have debts." "Well, you shall have 200,000 francs to pay them." Before dismissing him, he spoke of his past, his family, and the duchess, his mother : "She has got no great liking for me, eh ?" "No, sire," was the happy repartee, "so far, she has got no further than admiration !"[1]

---

[1] This delicate art of flattery, this form of polite but pungent frankness, had perished with the eighteenth century. The old society carried away

During the journey to Compiègne, I received orders to modify the usual etiquette. One morning the Emperor said to me at his levée, "No one ought to be on an equality with the Empress; henceforth, you will have all the fauteuils removed except hers and mine." As the Queens of Spain, Naples, Holland, and the Princess Pauline were of the party, I showed some hesitation. "Do as I command," said he; "in this point there is no difference between the Queen of Naples and Mme. de Rambuteau." Nevertheless, when I remarked that there should be some shade of difference, seeing that the Ladies of the Palace were often obliged to make shift with folding stools or banquettes, he agreed that chairs should be reserved for the Princesses. I promptly informed them of these orders, and apologised for being obliged to execute them. In the evening the Queens of Spain and Holland sat down quietly on their chairs, as if there were nothing unusual in the proceeding. "Pray, Monsieur, pray where is my place?" inquired the Queen of Naples very gruffly. I pointed to it, adding: "*The Emperor's orders!*" She wore a perpetual scowl during the rest of the journey. I had also charge of the entertainments, and, one night that Mme. Festa refused to sing, I bore her ill-temper patiently for a time; but finding my remonstrances were useless, I said: "Madame, those who disobey the Emperor sleep in jail. It would break my heart to have to take you there, as I should be unable to keep you company." She laughed, and sang like an angel.

Napoleon lived in great retirement. Save on the Fridays and Sundays when he held receptions, he worked the whole day. At five o'clock he drove out regularly. From time to time, he would cry: "To the right," "To the left," and the postillions had immediately to turn into roads that were often impracticable. Sometimes he started at seven

the secret of it, and fawning sycophancy took its place. Napoleon knew this, and said: "*I am heartsick of all this adulation which prevails around me. You don't believe it possible? Well, to be rid of this adulation, even in the camp, I have had to take as aide-de-camp a courtier and a clever man of the Old Court!*"

in the morning for Rueil or Courbevoie, and spent two or three hours in selecting such non-commissioned officers in the Guard as he intended sending to Spain. He usually unbuckled his sword and handed it to me, for I always followed him into the ranks. He questioned the private as well as the captain, and had notes made of all that he decided upon.

The Council of State met twice a week in the Grand Hall, which has since been used as a billiard-room. There was a fine painting by Prud'hon on the ceiling, *La Sagesse ramenant la Vérité*, which greatly amused these gentlemen, and over the fireplace there was a portrait of Bonaparte crossing the St. Bernard on a piebald horse. The artist had not drawn on his imagination, for the identical piebald horse was at that time turned out, and Napoleon used to visit him two or three times during summer to stroke him and give him bread. I was present at an important discussion which took place at one of the meetings on the National Guard and the organisation of the troops. M. Malouet maintained that the scheme was only conscription in disguise. The Emperor grew angry, exclaiming : " Monsieur, do you suppose me capable of resorting to trickery in order to mask my real intentions or of demanding a sacrifice of the country which has been hitherto undreamt of ! Undeceive yourself. I know France far too well to attempt any such step, and I know how to do her justice. If fortune were ever to betray me, far from concealing my losses, far from reducing my demands, I should on the contrary increase them. France would never hesitate to give me her last man and her last franc." The whole twenty-ninth bulletin of the following year was in these fateful words. On another occasion, when the subject under discussion was again the National Guard, and when the debate lasted from three till seven, although he had taken little part in it, he suddenly exclaimed : " Messieurs, the National Guard is the providence of shopkeepers ! Revolutions are made by arming the *canaille ;* they are prevented by arming the moneyed classes. When you want to obtain good legislation, keep this fact always present in your minds."

I remember another Council, at which the creation of the new nobility was canvassed. Napoleon spoke at great length : "In a revolution you only destroy what you replace ; that which you suppress, but do not replace, is not destroyed. In abolishing titles and privileges, you fancy you have accomplished a grand feat, whereas you have simply magnified the great historic names, without putting anything in their place. What does it matter to a Montmorency or a Rouchefoucauld that he is a Count, a Duke, or a Marquis ? Their name suffices them. But a title gives them an equal. Consequently, when I gave titles to my marshals, when I ennobled them with the names of their victories ; when I rewarded all their brilliant services, all their illustrious deeds ; I took care to bestow new titles on those belonging to the old nobility instead of restoring their old ones to them. And why ? In order to show that in my eyes true nobility could have but one source, one origin, and to prove my loyalty to the cause of equality, that equality of which France is so proud, and which (unlike *liberty*, which is the outcome of caprice) is not debasing but, on the contrary, elevating, because it gives to all alike the right to rise, and does justice to individual merit, I determined that from henceforward no one should be able to say to his subordinate, ' So far shalt thou rise and no farther,' and in so doing I achieved a popular success. I consecrated Equality—so to speak—from its starting-point, leaving talent, courage, and fortune to do the rest."

How well I remember all those discussions. They showed me how thoroughly Napoleon understood the pulse of the people, how well he knew the nation, and how skilful he was in turning this knowledge to his own advantage. He was always declaring that he had a great mission, that of effecting the transition between the past and the future. "I have dethroned nobody," he used to say ; "I found the crown lying in the mud, and in placing it on my own head I restored it to its former splendour."

He was fond of reviewing in thought his various destinies. " I have achieved the greatest success known to history," he said to us one evening. " Well, in order that I may leave the throne to my children, I must be master of all the capitals in Europe ! "

I cannot recall all his sayings, though they recur to me at intervals. Once, also at the Council of State, when we were discussing certain regulations for the University, he said : " Prejudices are great factors in governing, and we have destroyed too many of them ; I only wish I could create a few ; a prejudice is the current coin of more than one virtue. What a misfortune it is that every religious corporation should be dependent on a foreign spiritual sovereign ! If it were otherwise, I should hand over the education of France to the Congregations to-morrow. You will never find in the University so many traditions, such *esprit de corps,* zeal, devotion, and goodwill at so cheap a price ! "

I remember also the crushing onslaught he made one day on Portalis. I had noticed that, on his way to the meeting, he looked absent-minded and dissatisfied. He was scarcely seated when he broke out : " What must you think, Messieurs, of a man who, invested with the confidence of his master, summoned to his councils to enlighten him and lay before him all his various doubts and objections, should yet make common cause with his master's enemies, should possess secret information of their culpable plots, should be the confidant of the most serious plots on the part of a foreign sovereign, lending them the support not merely of his silence, but of his actual concurrence ? Monsieur Portalis, it is you whom I now denounce to your colleagues. Have you a knowledge of the brief of the Pope excommunicating the Emperor ? Have you given it credence ? Have you, instead of keeping the news secret, actually peddled it around ? Do you wish these gentlemen to sit in judgment on you ? " Portalis was thunderstruck. He could hardly stammer out some excuses and protest his good intentions. The whole

Council was astounded too. The Emperor continued :
"You will be good enough to retire, Monsieur ; you are
unworthy of my confidence. It is well for your good
father that he is dead ; your conduct would have killed
him, and it is only his memory which shields you against
my just anger."

All the Councils were not so dramatic. When the
regulation of the polder-land in Holland and Belgium came
up, the discussion lasted for more than three hours, and
yet we could come to no decision as to the share which
should devolve on the State, the assessments, the functions
of the superintending council, &c., for important financial
interests were at stake, and the Treasury might be seriously
involved. The Emperor appealed repeatedly to Cambacérès,
who, with his usual admirable coolness, answered : "What
can you expect ? They have no common sense ! " At
last Napoleon said to him : "So there is no one among
your young people who has a knowledge of the places
and a good idea of the business ? " "Yes, Sire, there is
little Maillard ; he is present now." "Stand up, Monsieur
Maillard," said the Emperor, proceeding therewith, with
his usual precision, to put a series of questions to Maillard
on the origin of the improvements, the successive regulations, &c. Maillard was a little confused at first, but,
soon recovering his self-control, he answered every question
modestly, laid his finger on the dangerous points in the
proposed measures, and demonstrated the advantages
of the old customs and how they might be adapted to
our administrative system so clearly, that his success was
complete. He was congratulated by the Emperor, and
appointed next day Master of Requests on ordinary service,
a post which, at that time, ensured a fortune to the holder.
Napoleon was absolutely unrivalled in his gift for discovering the right man for the right place.

Usually he spoke coldly and somewhat brusquely,
though always forcibly ; but at times he became im-
passioned and approached the sublime. I never admired
him so much as during a discussion in which the situa-

tion of Frenchmen authorised to serve abroad was to be determined. He maintained that no one could break irrevocably with the land of his birth, that the national tie can never really be severed, because the language, the memories, the relationships and associations of all sorts, forge indissoluble bonds between the individual and his country, and consequently the connection must be maintained and protected either by some law compelling him to return in the event of war with other States, or by the infliction of heavy penalties if he should fail to do so. Finally, the Emperor declared that these obligations were equally binding upon those absentee Princes who, in spite of being seated on thrones, still remained (in spite of their crowns) neither more nor less than French citizens in the eyes of France.

We had to carry out every order received from the Emperor with the greatest accuracy. Thus when, one day during the Empress's stay at Saint Cloud, feeling bored at being alone, she saw fit (as she frequently did) to invade the Emperor's study, she came into the ante-room, where I was on duty with Marshal Bessières, and desired me to announce her to Napoleon. I accordingly did so ; but though the Emperor received her at once, he gave me a sharp reprimand in the evening.

"It is unsuitable for the Empress to approach me through your apartments," he said to me. "Should she do so again, I forbid you to introduce her."

He made no exception for any one. I had received orders from the Minister of War to introduce the aides-de-camp of Massena, then in command of the expedition to Portugal ; they all brought bad tidings, positions evacuated, retreats, &c. After the fourth or fifth introduction, Napoleon flew into a passion, and, blaming me for what occurred, asked by what right I took upon myself to introduce couriers, and told me that I forgot my duty in usurping the functions of the aide-de-camp. Then he called abruptly for General de Lobau. The latter listened tranquilly, and replied, with perfect calmness : " Sire, I can only follow my instructions. From morning to night the Chamberlain is responsible for everything; from night to morning the same responsibility devolves on me. Revoke these orders if you will; otherwise, if fifty couriers were to arrive, I should not announce a single one, because that is Rambuteau's business. And now, your Majesty having given me other work to do, I will return to it." The Emperor made no reply. But on the five or six occasions during the day when I was obliged to enter his study, he took care to snub me severely. The next morning, he came up to me in high good humour, and pulling my ears, said : " Well, are you still angry ? Come, come, I know you are attached to me, and that you serve me well, and I am quite satisfied with you." Then he gave me two little taps on the cheek, and spoke of something else. It was the only time he was rude to me during the period of more than three years that I was attached to his service. He was really good-natured, and never failed in courtesy to us, even on the most trivial occasions ; as those who approached him would allow. For instance, if he wanted one of us, instead of calling or ringing for us, he either sent the portfolio-keeper or opened the door of his study himself.

On his return from the Council of State at the Tuileries, which held its sessions in the salon next the chapel, he traversed the grand apartments and the Galèrie de Diane. On the way, he talked of the meeting or of the business he had in hand. In the evening, when he had worked longer than usual, we found sometimes that the dishes had stood untasted on the table for more than two hours ; then he would banter me on the fine dinner I had had—far finer than his. I assured him of the contrary, declaring that the dozen lackeys who had waited on me in solitary state had so spoilt my enjoyment of the good things before me, that I had got through them as fast as I could. I remember a Lake Geneva trout, sent by the Mayor, and weighing forty pounds, which was served to us, because it was too big for his table. Our table stood at the end of the Galèrie de Diane, and had usually twelve or fourteen covers ; but if the Council was held, only two or three of us would be present at dinner, and if it lasted very long, I was often the only one at table.

The Emperor breakfasted at a little round table, generally on roast or grilled mutton, fried chicken, occasionally fish, vegetables, fruit, and cheese ; he always drank Chambertin. He always dined in private with the Empress, except on Sunday, when he gave a family dinner ; then the only guests were all crowned heads.   On the other hand, when there was a hunt, a magnificent déjeûner was laid out at the rendezvous, to which all those on duty and several other guests were invited ; the Emperor took advantage of this opportunity to show attention to certain important personages.

Frequently, he worked ten, twelve, fifteen hours a day, without any interval for rest or refreshment ; then he would say to me : " My legs are swollen, I need exercise ; write to Berthier."   Thereupon he would tire out six horses, take a bath on his return, dine, and then go to bed, sleeping eight hours on end, and recover strength enough to last him for a week.

When he was at Fontainebleau, Trianon, Compiègne, or Rambouillet, a score of persons were selected every day to dine at his table.   The Lady in Waiting, the Grand Marshal, and the Colonel-General presided over the guests. If there were any sovereigns present, they either invited such guests as they chose or sat at the Emperor's table.   But, on ordinary occasions, besides the table for those on service, there were several others ; the first, for the Grand Marshal, who breakfasted at it every day, and to which only the Lady in Waiting, the Ladies of the Empress, the Chamberlains, Equerries, Prefects of the Palace, the Colonel-General, and the Aide-de-camp were admitted.   The second was for colonels of the Guard, aides-de-camp, pages, &c.

Never was a great household conducted upon more strictly economical lines than those adopted by the Grand Marshal.   New candles were only given out to the servants when they produced the burnt-out ends of the old ones.

No fires were lit before the first of November. Our tables were splendidly served, but in our own rooms we could not order anything but cool drinks, Madeira, and rolls. Not a fruit, not a cup of tea, coffee, or chocolate. So that it was quite a pleasant excitement among the Ladies of the Palace to organise little collations. One hung up the *pot-au-feu*, another brought a ham or a *pâté-de-foi-gras*; each insisted on contributing a dish of her own, and no one cared to touch the excellent dinner provided by the Emperor, preferring her own humble supper, which had the savour of forbidden fruit.

Napoleon never expended more than twenty thousand francs on his wardrobe; and he was sometimes angry when that amount was reached. He always wore silk stockings, even with his boots, which were thickly lined. He seldom discarded the uniform of a colonel of the Chasseurs of the Guard, save when hunting or coursing; then he put on the costume de rigueur, always however retaining his grey overcoat. It was only on grand occasions that he donned his Imperial attire. He clung to the little hat, the only person who had the privilege of wearing one like it being the Prince de Neufchâtel.[1] When he insisted that the generals and marshals should wear richly embroidered and laced regimentals, even when not on duty, there was much grumbling. Berthier had his Constable's uniform made of velvet without any embroidery. When Mme. de Montebello expressed surprise at such strict etiquette, I heard the Emperor say to her : " Madame, under a monarchy certain positions ought to be independent of military rank or of fortune. Take the case of your son, for instance, who, as Duke of Montebello, will have the entrée to the Throne-room, no matter if he is a colonel or even merely a captain, whereas captains cannot present themselves at Court, and colonels are not allowed to appear in the Salle des Maréchaux. So you see, that something more than a mere uniform is necessary, since rank is specially recognised." The Prince-Cardinals, Grand Eagles, Dukes, Marshals,

----

[1] Berthier.

Grand Officers, Service of Honour, and the Ambassadors were allowed to enter the Throne-room; the Senators, Councillors of State, Generals of Division, Households of the Emperor and the Princes, Ministers Plenipotentiary, and First Presidents of the Courts of Justice, might invade the Hall of Peace; the Deputies, Brigadier-Generals, Prefects, the Institute, and the Mayors of the thirty-six good cities of France were received in the Blue Salon; while everybody else had to stop short at the Hall of the Marshals.

Every Sunday the Emperor walked to Mass, preceded by his Household. On his return, he would frequently stop and speak to some whom he wished to reward, or to others whom he desired to punish. One day, at Saint Cloud, he reprimanded a colonel, who, during the inspection of his regiment by General Charles de Lameth (the latter had recently been restored to his rank in the service), had treated the General with almost insolent levity. " So you permit yourself, Monsieur," said he, " to judge my acts, to criticise my choice, and disobey your chief! He was only to blame in one respect, namely, for not having arrested you immediately and sent you before a Council of War. An army cannot exist without discipline. You have failed in that : I deprive you of your regiment, and you may thank your former services that I am not more severe." The peremptory tone in which he spoke was terrible. Yet, imperious as was his manner sometimes, no one could show more delicacy in bestowing praise, although the commendation might be only a word or a smile, a gesture or a question discreetly put, but which were enough to show that he had a retentive memory, and were worth more than volumes of encouraging words.

His anger did not last long, especially with his soldiers, for whom he reserved his caresses, jests, and familiarities ; he was proud of them, proud even of their occasional pranks, which always savoured of high-spirited daring.

In 1812, M. de Mesgrigny, my brother-in-law, the Equerry on service, was riding beside his carriage, when an ex-Vendean officer approached with a petition, which he refused to hand to any one except the Emperor himself. Thrust aside somewhat roughly, he retired, but the next day he demanded satisfaction from M. de Mesgrigny : being a gentleman, he could not be refused. My brother-in-law consulted M. de Narbonne, who consented to act as his second. The meeting took place, and Mesgrigny was slightly wounded. The Emperor, at first, showed much irritation. He summoned M. de Narbonne before him, and asked him bluntly : " Since when, Monsieur, have my officers adopted the rôle of knights-errant ? " " Sire, since they have become as jealous of the honour of your House as they were formerly of their own name and epaulet ! " The Emperor's anger cooled ; he even bestowed a small appointment on the Vendean.

This duel reminds me of one which M. de Narbonne fought in his youth, and which he was fond of relating. He was then very much in love with the Marquise de Coigny, and his unsuccessful rival was M. d'Houdetot. One evening he was coming from her house, holding a rose she had just given him. M. d'Houdetot rushed on him, and, without further explanation, obliged him to draw his sword. Not wishing to drop his flower, he put the stalk between his lips, but, in the ardour of combat, he let it fall. While parrying, he stooped to pick it up. This unexpected movement threw his opponent off his guard, and his thrust missed the Count's shoulder. M. d'Houdetot received a wound that disabled him for six months, while M. de Narbonne owed his life to his flower.

But to return to the Emperor : his good nature never impaired his dignity. " With you Frenchmen," he said to us one evening, " it is absolutely necessary to keep one's distance. If you were permitted to shake my hand, you would want to climb on my shoulder." But he spoke without a touch of haughtiness or arrogance ; he was kind and unaffected, and loved the people as much as he detested the mob ; only the *canaille* found him pitiless. Thus, in 1811, there was a somewhat violent riot at Caen, connected with the corn supply. He sent General Durosnel, then Chief of Gendarmerie, to restore order. I was present when he gave his instructions. " Let your justice be quick and prompt, and make examples of a few so as to prevent the worst consequences. Women always believe in the immunity of their sex, and so are always in the van of seditions. Do not spare them ; send them before the provost-court, and if they are condemned, let them be shot with the others." And on this occasion three women were actually shot.

We attended, at Saint Cloud, the first night of M. Raynouard's *Les États de Blois*, which Napoleon wished to hear before authorising its representation. Before he prepared to retire on the same night, he forbade its appearance, and spoke at length of the drama and the historical events upon which it was based. " Henry III.," said he, " allowed himself to be driven into a corner, and the author proves that, but for the murder, a fourth dynasty would have sprung up then and there in France. But it is undesirable to stir up public opinion by such representations."

Some days later the incident of M. de Chateaubriand's address to the Academy took place. It was M. Daru who brought the manuscript to the Emperor on the following morning. The latter seemed to be plunged in thought during the whole day, evidently preoccupied about it. There was a reception, numerously attended, after the theatre. When he had dismissed every one, except those on duty, he reproached M. de Ségur, the Grand Master of Ceremonies, for not having reported the matter to him. " You literary people, you authors," he said, " seek material for your dramas in every direction. Little you care about disturbing a country, or reviving discord, provided you secure fame and success to yourselves. But I, who am bowed down with a heavy responsibility ; I, whose duty it is to allay hatreds, to lull certain memories to sleep, and to enlist all talents in the service of the country ; I, who do not ask men what they *have* done, but what they are *prepared* to do ; I, who place them between two stone-walls, with great rewards before them, and the whip over him who attempts to retreat,—do you imagine that I am going to let you destroy my work, and initiate dissension and civil war, merely because you are seeking literary effects? Undeceive yourselves. You speak of the death of Louis XVI. Does that calamity touch any one more closely than the Empress, whose aunt these people murdered? And after I have at length prevailed on her to overcome her most legitimate aversions; when the first persons I presented to her were Fouché and Cambacérès; when I have gone so far, in order to conciliate the country, will you set to work to resuscitate the past and thus counteract my efforts! Monsieur de Ségur, you should have warned me. It is absolutely necessary that I should know everything. Had the speech been delivered, I would have been merciless Either it will be modified, or M. de Châteaubriand will not be received." [1]

[1] It was not modified, and the author of *Les Martyrs* had to wait for the fall of the Empire before he could deliver it. Châteaubriand succeeded Marie Joseph Chénier. After hearing Napoleon, it is only fair to listen to Châteaubriand on the subject:—

"My discourse was ready. I was summoned to read it before the commission appointed to hear it. It was rejected, only two or three members being in its favour. You should have seen the terror of the fierce republicans who heard me, and who were appalled by the independence of my opinions. They shuddered with terror and indignation at the mere mention of the word Liberty. M. Daru took the manuscript to Saint Cloud. *Bonaparte* declared that if it had been delivered, he would have closed the doors of the Institute and *flung me into a dungeon for the rest of my life.* I went to Saint Cloud. M. Daru returned the manuscript, erased here and there, marked *ab irato* with parentheses and pencil strokes by *Bonaparte.* The lion's claw had scratched it everywhere. The beginning of the discourse was crossed out from end to end. It referred to Milton's views. Part of my protests against the determined effort to exclude literature from all share in public events was also ruled out. The eulogy on the Abbé Delille, which recalled the Emigration and poet's fidelity to the unfortunate royal family and to his unhappy companions in exile, was placed between parentheses. The eulogy on M. de Fontanes was marked with a cross. Almost everything I said about M. Chénier, his brother, and the expiatory altars that were being raised at Saint Denis was ruthlessly scored through. The paragraph beginning with these words: *M. Chénier adored liberty*, was erased with a double stroke. I religiously preserved the mutilated manuscript. Ill luck decreed that after I had left the Marie-Thérèse Infirmary, it should be burned, with a heap of other manuscripts."

Nevertheless, a copy apparently came into the possession of one of Châteaubriand's colleagues. See *Mémoires d'Outre-Tombe*, édition Edmond Biré.

He spoke for a long time. There were only seven of us present ; and no one dared open his mouth. I had had leave to go to Paris the next day, but on leaving the Emperor's presence I told the Grand Marshal I had no intention of doing so now, because Napoleon's remarks would certainly be repeated, and, being the youngest of the party, the blame would be laid on my shoulders. And sure enough, the very next day, Savary informed the Emperor that his words had been circulated abroad, and, as I had foreseen, I was the first upon whom his suspicions fell. He had to look elsewhere, however, as I had never left the Palace. Upon inquiry, it was learned that M. de Rémusat[1] had repeated everything to his wife, who at once ran to tell Châteaubriand. I have always been very grateful to the Grand Marshal, who was invariably kind to me.

I was on service during the entire winter of 1812. M. de Narbonne was aide-de-camp, my brother-in-law equerry, and my sister assistant-governess of the King of Rome. All four of us were lodged next to one another in the Black Corridor. Almost every evening the Emperor invited us into the Empress's apartments, where he would engage in long conversations with us. He was fond of talking, which afforded him a welcome distraction. He always spoke on serious subjects. Once the point at issue was the fate of Louis XVI. ; his integrity, his good intentions, his weakness, were discussed, and one of us insisted that if, at the beginning, he had struck off certain heads, he would have saved his own and the monarchy as well. "No," said the Emperor, "the King would not have averted the storm by getting rid of some of his enemies, for other enemies would have taken their place. When things are ripe for a revolution, men will always be forthcoming to finish what others began. The true reason is that the great majority consists of cowards, who try to discover which side is the stronger, so that they may join it and find safety under its protection. If Louis XVI. had had the courage to risk results, he would have inspired confidence by his resolution and strength of

[1] Prefect of the Palace and First Chamberlain.

E

will, and would thus have become a factor in the new ideas, for it is only when we are sensible of our own strength that we can afford to appear generous. In politics it is sometimes necessary to be in advance of public opinion. Place yourself at its head, and you can lead it where you will. But once allow yourself to be dragged at its tail, and you not only tread the same path but are even forced to go further than you would otherwise have gone."

Another time, Louis XIV. was under discussion ; the Emperor was visibly interested in the early years of his reign. I took the liberty of recalling that Louis XIV., in his *Mémoires*, had paid a tribute of filial respect to the Queen-mother for defending the royal authority during her regency and vanquishing the Fronde, never yielding either to the people, the Parliament, or the princes. He was pleased with this remark, and took the opportunity by enlarging on it of making certain pointed allusions to the regency of the Empress during his own absence, about which rumours were already being circulated. During all these conversations he encouraged us to speak candidly and freely, evincing the same unconstraint and frankness himself.

I did not accompany him on the journey to Holland, doubtless because, at the time, the Empress had refused to accept my father-in-law as Grand Master of her Household. Nor was I with him on the journey to Dresden, and for a reason, which will show what great effects flow from small causes. I was very intimate with Mme. de Bassano, and I tried to cement the friendship between M. de Narbonne and her husband, who distrusted Talleyrand. One morning, Mme. de Bassano said to me : " The Emperor intends taking Talleyrand with him to Warsaw ; but it is a great secret—he reproaches him for meddling in everything. Now, if it were noised abroad that this was the case, without the rumour being traced to us, such an indiscretion would have the effect of keeping him at home." I undertook to divulge the secret with as innocent an air as possible. In fact, that same evening, while playing billiards with Bubna, the creature of Metternich, Nesselrode, and Czernicheff, he began speaking of the list of those who were to accompany the Emperor, as if it were a thing already known, also of the fact that I was to be one of the party. Without appearing to attach the slightest importance to the matter, I said, carelessly, " And M. de Talleyrand also."

The next day his name was in every mouth. The Emperor was furious, and sent for him. " So my plans have been made public property ! " he cried. " Schwartzenberg, who visits you once a month, was with you yesterday, and half-an-hour later Kourakine was there in his turn. So it is you who divulged them." Talleyrand swore black and blue that he had not ; then, reflecting a moment, he cried : " Sire, it may have been Rambuteau ! You know how intimate I am with Mme. de Laval, who treats him as a child of the house. It is possible that I dropped some words when he was present. Besides, he knows everything that passes in your circle, and before now he has disclosed various things." So the Emperor was fairly beside himself, and ordered Duroc to exile me a hundred leagues from Paris. Duroc, however, as I have already said, was very fond of me. He sent for me, rated me soundly, listened to my confession, and, as at bottom he was not sorry that Talleyrand should be deprived of his chance of going to Warsaw, he pleaded for me and calmed the Emperor's wrath. I was only erased from the list, like Talleyrand, who was replaced by the Abbé de Pradt on this mission, that turned out so badly.

On the eve of the Russian campaign, M. de Narbonne was charged by Napoleon to convey his final proposals to the Emperor Alexander at Wilna, before the opening of hostilities. He was well received by the latter, who asked : " What does the Emperor want ? Would he force me to adopt measures that would ruin my people ? And, because I refuse, does he threaten me with war, because he imagines that, after two or three battles, and the occupation of a few provinces or of a capital city, he will succeed in making me sue for a peace of which he will dictate the conditions! He is mistaken." Then, taking a vast map of his States, he slowly unfolded it upon the table, and continued : " Monsieur le Comte, I believe that Napoleon is the greatest general in Europe, that his armies are the most warlike, his lieutenants the most valiant and experienced ; but space is a barrier. If, after several defeats, I retreat, sweeping the inhabitants with me—if I abandon the care of my defence to time, to the climate, to the desert— perhaps *I* may have the last word to say on the fate of the most formidable army of modern times."

This conversation struck M. de Narbonne so forcibly that he related it, word for word, to the Emperor, in the very terms in which I have set it down here. It apparently made some impression upon him, but the die was cast : he was determined to march at the head of all the nations of Europe—save England and Russia—gathered behind him, and to triumph over the one by crushing the other. Never was any expedition conducted under greater splendour ; well might the Emperor consider himself a second Agamemnon, and well, too, might M. de Narbonne say, apologising for his late arrival on a day when he was on duty : " Excuse me, Sire ; I fell amongst a throng of kings, and, in spite of all my efforts, found it terribly difficult to cleave my way through them."

I spent a part of the summer at home and at the Aix waters, where I met the Queens of Spain, Sweden, and Holland, Madame Mère (the official title of Napoleon's mother, the only title given her in all histories, French and English), the Duchesse d'Abrantès, and Princess Pauline. The latter was on a milk diet. I often attended her on her country excursions. Her milk was brought to her at regular intervals, and Mme. de Sémonville, with whom I lodged, supplied me with a lunch in a little basket, so that I might accompany her without being inconvenienced. We had a very fine fête on the lake. Talma was present—I often took parts with him at the Princess's villa, and frequently sang Blangini's nocturnes, both with the Princess herself and Mme. de Saluces. On leaving Aix we made an excursion to the Dent du Chat, where the Prefect gave us a grand déjeûner in the open air under the trees. We visited the state prison of Pierre-Châtel. There, on seeing a cell a little less gloomy than the others, I said to the director : "If ever, Monsieur, I should happen to be your boarder, remember that I hire this cell in advance, for the course of the Rhone can be seen from it." But such a painful recollection of this prison remained with me that, the following year, when I was asked to send twelve hostages to Pierre-Châtel, I flatly refused. After a short stay in Geneva we visited the glaciers. The Prefects of the Leman and Mont Blanc were added to our party, and five gendarmes in full uniform escorted our caravan on the Mer de Glace and as far as Montenvers.

As soon as the Emperor returned, I was at once recalled to Paris and resumed my service. The twenty-ninth bulletin had struck us with consternation ; on the other hand, the Malet affair showed us that the roots of power were not so deeply implanted as we had thought. But M. de Narbonne, on his return, soon convinced me of the magnitude of the disaster. The Emperor, who knew his integrity and candour, had ordered me to send him without delay to Fontainebleau, where he was to try to come to an understanding with the Pope. But his Holiness was leaving just when M. de Narbonne appeared. The Emperor was greatly agitated. He spoke in very angry terms of their differences, and added : "I have enough of all this ; if he will not listen to reason, let him keep his religion—I shall arrange mine with my clergy." "Sire, do not dream of such a thing," answered my father-in-law ; "we have not enough religion in France to divide it in two." This *boutade* calmed the Emperor, who then proceeded to question him upon the dispositions of the Courts of Germany, of which he had just made the round. M. de Narbonne did not hide the fact that everywhere the bonds of sub- mission were all but broken, and that even in Austria a formidable coalition was imminent.

Napoleon became very gloomy ; he had full confidence

in the fidelity of my father-in-law, whose behaviour he had
noticed so lately in that terrible campaign, particularly
during the retreat, in which his cheerfulness, his high spirits,
and his very elegance never forsook him for a moment.
He had observed him seated on a gun-carriage, having his
hair dressed and powdered, leaping from the horses that
sank under him in order to jump on to the hind-seat of the
Imperial berlin, next to Marshal Bessières.   Moreover, the
Emperor had seen my father-in-law distributing the sixty
thousand francs which he gave him at Moscow (of which
not a single sou remained to him at Wilna[1]) to the soldiers
of the Guard.   And he had noted how at every step he inspired fresh courage and vigour into the young officers, who
were half-dead with hunger and fatigue, till at last, filled
with admiration for him, he could not help exclaiming :
" There is something in the blood of your ancient nobility
which distinguishes it from my old veterans.   Their courage
is indomitable in presence of danger, but powerless in
presence of misfortune, which finds them feeble and disarmed ; your young noblemen, on the contrary, have an
inborn sense of honour and duty that sustains them even
when the struggle with destiny is hopeless."

The Marshals themselves, who could hardly be suspected
of much fellow-feeling for one another, much less for outsiders, had evinced their esteem for him, and to such a high
degree that Comte de Lobau and some other old aides-de-
camp and generals of the Guard (who had been hurt at
having to receive an aristocrat among them) said to me,

---

[1] It was not the first time.   At the beginning of the campaign the
Emperor had forbidden all private carriages.   Two days afterwards, observ-
ing a carriage that obstructed the way, he asked to whom it belonged.   "To
M. de Narbonne, the aide-de-camp," some one answered.   Without moving
from his seat he had it burned at once, but at the same time ordered Duroc
to send a thousand napoleons to M. de Narbonne, who was not rich.   Duroc
put the sum in a casket and a few books also.   When the casket reached
its destination, M. de Narbonne kept the books, but handed over the money
to a colonel of recruits to be distributed among them.   Some time later, the
Emperor said to him : "Well, you have replaced you baggage, I suppose.
You received the money?"   "Yes, Sire, but I thought I ought to keep only
the books, notably two treatises of Seneca which pleased me much, a *De
Beneficiis* and *De Patientia*."

after returning from Russia : " We used to think he was only fit to be an officer of the Crown, and now we are proud to have him for a comrade." [1]

As soon as I had an opportunity of talking with him, he said dejectedly : " Ah, my dear fellow, how many lost illusions ! About how many things I thought of writing to you, and yet I never traced a word of them ! But there are two men to whom, as a Frenchman, you should be eternally grateful, and for whom you should cherish the highest admiration : Ney and Caulaincourt ! " I was the more surprised at what I heard because he had formerly censured me merely for calling upon the latter's sister, and I asked for an explanation. " The one," he said, " has saved the army ; the other has shown himself the noblest servant of the Emperor. It would be impossible to discover any one more loyal, devoted, and intelligent, or a more perfect gentleman ; and yet, when he, Lauriston, Davout, Daru, and I insisted that the first campaign should end after Smolensk, and implored the Emperor to reorganise Poland and wait for the spring, the hot-heads of the General Staff dubbed us *the Russians !* As for Ney, he is the victor of Moskowa, but it was at the Beresina that he showed what he really is. History will never again record two such heroic deeds, and, but for him, not one of us would have returned ! "

" Illusions ! heroism ! " here are the last words of that woeful campaign. The Emperor himself acknowledged this. He said at the Tuileries, before Lobau, Davout, and myself : " How easily the best laid plans, the most care- fully studied preparations for future events may be foiled by unforeseen circumstances ! Commanding Europe, dis- posing of all its forces, I had believed that the right moment had come for invading Russia ; I wished to establish a

---

[1] It was surmised by some people that an allusion was made to M. de Narbonne in the phrase of the twenty-ninth bulletin : " *Those whom nature has created superior to all others retained their cheerfulness and their ordinary manners.*" When he was congratulated, after his return, upon this supposed reference to himself, he answered bitterly : " Ah, the Emperor can say what he chooses, but cheerfulness is rather strong."

barrier she could not cross and to retard her progress for a century ; and now, I have possibly advanced it by fifty years."

Before his departure for the Vienna Embassy, M. de Narbonne was on duty every day. Often, during the night, the Emperor would visit him in the first salon, where he lay on a camp bed. Sitting on the edge of the bed and forbidding him to rise, he would hold long conversations with him on public affairs.

One morning, I found him in bed, just at the very moment when his Majesty's levée was to begin : " The Emperor was with me until seven o'clock," he explained ; " he is anxious about the future. 'Narbonne,' he remarked, 'you will die a *Constitutionnel !* ' 'Yes, Sire, it was my first religion.' 'Well, my dear fellow, you must live longer than me, for I want you, as you well know, to rear my son. In spite of all your cleverness, you will make only an ordinary man of him, for superior men do not transmit their genius to their children. But a mediocre intelligence is all that a constitutional sovereign needs. When I have finished my work, all that will be required to preserve it will be a Government to counterbalance it ; the Senate should be made hereditary, and the Chamber of Deputies should have freedom of speech. But before this happens, the Senate must be purified by the agency of time, and an adequate number of great interests interwoven with the preservation of my work and of my dynasty. I shall need from fifteen to twenty years. With a representative Government influenced by personal feeling and dependent on mutual transactions, I should require forty, and then should probably fail.' "

My father-in-law started for Vienna, weighed down by sad presentiments. " I am sent there," he said to me, " just as a quack is called in when the patient is *in extremis.* Two years ago, I might have done much ; to-day, I am powerless to ward off evil." Nevertheless, nothing was omitted that could add to the splendour of his position. The Emperor decided that he should have the largest and most magnificent house in Vienna. In pursuance of his orders, I had forty-eight liveries made ; they were to be of the ancient colours of M. de Narbonne's house, red on red. I was also directed to provide him with twelve body-servants and stewards. A complete set of silver-plate, containing forty pieces, was made for his own table. He himself scattered money right and left. Why should he trouble himself about debts ? Had not the Emperor said, on confiding to him this supreme mission : " On your return, I shall give you a dukedom with a large revenue, and, as you have only daughters, you shall adopt Rambuteau."

The question was even mooted of attaching me to the Ministry of Foreign Affairs and sending me either to Munich, or to Vienna with him. But, as my title of Chamberlain prevented me from occupying a secondary position, I preferred a Prefecture. Besides, to secure the Emperor's favour, one must be useful to him. Now, all his aides-de-camp being generals, there was no place for me among them ; all the great diplomatic posts were also reserved for the military, for it is well to reinforce eloquence of speech with sabres ; consequently, promising as had been my début in the diplomatic line, I was condemned to make no progress. On the other hand, after being Prefect for a few years, during which I could easily distinguish myself, I should enter the Council of State, should then be under the eye of the Emperor, and thus the interest he already took in me would be redoubled. I had been thirteen months in his service. I had had the advantage of listening to his discourses, which I had thoroughly absorbed, and I had been present at the sittings of the Council of State, and had learned the lessons it taught me ; it was high time I should leave school and make use of all the advantages I had enjoyed.

My father-in-law fully concurred in my views. I was at first appointed Prefect of Montenotte ; but Brignole, Auditor of the Council, having also demanded a Prefecture, his mother (a native of Savona), who was a Lady of the

Palace and a friend of M. de Talleyrand, obtained a change, and I was named Prefect of the Simplon. This looked like a kind of slight, MM. de Grave and de Bondy,[1] who had not been longer with the Emperor than I had, having started, the one at Versailles, the other at Lyons ! But I took the matter gaily, and said to my friends : " I have to learn my trade, and I shall do so all the quicker if I am sent to a post where there will be nothing to distract my attention from my duties ; it is all for the best."

For that mater, M. de Bassano pointed out to me that, situated as I should be between Switzerland, France, and Italy, it would be in my power to render services that would attract attention. M. Roederer—to whom I had the good fortune to do a favour—who had arranged all the negotiations for Switzerland, as well as the Act of Mediation, and who had a thorough knowledge of all the men of the country, especially of those of the valleys, was kind enough to lend me his notes, which I read and copied, so that I set out reinforced with most valuable information, which proved exceedingly useful to me later on.

Sainte-Aulaire, my excellent friend, was included in the same promotion,[2] by that sort of fatality that continually associated both our destinies. He was two or three years older than I. We became acquainted in 1798, at Lemire's studio and at the dancing-rooms of Gaillet, where he paid assiduous court to Mlle. de Soyecourt, his first wife, whom he married in " spite of wind and wave." She was very wealthy, but the daughter of an extravagant mother, the Princesse de Nassau. For example, one day when the

---

[1] M. de Bondy was twice Prefect of Paris, in 1815 and in 1830. He was succeeded by Comte de Rambuteau in 1833.

[2] As Prefect of the Meuse. How great was their affection may be judged from his last letter to Comte de Rambuteau : " My dear Philibert, you are the oldest friend I have left; we have probably not much time remaining to us wherein to exchange marks of our mutual sympathy ; and, indeed, the occasions which elicit them are only misfortunes. Yours, however, console me. You have a good and noble heart. As yet the world has not quenched that generous sensibility which thrilled your youth. God preserve you, my old friend, and sustain your courage. We have had the same fortune on earth. Let us hope that we shall be united again in the other life."

Princess was giving a ball, and the bailiffs came to make a distraint, she bade them quite cheerfully, "to make themselves at home." "Take whatever you like, gentlemen," she said, "only please leave us the dishes until after supper."

He married again in 1808, the year in which I also was married. We were named Chamberlains in 1809 in the same gazette, we were decorated together, we were Prefects together, and were both returned to the Chambers by the Departments we had administered; we sat on the same benches, held the same political views, and, still united in a firm friendship, we both returned simultaneously to private life in 1848.

CHAPTER III

PREFECT OF THE SIMPLON

I WAS nominated in March, and started for my new post in the following April. I stopped at Geneva in order to see the Prefect, M. Capelle, and discuss with him the intrigues of which Switzerland was the theatre—intrigues which might have a serious effect on the inhabitants of the Valais, who were by no means reconciled to the French yoke, in spite of the magnificent present which France had conferred on them in the Simplon Road.

This road was undeniably a source of great wealth to a country so isolated hitherto, and, as it were, lost in its own mountains ; for henceforth it would serve as the most important line of communication between France and Italy.

But people are slow to sacrifice memories, customs, and, above all, prejudices, to the acquirement of even substantial advantages, and whatever wounds or merely modifies long-established constitutions is promptly resented. They neither recognise the beneficial results of innovations nor understand at first starting how to make the most of them, but are only aggrieved by the rupture which they entail with revered traditions, and the compulsory acceptance of new customs in the place of old. They can only grasp the unwelcome element of change, which at first always bulks largest in the introduction of fresh conditions without looking forward to the advantages of the future ; and the more backward or stationary a country may be, the more determined it will be to resist all efforts made for its improvement. Apart from this, it must be remembered that the aborigines are not always the first to reap the benefits accruing from radical changes in their condition, seeing that there are usually plenty of foreigners (sharper-witted than themselves) who are for ever on the look-out for windfalls, and run greedily to pocket all the gains to be snatched on the newly-broken ground.

It is the same with the new offices improvised by a new Government—rivalries, jealousies, regrets create distrust, if not hostility. If the mother-country wishes to overcome prejudices, she must send to the newly-annexed countries those only who are able to do credit to her— samples of her finest quality, if I may so speak. Alas ! too, too often has the contrary been the case. Our new possessions served at that time as a sort of refuge for officials whose negligence or incapacity necessitated their removal from the Home Provinces. Indeed, these posts were often conferred upon men whom the authorities preferred to send away in partial disgrace rather than punish by exposing their shortcomings and misdoings. I am quite sure, however, that where this was *not* the case, much of the dislike with which our deputies were universally received disappeared as soon as the people were convinced of the new-comer's personal merits and disinterestedness.

As for myself, I had no such difficulty to contend with from the beginning. My position near the Emperor, the name of my father-in-law, who, as Minister of War under the ancient régime, had frequent relations with the Swiss regiments and Swiss Guards, containing representatives of all the Helvetian families, my courteous manner, and the exceeding affability of my wife, placed me at once in an exceptional position. Mme. de Rambuteau, in fact, always gracious and simple, was only anxious to do good, and prove that the humble domestic virtues were as dear to her as to the rustic households around her ; and, by way of evincing her sympathy with her surroundings, would often adopt the customs, and sometimes even the costume, of the country.

But just then the political state of Switzerland was very grave. I was made fully acquainted with the subject by M. Roederer at Paris, M. Capelle at Geneva, and, especially, by M. Derville, my predecessor, who had lived in the Valais as Minister of France before being its Prefect, and knew the people well.

The Valaisan Republic was originally composed of twelve *dizaines* (ancient city districts), afterward Cantons, each forming a little State, in which three or four families contended for governmental supremacy. The Lower Valais still cherished its ancient hatred for the Upper Valais. We know that the former was subject to the latter before the Mediation of 1803 ;[1] nothing of the old rivalries was forgotten. Every one bowed before the present necessity, but all fostered the memories of their regrets or their hopes in the past, and the reverses we had just experienced gave new life to these unspoken sentiments.

I determined to adopt a waiting policy, to precipitate nothing, to risk nothing, and, whilst never forgetting to be on my guard, to use only kind and conciliatory measures. The Emperor had instructed me to keep him informed of all that came to my knowledge respecting the plots that were then hatching in Switzerland, Lower Germany, and Upper Italy. I succeeded in procuring some devoted and capable agents (one of whom was specially intelligent and rather ambitious, being anxious to leave his country, in which he had no chance of promotion). He gave me valuable information regarding the intrigues of our enemies, and put me in the way of securing an important correspondence which was to be exchanged between them and the malcontents of the Tyrol by way of the Furka Pass.

I had the emissaries arrested forthwith as smugglers by the Custom-house officers. They were stripped of everything they had with them, and even of their clothing. Their luggage was sent to me. After examining it care-

---

[1] The Lower Valais had always been subject to the Upper Valais from the fifteenth century to the Revolution of 1798, when the Swiss Cantons were reunited under the name of *Helvetia*. The *Acte de Médiation* of 1803, dictated by Bonaparte, restored their independence to the Cantons, but placed the Valais under a French protectorate as a distinct Republic, which was afterwards annexed to France, and formed the Department of the Simplon (1810).

fully, we at last found a document of the greatest importance : a ribbon of paper wound spirally round a stick, and
concealed under a layer of varnish. In this the insurrection
of the Tyrol was formally announced, and there is no doubt
but that the scenes of 1809 would have been renewed, had
not Bavaria joined the Coalition.[1] I hastened to forward
this information to Paris, and, from fear of offending the
Minister of Police[2] by appearing to throw doubt on his
vigilance, I addressed it directly to the Emperor's Cabinet,
as he had authorised me to do.

Shortly after my arrival in the Valais, I was visited by
the captain of the Gendarmerie, M. Debrosse, a brave and
worthy man, who had been for a long time a lieutenant
at Mâcon, and had served under my father-in-law in the
Gendarmerie of Lunéville. He came to warn me of a sort
of conspiracy planned at Brigue, where all the leaders of the
party hostile to France were to meet : MM. de Taffiner,
de Riedmatten, d'Augustini, &c., and especially M. de
Sépibus, ex-Grand Bailli of the Valais, and now Sub-Prefect,
as well as two Jesuits, Fathers Godinot and Siniot de
Latour. The instigator of the plot was General Reding,
who had been for long in the service of Spain, but who was
now living in retirement in Schwitz, his native country,
where he was a person of much importance, and was one
of the most active agents of the Coalition.[3] I replied
that I should start the next morning for Brigue, and that
I was going to write to M. de Sépibus to convoke these
gentlemen, as I wished to make their acquaintance. The
poor man turned pale : " Why, you are throwing yourself
into the jaws of the wolf ! " he exclaimed ; " I cannot, at such

---

[1] The Tyrol, taken from Austria and given to Bavaria by the treaty of
Presburg (1805), had risen at the summons of Andreas Hofer, an innkeeper,
and a man of extraordinary energy, who defeated the Bavarians, held our
troops long in check, and made a desperate resistance. After this bloody
insurrection, the Tyrol was annexed to the Kingdom of Italy (treaty of
Vienne), and formed the Department of the Haut-Adige.

[2] The Duc de Rovigo.

[3] As early as 1798 he attempted resistance. At the time of the Mediation he tried to raise several Cantons against the French intervention, and
Ney had to imprison him.

short notice, assemble an escort large enough to protect you,
and General d'Hénin de Cuvilliers, in command of the
Department, though lavish of compliments, makes such difficulties about the slightest thing, that he will not lend his
little garrison of two hundred conscripts without the order
of a Minister or General of Division." "An additional
reason, my dear Captain," I answered, "for going alone,
with only yourself and a single gendarme ; it will show
them that I mean no harm (I have never done them any) ;
and as they are, evidently, not ready for action, they will
listen all the more readily to me. Besides, the Emperor is
still in Paris, and the foreigners are far away ; so there can
be no question of a serious insurrection."

The same day I received a despatch from the Minister of
General Police, who, having been informed by his agents of
the same plots, directed me to seize twelve hostages and
conduct them to Pierre-Châtel. The recollection of this
gloomy prison, which I had visited the preceding year, made
me hesitate to arrest on suspicion worthy fellows whose only
offence was that of regretting the liberty and independence
of which we had deprived them. My fidelity and devotion
to the Emperor could not deter me from selecting the
means I deemed necessary for securing peace and obedience
in the country confided to my administration.

I arrived at Brigue, and found that nearly all the suspects
mentioned in the Ministerial despatch were there to meet me.
M. de Sépibus received me : he was almost an old man, tall
and upright, with grey hair. I recalled the impression his
features had made on M. de Roederer when the latter had
announced to the Valaisan deputies the union of their
country with France. He had stood erect, motionless as a
statue, unconscious of the big tears which rolled down his
cheeks, and not diminishing by a single gesture the dignity
of that mute sorrow. Among the notables thus assembled
were MM. de Courten, ex-officers of the Swiss Guards,
others whose names escape me, and the two Jesuits, full
of that subtle modesty and ability which made the one
Assistant-General of the Order, and the other Provincial of

the Province of Friburg. I spoke to them pretty nearly in these terms :

"Gentlemen, I am well aware of your regrets, your plans, and of your hopes. A stranger to this country and loyal to the Emperor, I have come among you in all confidence on a mission of peace and justice. I sympathise with your memories, but your unalterable attachment to them should not prevent you from listening to the counsels of prudence and reason. Have you foreseen the perils of an insurrection in a Department midway between France and Italy ? The ground upon which your cottages stood is still smoking from the conflagrations lit by General Turreau to avenge the French blood shed in the woods of Finges,[1] through which I have just made my way. Why expose yourselves anew to such cruel reprisals ? If I were a Valaisan I should doubtless regret my independence; still, you would surely be French rather than Piedmontese or Austrians. Do you suppose that because our success deserted us in Russia, it will abandon us for ever ? Well, have a little patience and, if we succumb in the great struggle in which we are now engaged, you will recover your freedom. But, whilst rendering full justice to your courage, let me tell you that it is not ten or twelve thousand insurgent Valaisans who will change the future. You will only incur for yourselves the worst disasters. I know you have just causes of complaint; I know that our Custom-house duties, particularly those on salt and tobacco, are vexatious. My position enables me to draw the attention of the Government to all abuses and injustices. I cannot, of course, either check or redress every wrong at a moment's notice, but I offer you my support and sympathy. In return I ask your obedience, which I will spare no effort to render easy for you. Relying on your loyalty and time-honoured valour, I have come amongst you without fear, hoping to touch your hearts, if I do not succeed in convincing your minds."

---

[1] General Turreau was an expert in conflagrations. It was he who organised the *infernal columns* in Vendée. As to the wood of Finges, a French company was ambuscaded there, May the 20th, 1799.

F

This appeal achieved a certain degree of success. A rather long conversation followed, which I cut short by inviting every one to follow me to the principal inn. Here a banquet had been prepared by my orders, which was much appreciated and lasted almost the whole day. On the morrow, I invited those named by the Minister to visit me, after having previously arranged matters with the Subprefect, who had won me by his frankness, and had made himself responsible for their intentions. I read to them the instructions I had received from Paris, and added : "I have taken it upon myself not to obey them ; and this step should convince you of my attachment to you, and the confidence I repose in you. But you will understand that such a proceeding on my part involves me in a very heavy responsibility. You must pledge me your word of honour to maintain peace and obedience throughout this district. Remember that, if a gendarme or Custom-house officer, or any Frenchman whatever, is assassinated, his blood will fall on my head, but that yours will answer for it. In that case, it would not be to Pierre-Châtel that I should send you, but before a relentless military commission. See to it, that you lack neither the will nor the courage to support me."

All gave me their word without hesitation, and all kept it—at least in regard to what concerned the peace of the country. And, frankly, what more could I have required ? My efforts were rewarded with the Cross of the Réunion.[1]

My assiduous attendance at the Council of State and my special studies had given me a general knowledge of the principles upon which the executive part of government should be based. But I had not yet mastered the practical details, and, firmly believing in the Emperor's maxim, that "to be a good commander, you must understand how to fulfil your own commands," I realised that I could only acquire a thorough knowledge of the different wheels of the machine by seeing them every day at work. With this object in view, I performed the tasks of the heads of the

[1] An Order founded by Napoleon in 1811, in memory of the reunion of Holland with France.

several offices, spending six or eight weeks in each office successively. I begged them to be quite candid in criticising my efforts, and whenever I succeeded in revising any correspondence correctly, or in the drawing up either of a report or a new Act, which would be brought to me later for my signature, I never hesitated to express my hearty gratitude to the man who had initiated me. At the end of six months I was well enough acquainted with the mechanism of the bureaus to be able to speak their technical language, question, consult, and decide in the most difficult cases.

Then I resolved to make a tour of my Department. My wife accompanied me to the St. Bernard during a heavy snowfall on July the 24th. Among my functions was that of Administrator-General of the Hospices of the St. Bernard, the St. Gothard, and the Simplon. To the St. Bernard the Emperor had annexed the Abbey of St. Maurice. The monks of the Hospice lived on fairly good terms with the canons of the Abbey, but they did not meet one another often, for it would have been as difficult to make the austere but active life of the St. Bernard Monastery acceptable to the canons, who were accustomed to the peaceful existence of their cloisters, as to render the silence of the cell tolerable to the mountain Fathers. The union of the two convents was, nevertheless, a measure that showed considerable foresight : St. Maurice afforded an asylum for such of the hospitallers as were worn out by the severe climate of these Alpine regions ; and who till then had had to content themselves with the chance of being nominated to some of the small livings in the valley of Entremont. The Emperor had also appropriated to the use of the Hospice the property of the Chartreuse of Pavia, which enabled them to enjoy a more assured income than that which they had derived from their collections in France, Switzerland, and Italy, and from the alms-box in the Church of St. Bernard. Here, later, they would be able to supply their own needs, and those of the seventeen or eighteen thousand travellers they received annually.

I was extremely interested in the ascent which I made of the St. Bernard, escorted by the two guides who had accompanied the Emperor during the famous passage of 1810, and by the same Father Prior who had led the march. They made me stop every moment to tell me of some detail or other connected with the expedition, or to recall some remark made by the Emperor. They took care to point out the spots where the artillery had to be dismounted, their ordnance placed upon the trunks of trees and hoisted by main force over the steep passes, whilst the gun-carriages, which were detached from their wheels, were transported on mule-back across the bridges.

The attachment of the monks to their monastery is extreme. I can still hear the affecting story of the Curé of Orsières, with whom I lodged the first night, who, with tears in his eyes, described his anguish at quitting this sacred abode, because his broken health made it impossible for him to remain there any longer. It was with the deepest respect that I entered this dwelling, the highest above the level of the sea in Europe.

Eight centuries ago, Bernard de Menthon founded this pious institution, where Christian charity has rescued so many victims from certain death. The whole Order happened to be assembled at the time of my visit. I concluded some rather important affairs to its advantage, one amongst others being the purchase of a spring of water in Lombardy for the Chartreuse of Pavia. The price, 150,000 francs, seemed at first exorbitant. But on closer consideration with regard to the rice-fields, I became convinced that it was a wise step, and would increase the agricultural income by some 15,000 francs.

I also saw the monument of Desaix, hidden by an altar, which the Chapter promised to have removed, so that every one might have a view of the last dwelling-place of our second Bayard, *sans peur et sans reproche*, and might remember the homage paid to his courage by the great man who was indebted to him for his finest victory.

The next morning, all the Superiors of the Order

expressed their thanks to me ; they had, they said, nothing to offer me but their prayers ; as, however, I had lost my father a short while before, the entire Order would unite to offer prayers for the repose of his soul ; this, they hoped, would be received as an evidence of their common gratitude. I was as deeply moved by so delicate an attention as I was by the service, which was celebrated the same morning. The grand voice of the organ amid the silence of the lofty mountains, the sepulchral gravity of the liturgical chants, rising from fifty breasts and intoning the Mass for the Dead, the darkness of the chapel whose windows were lashed by the snow, invested this ceremony with a religious grandeur which will live for ever in my memory.

I brought away with me a herbarium from Martigny, the gift of Prior Canon Muryth, a learned botanist. At St. Maurice I admired certain reservoirs traversed by an arm of the Rhone, and which were so limpid that the evolutions of enormous trout, from fifteen to twenty pound weight, could easily be seen at a depth of several feet. All one has to do is to select and catch his trout. These reservoirs form a part of the revenues of the monastery, which owns great fisheries on the Rhone, and supplies Geneva with the finest specimens exported from that city. I also visited the Val d'Illiez and the Val des Trois Torrents, the only part of the Catholic Valais where I found the industry, comfort, and cleanliness which is to be met with among the Protestants of the Canton de Vaud. I pushed on to the famous rocks of Meillerie, of which Rousseau sang.[1] These have since been blown up in order to make room for a splendid road in the form of a quay. A singular reception awaited me in the valley : the rocks

---

[1] It is near these rocks, *replete with that sort of beauty which only appeals to sensitive natures*, that Jean Jacques laid the celebrated scene which terminates the Fourth Part of the *Λouvelle Heloïse :* "Insensibly, the moon rose, the water became calmer, and Julia proposed that we should leave. The measured sound of the oars had a dreamy effect on my mind. Gradually the melancholy which afflicted my soul grew more intense ; vainly I tried to silence a thousand agonising reflections which awoke in my heart. I recalled a walk I had taken with her during our early loves. 'Gone,' I said to myself, 'are those days of the past,'" &c.

had been mined in more than two hundred places, and
when at a given signal they were all blown up, there
was such a terrific roar as they re-echoed from rock to rock
for more than a league, that the salvo of artillery which
saluted the Emperor on the dyke at Cherbourg was nothing
to it.

I had an important reason for inspecting these works,
undertaken by an Italian, M. Varci (who had already contracted for the works at Crevola and Isella), because shortly
before I left Paris, M. Molé, Director-General of the Department of Bridges and Highways, had strongly impressed
upon me the necessity of keeping an eye on the contractors.
The contracts were always made with the same men, and
they never offered discounts exceeding 3 or 4 per cent.   In
fact, shortly after my arrival, I was called upon to enter
into a contract for 150,000 francs, and that at once.   I
expressed my amazement that no means were adopted to
secure competition.   The chief engineer replied that it was
very difficult to induce persons who were unacquainted with
the country to send in any tenders, and that M. Moska
had had the monopoly of the contracts for a long time.   I
refused my signature, and adjourned the affair for a month,
during which I posted advertisements at Lyons, Milan,
and Turin; and also wrote to my colleagues in other
Departments, asking them to persuade some of the
large contractors to come and examine the estimates on
the spot.

M. Varci offered 16 per cent., and secured the contract,
to the great sorrow of the ordinary contractor, the engineer,
and the cashier, who no doubt had all been in partnership
for many years past.   Having no tangible proofs, I had to
content myself with exercising a rigorous surveillance for
the future.   At the end of two months, Varci asked for an
instalment of fifty thousand francs—a very reasonable request, for he had four thousand Piedmontese labourers to
pay.   This was refused.   He came to me, almost beside
himself.   I then sent word to the chief engineer to accompany me on an inspection of the works the next day;

after we had finished our inspection, he himself brought
me a voucher for an advance of 200,000 francs. "I am
willing to believe," I said, "that the ill-will of your subordinates is responsible for this trouble. But should such
a mistake ever occur again, I shall immediately report it to
the Ministry."

I acted in the same fashion toward the five hundred
Custom-house officers who were stationed along the line of
the Simplon. I had the good luck to find at the head of
the service a man of integrity and courage in the person of
M. Adine, who was a wonderful help to me, both by
reducing them to military discipline and by abolishing the
system of *agents provocateurs,* who set regular traps for the
poor people, who thus became the unhappy victims of design-
ing rogues. Many misdeeds had occurred in connection
with salt and tobacco. I had the proofs of one of these
where the cabin of a poverty-stricken family had been seized
and actually sold because *two pounds* of tobacco were found
in it! I announced loudly and firmly that I would
allow no such abuses, and my humane line of action
was rewarded. For when it became necessary to organise
a guard of honour, recruits from the best families in the
country volunteered to make up the requisite contingent.
I subscribed, and also persuaded others to subscribe, towards the expenses of the necessary equipments, and was
fortunate in obtaining officers' commissions for two of the
most distinguished and promising young men. Thus
the introduction of a measure which led to disastrous
results in other departments caused no disturbance in
mine.[1]

One of the questions that particularly engaged my
attention was cretinism, upon which—its causes, effects, and
the means of curing it—I had to furnish a report. I
collected all the documents I could. I requested reports

---

[1] In 1814, Napoleon commanded four regiments of *gardes d'honneur* to
be recruited among the bourgeoisie and equipped at their expense. They
were in reality hostages for the loyalty of the upper classes of the nation,
which was growing more dubious every day.

from the best doctors in Geneva, Lausanne, Berne, and Turin. I procured all the local information within my reach, and after carefully examining the statistics of the Valais, which, among its population of 75,000, counted 4000 cretins, I arrived at the conclusion that the water, so often accused of causing this hideous affliction, had absolutely nothing to do with it. In fact, on the plateaus and in the higher valleys, where the same water (that of the glaciers) was drunk, there had never been a case of cretinism ; and, if the children of the plains, when attacked by the first germs of the disease, were transported to the mountains, all its symptoms quickly disappeared.

It was proved to me that the extreme heat of the valleys, combined with the exhalations from the swamps, the lives led by the people in badly-aired, fetid houses, surrounded by dunghills, the food consisting almost entirely of salt meat, the scarcity of vegetables, and the abuse of a specially heady wine were the real sources of the scourge. The opening of the Simplon Road, the consequent influx of foreigners, the introduction of the potato, enforced attention to cleanliness in the dwellings, and proper drainage of the land were the measures I suggested for the gradual eradication of cretinism. I know that my report was highly appreciated at Paris, and quoted as the best that had hitherto appeared on the subject.[1]

I paid particular attention to the works executed in the Department, and laid the first stone of the Hospice du Simplon, a building large enough to receive five hundred persons. I was also specially interested in the admirable road that crosses the summits of the Alps from Brigue to Domo d'Ossola. A horseman can ride the whole length in eight hours, and it really resembles an avenue through a garden, with its two magnificent bridges, the one on the Ganter, the other at Crevola—the first opening, and the second closing this triumph of art over nature. I had a

---

[1] Long after, in 1860, Baron Larrey wrote to Comte de Rambuteau for a copy of this memoir, of which he had heard, and for which he had vainly sought in the archives of the Empire.

covered gallery constructed at the Schalbet, one of the most dangerous points of the route on account of the avalanches. At Crevola I saw the marble quarries from which the columns destined for the Arc de Triomphe at Milan were being extracted.

These gigantic monoliths measured thirty-four feet in length and four in diameter. Enormous holes, close to one another, were made in the rock in perpendicular lines, then plugged with dry wood, which was afterwards soaked with water ; the expanding of the wood was sufficient to separate the columns from the block. Their weight was such that the bridge of Crevola had to be shored up before they could be transported across it ; this bridge was five hundred feet high, built entirely of wood, and for military purposes, like the others. The great gallery of Gondo, hollowed in the rock, with vast openings on the torrent of the Saltine, which alone fills this deep gorge, is also a marvellous work, dedicated to fame by this commemorative inscription : " *Via Napoleone*, 1807-1812."

I visited Baveno, Belgirate, Arona, and the Borromean Isles, the latter seeming to me a dream of Ariosto realised. At l'Isola Matré I admired a magnificent laurel, as big as an oak, upon the bark of which Napoleon had himself cut the name of " *Bonaparte*," and which was destined to survive the fortunes of the great conqueror. I should have taken my wife with me to Milan, but I denied myself that pleasure, lest they should say in Paris that I was seeking my own amusement instead of devoting myself entirely to my duties. So I resumed my peregrinations through the Valais, not omitting to visit a single village, nor leaving the most secluded valley unexplored.

I heard Mass every morning before starting. The authorities and the inhabitants hurried from all quarters to receive me ; they barred the way with tables at which I had to sit down, seven or eight times a day, and drink the " wine of honour," offered me on a salver containing a huge tankard surrounded by little glasses. Politeness required that I should clink glasses with everybody and swallow the contents of mine at one gulp, saying first : " *Wollen sie mit mir trinken ?* " They are the only German words I have ever succeeded in retaining, and seemed to give great pleasure to my hosts ; I have certainly good reason to remember them. There is no more hospitable country in the world. Sometimes their hospitality was rather overwhelming, as, for instance, on one occasion when I arrived in a blinding rainstorm at Schinner's [1] house in Ernen, near the sources of the Rhone. At three in the morning I had to appear at a banquet offered to all the mayors and notabilities of the valley, who, you may be sure, showed heartier appreciation of the viands than I did—who had fifty-one dishes placed before me !

During one of my excursions an old man was presented to me as being the best marksman in the district, and it was told me boastfully that, at the skirmish in the wood of Finges with General Turreau, he had brought down seventeen French officers, just as if they had been so many chamois, aiming at them from the top of a rock. I visited the sources of the Rhone above Oberwald ; and have a vivid recollection of a little plain I saw entirely covered with splendid trees, which compared well with the larches I had noticed in the valley of Binn. Those in the latter had a girth of fifteen feet, and were a hundred and twenty feet high ; but the wild and beautiful gorges in which they grew were inaccessible, and it was impossible to transplant them without injuring them. The impression made on me by the majestic forests and the study of the soil—which, as I discovered after, resembled that of our mountains in the Charollais — developed my taste for plantations, to the making of which I have devoted myself for the last thirty years. May they continue to grow and provide shade for me in my declining years !

At Saint-Nicolas, in the valley of Viege, the wife of the Mayor was confined during my stay, and I was requested to

---

[1] He belonged to the family of the famous cardinal, Cardinal Schinner, better known as the *Cardinal of Sion*, who was the very soul of all the Swiss intrigues against France under Francis I. during the Italian wars.

stand godfather to the child. I was somewhat embarrassed as to the nature of the present I should offer on the occasion, but the Sub-prefect assured me that a few napoleons would not come amiss. Nor did they, but I have never heard of my godson from that day to this. These frequent excursions, my endeavour to promote justice and the welfare of the people in every way, the numerous receptions we held, where we never stinted the good cheer of Paris or the generous wines of France, the presents made on appropriate occasions, particularly the silver prize-cups offered at the shooting matches during the local festivals, and, above all, the gracious kindliness of Mme. de Rambuteau, who took care to be constantly seen in the Valaisan costume, and finally, our visits to the mayors, all alike won us universal good-will. "Why can't we have you as our Grand Bailiff?" these worthy fellows would often ask me. I was very much flattered by this general good feeling towards me, which helped them to forget for a time their memories and their regrets.

The time was passing in this pleasant fashion when tidings of the death of my father-in-law reached me, and greatly distressed me. He had been attacked at Torgau by typhus, which carried off seventeen thousand out of the twenty-two thousand soldiers he commanded. He had devoted every moment, night and day, to attending to the needs of his men, visiting in the hospitals, and going from the infirmaries to the ambulances, when an unfortunate fall from his horse obliged him to take to his bed. Then in his turn he succumbed to the disease from which he never recovered. I have already mentioned the forebodings with which he accepted the Embassy to Vienna. He was not deceived as to the success of his mission. His intimacy with the high Viennese aristocracy soon made him aware of the plots brewing against us ; but for all that, he did not strive the less valiantly in the Emperor's interests. I heard Count Roger Damas (who was in Vienna at the same time, as an agent of the Bourbon Princes) declare, towards the end of 1814, that : "M. de Narbonne was the ablest and most

inflexible of our adversaries." For that matter, Napoleon
has done him justice at St. Helena.[1]

When the negotiations were opened at Prague, he was
sent there with Caulaincourt, but the Emperor of Austria
refused all communications with these plenipotentiaries ; he
made strong representations to M. de Metternich : " His
Majesty refuses to receive the French Ministers, but M. de
Narbonne will be always welcome," was the answer. And,
in fact, united with Caulaincourt in the same noble and
loyal devotion which had but one single aim—to obtain at all
costs the honourable peace so greatly needed by them—they
succeeded, by their common efforts, in gaining the Rhine
and Italy, whilst M. de Narbonne himself was charged to
carry this ultimatum to Napoleon. On meeting the
Emperor at Dresden, he used all his endeavours to persuade him to accept the conditions.

" Sire," he said, " France has given you her last man
and her last crown. You have thirty thousand men on
horseback, but they do not form a body of real cavalry ;
your regiments are filled with conscripts, brave, but not
inured to war, who may win a battle, but cannot stand a
reverse or a retreat. Your two hundred thousand best
soldiers are prisoners, or scattered in distant fortresses.
The first check we experience will mean ruin for France
and for you, for now we have the whole of Europe against
us. A peace, though it were only a truce, would save
us. Conclude one, even if only for two years. During
that time you can consolidate all the elements of your
power ; we shall be able to achieve disunion among our

---

[1] In the *Mémorial*, t. iii. page 75, we read :

" Before M. de Narbonne's embassy to Vienna we had been the dupes of
Austria ; in less than a fortnight he had got to the bottom of everything,
and M. de Metternich was very much embarrassed by this nomination.
Nevertheless, see what destiny can do ! His very success was, perhaps,
the cause of my ruin ; his talents were, at least, as injurious to me as they
were useful. Austria, seeing that she was unmasked, threw off the veil and
hurried on her preparations. If we had shown less perspicacity, she might
have acted with more reserve, and more slowly ; she might have continued
to exhibit the indecision that was natural to her, and, during that time, other
chances might have risen."

The Emperor was the prey of illusion to the very end.

Hélio & Dujardin. Paris.

The Comte Louis de Narbonne.

enemies, and you will try your fortune anew. There is at present no other way open to you to procure the happiness, nay, the safety of France. Peace is necessary, and it is my devotion, my loyalty to your person, that makes me ask it of your Majesty on my knees."

The Emperor, alas! refused to listen. He sent M. de Narbonne to Turgau, either to punish him for his hopelessness or to keep him within reach if events should render negotiations necessary. Before leaving, he wrote me a farewell note which ended with these words : "I thank you for having been a good son, and to acquit myself of my debt to you, I bequeath to you my mother." I was faithful to the trust so long as she lived ; I was the devoted son of that venerable mother of the best of men. The Emperor himself was not insensible to this loss. He granted the widow a pension of 6000 francs, the maximum that could be bestowed on the wife of a lieutenant-general, and he sent his aide-de-camp, M. de Flahaut, to offer a pension of 24,000 francs to the mother, the first year payable in advance. Later, during the Hundred Days, he commissioned the Grand Marshal, Bertrand, to inquire if she had received her pension. She was obliged to answer in the negative, and he had it paid immediately. As for myself, I have said enough in the course of this narrative of all the claims which M. de Narbonne had on my gratitude to make the reader understand the depth of my sorrow far better than any words of mine.

Alas! to domestic misfortunes were added those of France, which surpassed our gloomiest forebodings. After the battle of Leipzig, the King of Naples, on his way back to his States, crossed the Simplon and slept at Sion, where, on the pretext of fatigue, he refused to see me. I had a sad presentiment of his approaching defection, for the office I had held near the Emperor's person and my position now as Prefect of a frontier Department were quite enough to explain to me the real reason of this refusal.

Some days later, I was informed that the remains of the army of Italy were also crossing the Simplon. They numbered 18,000, and had to make seven halts on my territory.   Good heavens ! what a condition they were in. When I saw them again I could hardly realise that the were the splendid regiments which, on setting out, bid fair to rival the Imperial Guard !   Now, every single detachment was made up of soldiers each bearing different arms and taken from different corps, there was no discipline, and even the officers were as demoralised as the men.   A successful effort was made, though with great difficulty, to organise a service of supplies for each passage ; then came a snow-fall of from ten to twelve feet, and, after twenty-four hours, all communication was cut off.

Just as the head of the column had reached the Simplon village, an avalanche descended, levelling several houses and killing seventeen horses and five postillions ; the barrack of the Gendarmerie, built against an ancient tower, was carried away and the gendarmes were buried under the snow ; two children were found crouching under a table, and providentially saved ; many soldiers disappeared in the whirlwind of snow, others were fortunate enough to find shelter in the houses of the road-menders, where they were closely packed together, for there were nearly 17,000 of them on the mountain road.   One of the most interesting of the victims was a young colonel of the Italian Guard. His wife and mother had come as far as Domo d'Ossola to meet him.   He had stopped at the Schalbet station, and scarcely a half quarter of a league separated him from the Hospice.   Without concealing from him the risk he must run on account of the constantly recurring avalanches, he was assured on leaving the Hospice that he would find the road passable to Issel and Domo.   He determined to attempt the passage with a dozen of his pluckiest men, but a terrible snow-drift hurled them into an abyss, where their bodies were afterwards found.

I received all these sad tidings at the same moment.   It was necessary, therefore, to provide for the support of 15,000 soldiers drawn up in the valley, and to forward provisions to those who had found shelter on the mountain, as well as to open up a passage for the army through the snow. I had 200 sappers and from sixty to eighty mules, but the public coffers were empty and the stores likewise. I made the journey several times between Brigue and St. Maurice in order to obtain from the local authorities, and especially from the inhabitants, corn, wine, meat, and fodder. I explained to them their obligations to help us, by pointing out to them that what they refused to supply voluntarily could be taken from them by force. They all responded to my appeal—not only those of the great valley, but also those who dwelt in the more remote defiles. As in this country every one lays in a supply of provisions for six or eight months, and sometimes for a year, I had no trouble in providing for the most pressing needs.

I had more trouble in maintaining order and discipline, in spite of the presence of so many officers, because of the mixture of troops from different regiments, and constantly I had to calm down quite serious quarrels. But my greatest trouble was in dealing with the sick. In fact, 1200 men had typhus, and I had no establishment ready to receive them. A certain number were cared for in the Abbey of St. Maurice, and also in Sion; but the great majority were left at Brigue, where I concentrated all my efforts, transforming the immense convent of the Jesuits into a vast hospital. At first the patients had to sleep on straw, but afterward my good Valaisans brought me mattresses and feather-beds from all parts. My Custom-house officers acted as nurses, with a devotion which cost the lives of several of them, as well as of four army doctors.

On the other hand, with the half of the engineers I was enabled to re-open communications; they had become so difficult that at first my messages to the neighbouring villages, either giving orders or asking or offering help, cost fifty, and even sixty, francs. Only imagine the condition of those troops in the mountains, packed into houses intended to accommodate barely twelve or fifteen persons and occupied now by two or three hundred, with 15 feet of snow all around! For a whole week I could not spare the time to go to bed ; I slept in a carriage or on a sofa, ready to start at any moment to the spot where I was needed. At last, the road was so far repaired that the army could descend into Italy, after having rehearsed the terrible experiences of the Russian campaign at the very doors of their native land.

The news from France became more and more deplorable ; the retreat of our troops from the Rhine, the coalition of all the powers of Germany, who from recent allies were now transformed into foes, made the *personnel* of the annexed Departments feel hopeless. Already the Hanseatic cities, Westphalia, and Holland had severed the ties that united them to France ; Switzerland was, to a great extent, devoted to the Coalition, and there could be no doubt as to the reception the ancient Cantons, under the guidance of the old families, who were all hostile to France, would give to the allied armies.

From the end of September I had been advising the Ministers, and even the Emperor, of the plots and intrigues devised against us. Berne and Friburg swarmed with English agents, who not only did their utmost to bring about a separation, but fomented insurrections in Piedmont and Lombardy. I had the good luck to be able to warn my colleague, Alexandre de Lameth, Prefect of Turin, of these proceedings, and so helped to foil them. As to the Valais, I was pretty well satisfied with matters as they stood. Of course, I could not conceal from myself that many amongst them cherished their own plans and hopes ; but the people trusted me—nay, more than that, they gave me plain proofs of their gratitude ; they had followed my advice to wait, and not forestall events ; and, to the last hours of my administration, I had precious evidence of their sympathy.

But it was clear that the invasion of Switzerland was imminent, and I had to think of retreating. Deputies came to me from the two highest districts in the Upper Valais, and invited me to stay amongst them : " You have been," they said, " a father to us ; we will not suffer a hair of your head to be touched." A still more direct step was taken with regard to me by the President of the Little Council of the Canton of Vaud. I had had a good deal of communication with this Canton ; its independence had been proclaimed by France, and it was devoted to the Empire. There was nothing the inhabitants dreaded so much as to fall anew under the yoke of Berne, and with good reason, as its seizure by the Bernese oligarchy had only been prevented by the intervention of the Emperor Alexander, at the solicitation of General Laharpe, his ex-tutor.

Now, at the moment which was so fatal to our arms, the President asked me for an interview at St. Maurice. There he told me that the Canton de Vaud was disposed to take up arms, and that it could put twelve or fifteen thousand men with fire-arms in the field, but that, in that case, it must receive immediate support, and that if a division were sent from Lyons or Marseilles, he would be responsible for everything ; and I might rest assured they would offer a stout resistance.

I could not help expressing my surprise that he should address himself to me rather than to the Prefect of Geneva. He answered : " My colleagues and I know that you are incapable of deceiving us for your own ends, and that you will frankly tell us the truth." He was right. I did not hesitate to tell him the true condition of things. I said we were absolutely unprepared ; after repeated and urgent demands, they had sent me eight cannon and two howitzers to protect the Simplon, but not a single artilleryman, not a single soldier ; all our forces consisted of three hundred conscripts, a few gendarmes, and five hundred Custom-house officers. The Army of Italy, then operating on the Adige, was far away from us ; Turin, Lyons, and Grenoble were denuded of troops. I was therefore forced to renounce the hope of seeing a portion of Switzerland take up the defence of its neutrality ; and, moreover, I had neither instructions nor orders on this subject.

The Allies were approaching ; the Minister of France at Berne and my colleague at Geneva kept me informed of the progress of the invasion ; already Bulle, Châtel-Saint-

Denis, and Vevey were occupied. The proclamation of Prince de Schwarzenberg, enjoining all administrative officials to keep their posts, made my duty quite clear to me. I could not obey the enemy; I must therefore leave. My plan was to march the Custom-house officers and gendarmes of Brigue along the Simplon, and to withdraw the guns by the same route. Monsieur Hénin de Cuvilliers protested against this step. He had never asked for the cannon to be sent to Sion, he maintained. Consequently, if the enemy should seize them in that town, the responsibility for the loss could not devolve on him, as it certainly would if he allowed the guns to be removed on his own authority without having a sufficient force to protect them; and, finally, in accordance with the terms of the military regulations, he should spike the guns and retire. I had no power to oppose this decision.

I had at first resolved that we should start for Geneva on the 24th of December, by way of St. Maurice; but being assured that our little band would need at least three days to make the journey, during which it would be exposed to great danger, after consulting with the chief officials, I proposed to the General that he should head the column and effect a retreat by way of Chamonix. It would be more fatiguing, but safer. He replied that his official duties ceased at the boundary of the Department, that a major ought to suffice for the command of half a battalion, and that it was not his business to take charge of Custom-house officers, gendarmes, and civilians. This refusal entailed great obligations upon me. I could not remain deaf to the urgent solicitations of eight hundred Frenchmen thus left to themselves, and so, in the very depth of winter, without money, without resources, we had to cross fifty leagues of mountains, travelling through the snow and over impracticable roads, always with the additional risk of encountering insurgents or enemies on the way. I became the guide and leader of the party, being convinced that by sharing all its toils and sufferings, I should, at any rate, insure its confidence.

From Martigny, where I had assembled my people, I sent letters to the mayors and curés of Vallorsine, Le Tour, Argentières, and Chamonix, asking for their aid when we should reach these towns. We set out at noon on the 25th of December, a beautiful sunny day. I took care to have double rations of bread and wine distributed, so as to keep up their spirits ; indeed, I made over the contents of my cellar so entirely to them, that on the march I was obliged to beg, now and then, for a few mouthfuls of sherry for myself.

Two women insisted on sharing our dangers—one, the wife of a Custom-house official, whose courage was greater than her strength, and whom we had to leave behind with the curé of Vallorsine ; the other, the daughter of the Tax-surveyor, who refused to abandon her old father. Clad like a man, she followed us gayly, and, thanks to her twenty years, her vigour, energy, and the care we took of her, she arrived safe and sound at the end of our six days' march.

The snow was so thick that it measured fifteen feet at the Trient and the Col de Balme. We reached Trient at midnight, preceded by guides with lighted torches, whom we followed in Indian file, for no one could remain on horseback. I had even been obliged to get off my mule. The gendarmes brought up the rear, but by way of relieving the young soldiers, who were uninured to fatigue and over-burdened with the weight of their arms, provisions, and munitions, I organised a platoon of guides who were to follow *en queue* and help the stragglers. It had been agreed that they were not to receive their wages until our arrival, and then only on condition that no one was missing from the roll-call. Our experiences in the fifteen or twenty châlets along the Trient were rather unpleasant ; the snow was packed up around us as high as the roofs, which we feared every moment would be staved in by the horses we had tethered on them. Outside, it was about 12 degrees below zero.

When we entered Vallorsine the next day, it was a touching spectacle to see how all the priests of the neighbouring parishes had come with their parishioners to meet us, and to do all in their power to clear a path for us. Early in the morning they had assembled their people in church, saying, " My children, we are gathered together to pray to God, but no prayers can be so pleasing in His sight as the help we give our neighbour. A large number of people are on their way here, struggling through the snow ; let us go and give them all the assistance in our power." Ah ! where should we have been without their help in that plain called the Val des Morts (Valley of the Dead), which lies between Vallorsine and Argentières, and where we found eighteen feet of snow ! In spite of the trench opened by the inhabitants, we sank up to the waist, and marched between dazzling walls six feet high. "If a breeze were to spring up," said the parish priest of Le Tour, "not a man of us would leave this spot alive."

I do not know what would have become of us but for these good people ; yet they would accept nothing, not even those who received us with the kindest hospitality in their houses during the night ; the only thing I could do was to leave tokens of our gratitude in the alms-boxes of the churches.

On the evening of the second day we reached Chamonix, fairly worn out ; on the third we were at Salanches, and I was in hopes of entering Geneva on the day following, when I heard that the Austrian outposts were close to the city ; I resolved, therefore, to retreat in the direction of Chambéry.

At Ugine, where I arrived with the vanguard, we found an excited crowd, which was evidently hostile to us. I had written to the Mayor, asking him to procure supplies for us ; he had done nothing of the sort. At first he tried prevarication ; but presently, taking hold of one of my uniform buttons, he said : "The French are thieves, and you won't get anything here except for ready money." This insolence might have cost him very dear, for my gendarmes had already flown at his throat, without heeding the murmurs of the crowd, and I had the greatest difficulty in calming them for the moment. But when the rest of the column arrived, the news spread like wildfire through all the ranks, and I realised that, if we remained in the town for any length of time, I could not answer for its safety. So I had a fire lit in the square, a table set for the Staff, bread and wine distributed, and, after an hour's halt, we set out for Saint-Pierre-d'Aubigny, where we arrived at ten in the evening, after a march of fourteen leagues in seventeen hours. There, at any rate, we were better treated, and my men had some rest.

The next day we were at Montmélian; there I found a carriage, and started for Chambéry, where my colleague took the necessary measures for assuring the future welfare of my caravan. From what a responsibility was I thus relieved! I learned all the news from him, and that M. Capelle, Prefect of Geneva, was at Fort l'Écluse. As it was very important that I should see him, I travelled on the stage-coach to Frangy, accompanied by my calash, in which my secretary-general had journeyed to Chambéry, where he was awaiting me. No doubt we might have exchanged places. But oh! the intense satisfaction I felt in having successfully piloted my little band into port, and myself set them the example, which they had the right to expect from me.

Surely that was well worth a carriage!

At Frangy I took a guide for Fort l'Écluse, who was to lead me by a cross-cut. But I found that I was likely to encounter an Austrian outpost on the way, and so, hiring a cart, I retreated with all possible speed.

At Bourg, I mentioned to the Prefect the importance of sending succours to Fort l'Écluse and Bellegarde. But neither he, nor his colleague at Mâcon, nor, in fact, the Prefects of the neighbouring Departments, had received any orders whatever, and no one thought of anything but of packing up his belongings and making ready for flight. I confess I was thoroughly astonished and bewildered. I had thought it natural enough that my Department, which had been incorporated with France by sheer force, should evince its ill-will, but it was totally inconceivable that, at the news of the invasion, all France should not arise as one man! Nor was I greatly surprised at being left to myself like some forgotten sentinel ; but that ten days should be allowed to elapse after the passage of the Rhine by the Allies without a single measure being adopted, without a single decree issued, without a single order transmitted to the Departments from the Ministry of the Interior—*that* was simply inexplicable. I expected to see France bristling with bayonets, and I found Prefects strapping their trunks ! I suffered as much grief and shame as if I had been myself responsible for such weakness.

I entered Mâcon on the 1st of January 1814,[1] seated on two bundles of straw, without a servant, and in the clothes I had worn during the preceding ten days. My wife had just arrived from Paris two hours before me. The Emperor had received her at the moment when he learned of the invasion of Switzerland and the passage of the Rhine. These sad tidings did not lessen the friendliness of his reception. He repeated that he should never forget the children of his friend M. de Narbonne ; that he was perfectly satisfied with me, and should always be delighted to find me employment in some other post, adding that all our family might count upon his affectionate protection. Before a week had elapsed, I was appointed Prefect of the Loire.

[1] On the day of his arrival at Mâcon, Comte de Rambuteau sent to the Minister of the Interior a detailed report of his splendid retreat, with sundry incidents connected with his administration which he has not mentioned in his narrative. He also gave his reasons for selecting the route to the Col de Balme, the most difficult, but the only practicable one, both on account of the piles of snow on the St. Bernard and the approach of the enemy by the St. Gothard, thus preventing all attempts to march along the Simplon Road.

CHAPTER IV

PREFECT OF THE LOIRE

AFTER my nomination on the 7th of January 1814, I hastened at once to my post, for the impending invasion, far from discouraging me, inspired me with new courage. To a certain extent the Emperor's misfortunes, in some sort, enhanced his glory and increased my zeal and devotion to his person. Full of confidence in his genius, I was determined not to lose faith in his good fortune, and, in any case, I was only the prouder of serving him in his reverses. I now recalled a saying of Duroc, the Grand Marshal, at the time when I was Chamberlain. One day I expressed a wish for some position which would be more useful and important than that which I held near the person of the Emperor: "Have patience; we shall have plenty of fighting before long; then there will be hot work for everybody!" I very soon realised this during my retreat over the Simplon, and I was burning for revenge!

So I started, full of ardour, for Lyons, of which Marshal Augereau had just assumed the command. I met Cardinal Fesch a few stages from the city: "Why, where are you going, my dear fellow?" he cried, as soon as he saw me. "Do you want to fall into the midst of the enemy?" "Monseigneur," I answered, "when did your Eminence leave Lyons?" "This very morning." "Then I am sure to be safe for, at least, two days." He was not offended by the tribute I paid to his prudence, and wished me good luck.

At Lyons I found the Marshal in despair. "I am sent," he said, "to command the army at Lyons; the Emperor speaks of 20,000 men; I have not four thousand! And it is I, an old veteran of the Army of Italy, who am selected to surrender the second city of France to the enemy!" He had tears in his eyes. I reminded him of his past glorious services; I extolled the good-will of the people, I spoke of the approach of several regiments belonging to the Army of Spain; and lastly, I insisted on the instinctive hesitation, the uncertainty, and timidity that were sure to mark the first attempts of the Coalition, which (as I firmly believed) would be sure to inspire our troops with a certain degree of confidence in themselves. In short, he consented to put on a bold face, and, setting the National Guards in motion, succeeded in intimidating General de Bubna, who was advancing on the city. But in spite of all this, our outposts were so severely repulsed by a reconnoitring party of cavalry, that the Marshal said gloomily: "If our enemies were Frenchmen, Lyons would have been taken this very day!"

We discussed all the plans to be adopted at Saint-Étienne for the manufacture of arms, the dépôts of the different regiments that were to muster there, and the recruiting and mobilisation of the National Guard. Then I set out for Montbrison.

Whilst passing through Roanne, I had acquired some useful information as to the situation of the country and the administration of my predecessor, M. d'Holvoët. He had been entirely unable to prevent abuses, particularly those connected with the conscription; and so, either from idleness or from prudence, he had seen fit to hold himself aloof from such matters, and thus escape all the responsibility which he might otherwise incur.

Two days after my installation, I wrote to the Minister of War,[1] with whom I was personally acquainted :—

"Monseigneur, I am always ready to give my fortune and my life for the service of the Emperor; but there is one sacrifice beyond my strength—it is that of honour. When a person is obliged to make all sorts of demands with a view to the safety of the Fatherland, when the

---

[1] General Clarke. His daughter had married M. de Fézensac, a cousin of Mme. de Rambuteau.

ordinary guarantees of the law are more or less inverted, the executive power should be sheltered from all reproach, and even from the slightest suspicion. Now, having been placed only quite recently at the head of the Department of the Loire, though I cannot furnish you with any proofs, yet I am none the less convinced that the Council of Revision sells its resolutions ; and I must warn you that it is therefore impossible for me to co-operate with it, and in consequence I demand a fresh election of its members ; if I cannot obtain this amount of justice, I shall be compelled to send in my resignation."

A military courier brought me the reply of the Minister, who charged the Marshal to replace the Commander of the Forces in the Department, the Sub-intendant and the captain of recruits. The Marshal sent me a blank nomination form, in order that I might choose a general on the spot from those who were on the retired list. I at once sought the Marquis de Rostaing at his château ; he had gone through the American campaigns with M. de Lafeyette. He had known M. de Narbonne, and even served under him. I begged him to give his judicious and far-seeing support to the first acts of my administration, which would make an excellent effect on the whole country. He consented, and I had good reason afterwards to congratulate myself on his support. The members of the Council General and the important people of the Department gave me a helping hand, along with an absolute confidence that were extremely useful to me.

I paid particular attention to the decisions of the Council of Recruiting ; I noted them all with my own hand every morning ; I nominated the physician who was to have charge of the examinations during the day. I had 2500 conscripts, and, after they had been thoroughly inspected, it was discovered that there were only 1900 men fit for service. I abided by the decision, believing that it was my duty to furnish soldiers for the army and not for the hospital. I informed the Minister of what I had done, and he approved it. Before me, it was the

custom for the authorities to enlist conscripts in excess of
the contingent demanded, fearing that otherwise they might
not appear sufficiently zealous.

I visited Saint-Étienne several times ; I took all the
necessary steps for accelerating the work of manufacturing
arms, and we were enabled to deliver eight hundred guns a
day, the sole resource of the Army of Lyons, and even of
the South. Consequently when, through fear of the
invaders, the Minister of War ordered the factory to be
dismantled, I supported Marshal Augereau in resisting this
extreme measure, which he wished to defer till the last
moment.

My exceptional situation was constantly imposing new
duties upon me. I wrote out my own orders, which I took
to Lyons and laid before Comte Chaptal, ex-Minister of
the Interior, recently sent thither by the Emperor as Commissary Extraordinary. The first time I explained to him
my methods for supplying the needs of the army out of
the Department, he did not allow me to finish : " My
dear friend," he said, " you know as much about the matter
as I do, and, besides, you have the advantage of youth
and activity. I will sign blindly whatever you submit
to me."

He quite agreed with the arrangements I had made for
the work of manufacturing arms, and on the necessity of
devoting the money collected in the Department to that
purpose ; he considered I was justified in the circumstances
in requisitioning the products of nature, and authorised me
to dispose of all the departmental and communal funds, and
even those of the hospitals, the sums so used to be reimbursed hereafter. He did so because I had to meet very
large expenses ; the organisation of the mobile National
Guards, the works of defence undertaken by the Department
of Highways and Bridges, the obstruction of the march of
the enemy, and the concentration of arms and munitions.

On the other hand, Marshal Augereau demanded four
hundred horses for his artillery. When he began to enter
into a multitude of details as to how I should set about

procuring them, I said : "Monsieur le Maréchal, you may order your dinner, but you will kindly leave me to do the cooking. I should be quite incapable of leading one of your divisions, but I know how to manage my Department. If I were to follow your suggestions, it would entail my bringing some three or four thousand horses to the county-town. Most of these would probably be so unfit for the service, that I should have a great difficulty in picking out the requisite number, and even then the chances are that those I selected would prove unmanageable on the very first day, would break their harness, and leave your gun-carriages on the road. Only give me 240,000 francs, and I will undertake that you shall be well served." He consented.

I summoned the principal horse-dealers of Lyons and Saint-Étienne, and said to them : " I know that my col-leagues offer you seven, eight, even nine hundred francs a horse, and that you serve them badly, because you don't know when you are to be paid. I will give you five hundred francs, but the horses must be perfectly fit for artillery, remount and carriages. They will, moreover, be examined by military officers. The half of the price will be lodged with a banker ; the other half will be paid you in a fortnight after the sale. I know that a great number of beasts are available, in consequence of relays and stage-coaches having ceased to ply on account of the advance of the enemy. You will therefore have no difficulty in accept-ing my terms. I shall rely upon your doing so."

They accepted my proposal, and I pursued the same plan with the saddlers who supplied the harness.

As I had nearly 3000 conscripts at the dépôt, I was able to make a selection of those who understood the manage-ment of horses, so that within three weeks I furnished no less than one hundred teams to the Marshal, without which he would never have effected his advance on Franche-Comté. At the same time, I organised provisional squadrons and battalions among the refugee soldiers in the seven dépôts ; and this was the nucleus of the little Army of the Loire of which Montholon took command when he arrived later as Commander of the Forces in the Department.

I had also organised the service of requisitions, which were fairly divided by a commission of the Council General between the several communes according to their resources, so that, for two months, I was able to distribute 14,000 rations daily, and send assistance in grain and coal to the Army of Lyons. I was equally successful in paying for the work on the fortifications thrown up before Roanne and Rive-de-Gier, thanks to the devoted aid of M. de Tardy, ex-officer of Engineers and member of the Council General, and of M. Populle, Mayor of Roanne.

I was not less active in organising the National Guard, which was largely recruited from soldiers on the retired list. My next step was to obtain the *matériel* part of the defence, namely, fire-arms, ammunition, &c. I discovered that my Department could boast of four pieces of ordnance, which dated from the Revolution ; these, at my urgent request, were supplemented, by my colleagues in the Allier and Puy-de-Dôme, who after similar searches sent me ten guns, but without carriages. I had some caissons constructed, monopolised all the ammunition of the Department as well as a quantity of powder which was brought from Lyons to Saint-Étienne, so that I had fifty charges for each of my guns and 250,000 cartridges at my disposal as well ; I requisitioned all the lead for sale to make balls.

As for fire-arms, as I was forbidden to touch those manufactured solely for the army, I called the principal gunsmiths together, and said to them : " In the Loire and in the neighbouring Departments there are plenty of rifles belonging to private individuals, besides all those that you have in your shops. Now if you will put these into good repair, I will undertake to give you twenty-seven francs for each, provided they have been inspected and passed by one of the artillery officers, who are official experts in the manufacture of arms." In a few days I had eight thousand, and was thus enabled to equip two battalions of the mobile National Guard as well as of the stationary National Guards, whom I succeeded in mobilising and converting into regulars.

Later on, instead of despatching their units to the defence of Lyons, who would have been practically useless, I mustered a contingent of two thousand in the barracks. These were commanded by officers on the retired list (to whom I granted an indemnity from active service in the event of a campaign) as well as by non-commissioned officers selected from the veterans who had been "called out." My little band, who were well fed and well treated, behaved excellently, and when the moment came for me to present them to the Marshal about the beginning of March, I had not a single desertion. He reviewed them at once, and was so extremely delighted with them that he assured me afterwards that he felt he was dealing with old and experienced soldiers. Some days afterwards he sent me the Cross of the Legion of Honour, an award which was confirmed by the Government.

The boatmen of the Loire, who were also organised as a National Guard, were very enthusiastic. They defeated several detachments of the enemy that had returned into the district, making a number of prisoners, whom they brought to me ; and these little successes infused such confidence into the brave people of the district that they vigorously repulsed a sudden attack on Roanne and Charlieu, so that the Department of the Loire could still hold its own, although Mâcon in the Seine-et-Loire had been occupied since the 15th of January.

This was the moment when General Montholon assumed command. Finding four or five thousand bayonets at his disposal, he made his arrangements to reinforce Augereau, and thought fit to advance on Franche-Comté. I have always regretted that he did not prefer the right bank of the Saone, which would not only have covered his march and safe-guarded his flanks, but would also have afforded free communication with the Departments of the centre, thus enabling him to form a junction with one of the corps of the Grand Army under Lyons. Instead of this, he exposed himself to be taken in the rear by the Austrian force which was descending from Langres on Dijon, Chalon, and Mâcon, and which soon obliged him to fall back on Lyons, whose defence was becoming more and more difficult on account of the number of assailants.

Thereupon I visited the Marshal, in order to express to him my anxiety as to the fate of Saint-Étienne in the event of his being driven to evacuate Lyons, and the situation in which I should find myself, in spite of the measures taken to protect Rive-de-Gier and to retard the march of the enemy. He promised to move a division on my line of defence, and gave orders to that effect to M. Ducasse, his principal staff-officer, in my presence. But, as in every serious affair, it is better to take three precautions than one, I left at Lyons two reliable agents, who were to keep me informed of all the operations.

I believed that Augereau could still hold out for ten days or so. Great, therefore, was my surprise when one of my agents arrived at nightfall, not twenty-four hours later ! He was one of my horse-dealers, who, enheartened by the hope of a reward, had screwed up the necessary courage and shrewdness to make his way through the enemy's out-posts. He reported the retreat of the Marshal, whose whole army he had seen defile on the bridge of La Guillotière *en route* for Isère, and not a single regiment, not a single battalion taking the road to Saint-Chamond.

In plain words, I was utterly unprotected. But I imme-diately issued orders for the handful of troops quartered at Montbrison and on the banks of the Loire to march with all speed on Saint-Chamond. I sent information of what had occurred to Montholon at Roanne, I mobilised all the National Guards, and galloped in the dead of night, through pouring rain and along abominable roads, to Saint-Étienne. As soon as I arrived, I ordered four cannon to be despatched to Rive-de-Gier, with the men of two dépôts and all the National Guard that could be mobilised ; then I directed the tocsin to be rung uninterruptedly in thirty or forty communes : so that in less than twenty-four hours the lines which covered Rive-de-Gier were put in a state of defence. This rapid concentration disconcerted the enemy, already embarrassed by its occupation of Lyons and by the necessity of watching Augereau's army, which had fallen back on Vienne. It limited its operations to making a few reconnaissances, but did not venture to push forward to Rive-de-Gier.

This state of affairs lasted for ten days, and it is needless to say that I made the most of each day. All the important fire-arms factories were dismantled, their machinery taken to pieces, and the transportable *matériel* carried to the mountains. Thus I saved 120,000 guns, so that the task of equipping the troops could be resumed after the evacuation ; and, as reconnoitring parties were now advancing as far as Montbrison, I made Saint-Bonnet-le-Château the chief town of the Department, where all the heads of the Administration rallied round me.

My wife and children, who had joined me shortly before, were in safety there ; they had spent a part of the winter in Rambuteau, which was in the hands of the enemy, and had been even threatened with being kept as hostages, with a view to preventing us from offering any further resistance. However, the movement of Augereau on Franche-Comté, which caused the Allies to fall back, had released them, but only for a time, and now I had to seek another refuge for them. Mme. de Montholon and her children were with them. They were all placed under a good escort, along with the money-chest of the Department, and started out for their new residence. At nightfall the leader of the detachment wished to spend the night at Saint-Rambert in the plain. My wife opposed this vigorously, urging their danger, reiterating my imperative orders, and demonstrating the responsibility that would be incurred if the money of the Department fell into the hands of the enemy. In consequence of her remonstrances the party pushed on for Saint-Bonnet, and it was lucky it did, for that night Saint-Rambert was occupied by the enemy.

After the capture of Saint-Étienne I went to Roanne,

hoping to prolong its resistance by means of a diversion agreed upon between Montholon and me. Knowing exactly the strength of the enemy, and feeling sure that we could rely on the temper of the country, we were convinced that, if two columns started from Roanne and Tartare, they would drive the Allies back to the suburbs of Lyons, whilst a third column, commanded by the Colonel of the 60th Regiment of the Line, would operate on Charlieu and march rapidly to Mâcon, where the grand park of the artillery of the Austrian army was but feebly guarded. The people of the Charollais and Beaujolais would have followed us *en masse*, and the success of our surprise would in two days have disorganised a part of the troops opposed to Marshal Augereau, who had the better chance of resuming the offensive, and, perhaps, re-entering Lyons, bècause he had just been reinforced by detachments of veterans from the army of Marshal Suchet.

Our movement was already in operation, and Montholon was within three leagues of Lyons, when he was informed that Augereau had retired behind the Isère and burned the bridge, and that in two or three days General Hardeck, with 22,000 men, would be before Roanne.

In this case resistance was no longer possible. Nevertheless, we had not allowed ourselves to be disheartened by the news of the capture of Paris, and I had made every effort to respond worthily to the first proclamation of Marie Louise ; but was I justified in uselessly sacrificing a town which, for the last three months, had given the noblest example of patriotism ? I therefore charged the Mayor and one of the colonels to treat with General Hardeck. He knew our situation, and had admired the courage of our little army, and now he granted us the most honourable conditions. All the troops had permission to retire to Auvergne with arms and baggage ; the inhabitants were to suffer no annoyances of any kind by way of retaliation for the defence they had made and the skirmishes in which they had taken part ; neither would any war-tax be levied on the town and its environs. The capitulation was signed on the 10th of April.

I joined my wife at Ambert, where I learned the abdication of the Emperor. I then proceeded to Clermont to request a passport from General Hardeck. He proposed that I should return to Montbrison, where the Prince of Hesse would accompany me and re-establish my authority; but I had no difficulty in making him understand that I must go to Paris and receive instructions from the Government. 1 accordingly set out immediately with my wife.

I shall never forget the painful spectacle presented by that long route, lined at intervals with foreign troops and with the enemy's encampments, through which we were perpetually passing. Nor can any words describe the gloom and silence of Fontainebleau, nor the pitiful condition of the *débris* of the Guard, and the intense melancholy which pervaded the surroundings of the Château. One seemed to feel oneself literally in the actual presence of death.

I was most anxious to receive the Emperor's last orders. "Farewell," he said; "you have served me faithfully, but you belong to your country. Go to Paris, and do your duty, but do not forget me."

As soon as I arrived in the city, I called on MM. de Jaucourt, d'Alberg, and Montesquiou, members of the Provisional Government. I told them where I came from, what I had done, and asked what they wished me to do. "Save France," was the answer; "and, to start with, tell us what is happening in the provinces through which you have just passed, for we are really ignorant of everything outside Charenton."

I very soon put them *au courant* of everything. We then discussed the armistice, and they told me that the course of the Loire would be taken as a line of demarcation between our troops and the foreign armies. This, I represented, would not only relinquish Saint-Étienne to the enemy, but such a boundary would prove delusory, because during spring and summer the river is fordable at almost every part. I further represented the impossibility of stationing the army corps there which they wished to con-

H

centrate in that direction ; I insisted that the line of the
mountains resting on the Rhone, Allier, and Loire would
be far more suitable, and, finally, my suggestions were so
far appreciated that my presence was commanded on the
evening of the 22nd of April, in the Cabinet of the Comte
d'Artois, Lieutenant-General of the Kingdom. I then said
to him : " Monseigneur, in the situation in which you are
placed, your enemies of yesterday are your friends to-day,
whilst your friends have become your enemies. All that
France lost lately you took from the Emperor ; all that it
surrenders to-day you take from the King." Unfortunately
I was only partially listened to, but the line of defence was
rectified in accordance with my suggestion, and I received
orders to set out immediately for the Loire, from which
the Allies were obliged to retire on the 30th of April, and
give place to a part of the Army of the Alps.

I had conferred previously with MM. Louis, Beugnot,
and the Abbé Montesquiou. The latter tried to disgust
me with the career of a deputy-governor : " The husband
of my niece," he declared, " should seek something better
than a mere surveyorship." Therewith he urged me to
enter the Gardes du Corps, which was about to be revived.
I answered him gratefully, but firmly.

" How can I," I asked, " at the age of thirty-three, and
at the very moment when peace is proclaimed, assume
epaulets which I never won on a field of battle ? And
though I am still willing and able to serve my country, I
am not disposed to change the livery which, rightly or
wrongly, I have always worn hitherto."

I left my wife in Paris, and hastened to return to my
post for many reasons. In the first place, I already saw the
dawn of a reaction against which I wished to defend those
who had so courageously supported me ; in the next, I
thirsted to get away from the capital, where I was sick of
witnessing so many recantations ; for the triumph of the
foreigners distressed me far less than the sight of the
Frenchmen who truckled to them, by boasting how they
had played the part of traitors the day after our misfortunes.

I was very glad to be able to find a refuge among those simple folk who, till within a fortnight, had never despaired of France, and whom I was now determined to protect and succour. I found myself the butt of the malevolence of all those who hoped to gain importance for themselves by opposing me ; but I let them talk as much as they liked, steadily ignoring their foolish insults, which I requited with silent disdain, devoting all my attention to business.

Five regiments, consisting of between eighteen and twenty thousand men, had been ordered to the Department. It was necessary to provide them with quarters and victuals. For this I had to use my best efforts. I had asked M. Louis : " Can you get on without the *droits-réunis* (united duties)[1] the suppression of which was announced in the first royal proclamation ? " He did not conceal the fact that he thought it impossible. " Then," I said, " I shall restore them, for I do not wish my people to accustom themselves to an illusion more difficult to destroy than to provide against."

In this matter I could depend on my staff, which I found intact ; it had full confidence in me, and the habits of obedience and discipline in which it had been trained were not likely to have suffered by less than four weeks of foreign occupation. I availed myself of its aid in spreading details concerning the new condition of affairs, besides information concerning our obligations, the wants of the army, the imperative necessity of collecting the taxes, and thus avoiding the renewal of requisitions and arbitrary assessments. To prevent the dispersion of the workmen, I persuaded the merchants of Saint-Étienne to subscribe money enough to purchase 15,000 pounds of bread daily, which I doubled at the expense of the Department ; and when an attempt was made to stir up the working-people on account of the *droits-réunis*, I appeared at their meetings, accompanied by some merchants and officers of the National

---

[1] Taxes collected on objects of general consumption—drinks, &c. They were abolished by the Revolution, but revived under Napoleon. Louis XVIII. promised in the Charter to suppress them, but did not keep his promise.

Guard, and addressed them as follows : " Was your wine cheaper when the *droits-réunis* were abolished during the foreign occupation ?   No, the only persons who profited by their suppression were the vintners.   How can I feed you if the taxes, my sole support, are not collected ? "

They listened calmly, and I quelled two riots without having recourse to force, as I could and should have done if I had not gained my object by persuasion.   I must also acknowledge the valuable aid I received from the *prud'hommes*,[1] who had an exceedingly delicate task in the circumstances.   The time fixed for their re-election had arrived.   I went to Saint-Étienne, and requested the mayor to appoint me President of the Board.   The reasons I put forward, coupled with my recent entreaties, induced them to accept a new warrant, and in years to come the recollection of their devotion to me on this occasion stimulated my efforts to establish this useful institution in Paris.

Meanwhile, the expected troops had arrived ; they were two fine regiments, consisting of ten battalions, the 16th, 29th, and 24th of the Line, the 4th Hussars, the 12th Dragoons, and a detachment of artillery which had just returned from Spain, where they had formed a part of the army of Marshal Suchet, and who were smarting under the reverses in which they had not shared, and the change of Government.   It was rather difficult to preserve peace among them.   I kept open table for the seniors and principal officers.

I was informed by the Treasurer that, instead of the month's pay which had been promised, he had received only 50,000 francs.   I immediately sent for the Receiver General, who had more than 300,000 francs at his disposal, but he informed me that the tradesmen of Saint-Étienne had bills of exchange of long-standing on the Treasury for more than 240,000 francs.   The situation was serious. The commanding officers of the different corps had already warned me of the difficulty they had in controlling their men.   What would happen if the men were not paid ?

[1] A board of arbitration consisting of masters and workmen.

On the other hand, how could I promise the credit of the Treasury by presenting a draft it was unable to honour, at the very moment that a new Government was established ?

I repaired to Saint-Étienne, convoked the Chamber of Commerce and the leading merchants, and laid the situation before them, emphasising my temporary poverty and the imperious necessity of paying the troops if we were to avoid serious trouble. They gave the matter their immediate attention, the result of which was an undertaking to suspend the presentation of notes for twenty days, and to agree amongst themselves to redeem the securities of those who could not wait so long. In return, I formally pledged myself to have the incoming taxes of the Department placed to their credit until there was a complete liquidation. I then proceeded to the Receiver General's office with two gendarmes, where I deposited an official report recording that I had broken the seals of the Treasury, and taken 250,000 francs, independently of the sum paid the Treasurer, and, as soon as the operation was finished, I wrote the full details to the Ministers of Finance, War, and the Interior, all of whom entirely approved of my action.

One of my earliest projects was to re-establish a commission for liquidating the requisitions and forced sales of supplies ; it was composed of members of the Council General. During the whole duration of their labours I gave them the hospitality of my home. I persuaded the Government to allow me to use the *centimes extraordinaires* of the Department for this liquidation, which was concluded by a final payment of 1,780,000 francs, 25 of which were paid for fifty hens, estimated at 50 centimes per hen, thus proving that the poor man's hen was estimated as highly as the rich man's ox.

All the same I still remained a victim to the intrigues of the new Royalists, who believed they were enhancing the glory of their principles by compassing my dismissal. I had defended the country against their friends the Allies ; and this was an unpardonable crime. But that was not the judgment meted out to me in Paris where the Abbé de

Montesquiou, Minister of the Interior, said to my wife :
" I have carefully scrutinised your husband's conduct. I
find it entirely free from blame, and this is an additional
reason for not transferring him to another Department at
the present moment. But if he does not feel comfortable
at Montbrison, I give him *carte blanche* to make Roanne or
Saint-Étienne the chief town." I refused, because I did
not wish to appear apprehensive. There was no doubt that
Saint-Étienne was a much more important centre. I was
constantly obliged to be there. Moreover, I was convinced
that the change would some day become necessary ; but as
I was equally convinced that it would involve the ruin of
Montbrison, I did not wish to incur the odium of making
it, and preferred enduring any amount of fatigue and worry
to the adoption of a measure which, as matters stood, would
seem the outcome of my own selfishness.

It was at this time that, being advised of the approaching arrival of the Duchesse d'Angoulême, who was just
then at Vichy, I thought it my duty to pay her a visit and
receive her commands. I knew she was surrounded by my
detractors, but I preferred to go and meet the danger rather
than to await it. Accordingly I set out from Roanne,
where I had just received the Dowager-Duchesse d'Orléans,[1]
who actually begged me to ask an audience for her, although
she did not conceal the anxiety and embarrassment which
such an interview would cause her. As soon as I entered
Vichy, I called upon the Duchesse de Séran, her Royal
Highness's Lady-in-waiting. She had known the Duchesse
de Narbonne, my wife's grandmother, and, profiting by this
circumstance, I begged her to obtain a private audience for
me ; my request was granted.

I found the Princess alone with Mme. de Séran.
Though not exactly beautiful, she had a noble presence
and was very dignified, and the profound pity which I felt
for the misfortunes she had borne so bravely seemed to
invest her with an aureole, and only increased the respect

---

[1] The Duchess-Dowager, wife of Philippe d'Égalité and mother of Louis
Philippe.

with which she had always inspired me. Consequently it cost me no effort to approach her with the greatest veneration.

I told her that, on hearing of her impending visit to my Department, I had considered it my duty to pay my respects to her : "Having been informed that your Royal Highness had expressed some unwillingness to meet me, owing to the calumnies of certain persons desirous to injure me in your good opinion, and feeling that only those enjoying the confidence of your Royal Highness should occupy positions similar to that which I hold, I hasten to lay my resignation at the feet of your Royal Highness, should you deem me unworthy of your esteem ; for, indeed, I feel no special attachment to my post, which I only retained at the express desire of M. de Montesquiou and in obedience to the formal orders of Monseigneur the Comte d'Artois ; and which I would gladly relinquish rather than incur the misfortune of displeasing you by retaining it."

The Duchess replied that my well-known devotion to Bonaparte justified her prepossessions and her fears. "Madame," said I, "I was not reared in a spirit of either hatred or opposition to your family. For three centuries all my ancestors served yours ; and many of them died on the field of battle. Whilst still too young to defend you, I shared the prison of my relatives. Later on, it is true, I entered into engagements with the great leader of my country, whom I served in the days of his victories, and I did not desert him in the day of his reverses, but defended the post assigned me until the last moment. You reckon these acts as crimes ; I am ready to expiate them by resigning my office, but not to disown them." The Duchess then put several questions to me concerning the Department, the troops, and the population, which I answered frankly, and she added : "Now, Monsieur, I feel that I know you ; and, far from desiring your dismissal, I request you to remain, and shall report favourably of you to the King ; furthermore, to prove what confidence I repose in you, I commission you to draw up a list of the changes you would wish to have made in the official staff of your Department." As regards any changes which I might desire I answered : " My reply, Madame, is contained in a single word, *None*." Then she fired up.

" I have been warned," she cried, " that my kindness would be misunderstood, and my advances repulsed by the creatures of Bonaparte———" I let the torrent run its course. When she had finished, I said, with perfect calmness, " I must beg your Royal Highness to reflect that nothing but a strong sense of duty would induce me to risk your Royal Highness's displeasure at the very moment of receiving a favour from you, for which I should never have dared to hope. But as regards my good people in the Loire Department, their only fault has been that of both trusting and obeying me implicitly. What justification, therefore, could I have for persecuting those whose sole offence lay in their obedience to me ? When the King confided 400,000 of his children to my care, it was in order that I should hold out my arms to them and guide them to his feet, not that I should place myself at the head of some that I might punish the others with stripes. There is no one at the present moment of sufficient importance to be considered dangerous ; we must therefore wait and note the conduct of each. Should any fail in fidelity and obedience, I shall be the first to execute justice. But a massacre of the innocents is more than unjust and dangerous ; it is useless so long as everybody is able and willing to obey." This language gave her food for reflection ; at any rate it showed her that if she wanted any one to be deposed from their office, she must begin with me, or else pardon everybody.

I had the honour of dining with Mme. and M. de Frondeville, the Prefect of the Allier, and I sat next to her. He wore the new blue uniform, quite plain, with only a simple fleur-de-lis worked on the collar. I was still wearing the uniform of the Empire, which was covered with embroidery. After looking at us both, her Royal Highness exclaimed : " Really, I am quite sorry for you, Monsieur de Frondeville, but you look as if you were only Monsieur de Rambuteau's aide-de-camp." I held my tongue, but I thought to myself that the embroideries would soon be back again, and that I had no need to be in such a hurry to discard my uniform.

Did not the Abbé de Montesquiou, influenced by his attachment to old traditions, propose to garb the Prefects in the black coats and short mantles of the Intendants of bygone days ? He discussed the matter with Mme. de Rambuteau, who answered : "Why, how could you expect my husband to review the National Guards in such a costume as that ?" And, indeed, it was imperative to abolish the superannuated etiquette belonging to a dead past which it was impossible to resuscitate.

I had also the honour of riding beside Madame la Dauphine. She had an air of great distinction, and managed her rather mettlesome steed with boldness and grace. We passed a regiment of dragoons, drafted to Vichy, who cried : "*Vive Marie Thérèse !*" Of course, I assured her that these brave fellows would follow so worthy a leader with equal enthusiasm, and would gladly lose their lives in her defence. She brought her horse to a sudden standstill. "You may think I am jesting, Monsieur le Comte," she said, "but I assure you that I would rather a thousand times perish at the head of a French squadron than be condemned to eat the bitter bread of exile once more." I could read in her eyes the promise of all she was to achieve later at Bordeaux, and it never occurred to me to entertain any doubt as to her tenacity of purpose. But my respect for her misfortunes and my admiration for her courage made me long to discern some trace of kindly sympathy and gentleness existing in her character.

On returning from our ride, the Duchesse d'Orléans was announced. I wished to withdraw, but the Princess bade me stay. "Remain," she said, addressing Frondeville and myself; "I consider you as belonging to my household." We took our places behind her. The widow of Philippe d'Égalité was introduced by Mme. de Séran with the same ceremonial that used to be customary at Versailles.

They had not seen each other since 1790. The Duchess was trembling, and, after making two or three steps forward, she fell upon her knees, stretching out her arms and crying : "Pardon, Madame, pardon ! " as if twenty-five years had not elapsed, and as if a common affliction did not await them in the future. Madame remained impassive ; she let the Duchess drag herself two or three steps on her knees ; then, holding out her hand to be kissed, she said : "Rise, Madame." They then sat down, and exchanged a few commonplace phrases, and therewith the audience ended. The Princess had not uttered a single kind word.

I left in the evening, filled with compassion for such a sad career and full of respect for such a strong and determined character, but regretting nevertheless the entire absence of all that was tender and womanly.

I made all the necessary preparations for the reception of Madame at Roanne, and went to the frontier of my Department to meet her. She received my wife most kindly, took her by the hand, and said to the Duchesse de Séran : "I present to you Mme. de Rambuteau ; you remember the little de Narbonne—she is one of our own people. . . ." She was very dignified at all the receptions, adopted my suggestions in making her official replies, and was present at all the balls and banquets ; but she was never gracious, and showed no desire to please.

She left on the next morning, and I escorted her as far as Tarare. As I was taking my leave of her, she said : "Pray, where is M. de Bondy, the Prefect of the Rhone ?" When I made excuses for my old colleague, who was doubtless obliged to remain at Lyons, she retorted : "I can easily tell, Monsieur le Comte, that I have left your Department by the difference of my reception here." At Lyons, the Maréchale Augereau presented Mme. de Mesgrigny to her, saying that she was my sister. "Madame," she replied, "write to your brother that I was much pleased with the manner in which he received me, and that, in my opinion, no one serves the King better."

By going to Paris, whither she had invited me, I should

have been able to cultivate this budding good-will ; but what I heard in confidence from Comte d'Agout, as well as from some of the principal officers of the Comte d'Artois, warned me as to the price I should have to pay for this advantage. I should have to disown my past, break all the ties of old friendships, bury my memories, adore what I had hitherto condemned, and be ashamed of what I had loved. I possessed neither that sorry courage nor that ambition which enable one to adapt oneself to every change, if it be profitable to do so. I was resolved to serve the new Government loyally, but I felt that the nation could only be won and kept by conciliating its existing forces ; for this reason, I wrote to M. de Montesquiou, at the time of the famous speech on the straight line and the curve :[1] "I can reconcile my entire Department to the King, I can assure him the obedience of the troops ; but to win men's hearts, after such language as that, is beyond my power, and to use it is to betray the Royal cause."

About the same time, Comte d'Artois came to Lyons. As the Prefect and even Marshal Augereau lay under suspicion, I was summoned thither in order to acquaint the Prince with various facts of which it was not proper that he should be ignorant. It was a rather singular mission for me, the bugbear of the Royalists ; but I only thought how best to fulfil my duty by letting the Prince hear the whole truth.

Monsieur was well received. His affable and courteous manners, and a few well-sounding phrases referring to the valour of the Lyonese during the siege, won over his hearers. The first person I met was Marshal Ney, whose loyalty was so extravagant that he was half-inclined to find

---

[1] Discourse on the 13th of September 1814, when Comte Ferrand, a fierce Royalist, made a vehement attack on the purchasers of national property : "At the epoch of the Revolution," he said, "there were two categories of Frenchmen, the *émigrés* and the *regnicoles* (stay-at-homes) ; the first never intended to be separated from France, the others eagerly desired the return of the King. On the Restoration, both found themselves in the same position. But the *émigrés* had gained this point *by following a straight line, without ever deviating from it,* while the *regnicoles* had only reached it *by adapting themselves more or less to each revolutionary phase.*"

fault with the simplicity of our sincere and honest submission to the new régime. I saw also the Ducs de Maillé
and Fitz-James, whom I had known long ago. The latter,
having owed certain obligations to M. de Narbonne, wished
to be useful to me. On presenting me to the Prince in
the evening, he said : "Monseigneur, I assure you that,
though some may act in the comedy of loyal devotion to
you, after having spent themselves, body and soul, in the
opposite cause, such is not the case with Rambuteau."
"Indeed !" I hastened to add, "I beg your Royal Highness to believe nothing of the sort ! Now, as then, I have
always been loyal, and I cannot give better pledges for the
future than to remind you of my past fidelity."

Monsieur asked me several questions about Lyons ; its
commerce, its works, its monuments. I satisfied him as
well as I was able, occasionally mentioning the Emperor, to
the great embarrassment of Fitz-James, who nudged me,
whispering : "Take care, my dear fellow, don't use that
word in presence of Monseigneur." I turned round
quietly, saying out loud : "My dear Édouard, there has
never been a lackey in our family, consequently, I could
never have been the lackey of M. Bonaparte." "That is
a very proper answer," replied the Prince, to whom I
must render justice : "M. de Rambuteau is right, and I
esteem him the more for that reply."

He proved that this was the case on the morrow by
taking me to his study and questioning me on several points,
especially on the national property. "Monseigneur," I
answered, "I do not possess a sou of national property ;
on the contrary, if it were restored to the original owners,
I should add sixty or seventy thousand francs to my yearly
income. But, having the honour to serve you, I would
prefer to offer you the half of my patrimony that has been
left me, rather than see you embark on a struggle which
would be very likely to cost me the total."

He spoke then of the National Guards, the *droits-
réunis*, the religious opinions of the country, and of Cardinal
Fesch, whom he detested. I did not conceal my opinion

that the latter had much influence over the clergy and people, although my colleague Capelle had shown me that very morning his report, in which he affirmed that the people had only one desire—to get rid of its Archbishop. But Capelle had written to this effect with the view of making a favourable impression on the Prince, whereas I had spoken in the Prince's interest, without caring whether I pleased him or not.

The consequence was that the Comte d'Artois told M. de La Roche-Aymon, one of his gentlemen, who had asked him if he was satisfied with me : " He is an honest and capable man, but he is a child of the Revolution." M. de La Roche-Aymon was sorry, as he was well disposed towards me for the sake of his aunt, who had married my father-in-law's brother.

How right was La Fontaine in preferring a *discreet enemy* to *an imprudent friend!* When sitting beside a colonel of Gendarmerie at a déjeûner given by the authorities of Lyons, an over-zealous courtier asked this officer if he had been long in the army. " Yes, Monsieur," was the answer. " Oh, but then what a number of émigrés you must have shot ! " The blood surged to the face, not only of the colonel, but of every military man present. In vain did his Highness try to heal the wounds so constantly made by the tactlessness and exclusiveness of those who wished to be considered the only pure Royalists in the kingdom. He did not succeed, and his stay at Lyons, far from winning support for the new régime, awakened regret for the past, and widened the gap between it and the present.

The Prince desired to visit Saint-Étienne. I arranged that he should have a good reception ; Guards of Honour had been organised ; those furnished by the city, commanded by the director of the great arms' factory, were superb ; every town and village had sent detachments, more or less numerous. The 20th and 24th of the Line, forming six battalions, were the élite of the eighteen battalions of which they had formerly made a part ; they were veterans of the army of Suchet, and as fine-looking as the old Guard.

"They are the first regiments," said the Prince, after the review, "with which I have been pleased." "It is because, Monseigneur, for the last three months I have diligently instilled into them that you consider everything they have done for France as done for yourself, and that the bravest are simply the eldest sons of the great French family ; and, moreover, when they drink to the King's health at my table, they drink to no health but his."

In order to show him the successive operations in the making of a gun, we had its different parts displayed in twenty-four workrooms, like the plates in an encyclopædia. He could then embrace at a single glance, so to say, the different phases and the progress of the labour.

At Rive-de-Gier he was received by the Mayor, who had distinguished himself at the siege of Lyons as well as against the Austrians ; he invested him with the Cross. At Saint-Chamond he also visited the great factory of MM. Dugas, who initiated him into the most secret processes, notably that of the watered finish of the ribbons of the Order. At Saint-Étienne he also decorated the chiefs of the National Guard, the directors of the factories, the Sub-prefect and the President of the Tribunal of Commerce ; and I obtained six Crosses for those who had best supported me in the defence of the Department, and when, as I had nothing to say with regard to another request which was strongly seconded, he expressed his astonishment, I answered : "Monseigneur, the honours I have solicited are for services rendered either in defence of the country, its administration, or for the purpose of enriching it by labour : all I ask for is justice ; it does not lie within my province to ask for favours."

M. de Tardy (whose zeal in the defence of Roanne I had admired) had the singular notion—singular, at least, at that time—of wishing to be created a Marquis. I did my best to aid him in his ambition, and I succeeded. I mention this detail, because it was the only title granted under the First Restoration. As for myself, it did not become me to ask for anything. Doubtless his Royal Highness might have taken the initiative ; but it was not for me to suggest it to him. The Emperor had bestowed the Cross of Re-union on me when I was at the Simplon, and Marshal Augereau had procured me the Cross of the Legion of Honour ; the latter I kept for twenty years.

Nevertheless, the Prince showed that he was well pleased with his journey. I had been careful to provide for all his habits and tastes : at each relay he found a platter with a consommé and a bottle of Bordeaux ; and every evening a bath was ready beside his bed. His most insignificant likes and dislikes had been communicated to me by M. Bourlet, his first valet-de-chambre, and I was determined to prove to him that a good Deputy-Governor may be also an attentive Amphitryon. He was not called upon to spend anything ; the Department and the towns paid for everything.

At Saint-Étienne the ladies of the city sang a cantata, followed by a ball and illuminations : a monstrous fleur-de-lis, formed of burning coal, was outlined on a steep slope of the mountain ; two hundred carts of coal, presented by the mining companies, were employed for the purpose. Monsieur expressed his thanks to me for the reception, and was delighted with the enthusiasm of the people. " What a different city this is from Lyons ! " he said to me. " Lyons, indeed ! What a city ! Seventeen compliments, and not a chamber-pot ! "

I have said that the favourable impression made by the Comte d'Artois at Lyons had been very ephemeral. As the Department of the Loire is to Lyons what the Seine-et-Oise is to Paris, I was very well informed as to the public feeling which was prevalent just then. For this purpose, when he made his second journey, six weeks afterwards, in order to arrive at the real opinion of the people, I disguised myself in a greatcoat, with my hat slouched over my eyes, and mixed with the cortége on the way to La Guillotière. What I heard surpassed all that I knew already.

At nightfall, after dinner, his Highness took me to the balcony, beneath which were two or three hundred people, most of them hired by the police, who cried : " *Vive le Comte d'Artois !* " The Prince said to me : " Look at these good people ! See how they love us ! " I did not venture to undeceive him at the moment or tell him all that I feared. But the next day I gave him a little lecture on the skilful treatment of public opinion : " It was always necessary to consult it, even in its faults and errors ; always necessary to avoid wounding it in its prejudices ; as it was so much easier to guide it than to coerce it."

He listened, but did not believe me ; Princes have not a keen scent for the truth. Thus, being apparently convinced that his reception in the Loire had not been a heavy burden on the Department, I was obliged to say to him : " If your Royal Highness merely refers to the amount of money that was spent, it probably does not exceed fifteen or twenty thousand francs ; but if you deign to consider that three or four thousand men equipped themselves at their own expense as National Guards, that more than three hundred went to the expense of costly uniforms as Guards of Honour, that the entire population of an industrial district stopped working for three days and spent more than a week's wages, you will see that these festivities cannot be renewed without causing considerable loss."

A short time afterwards, Marshal Augereau was recalled, and Comte Roger Damas named Governor of Lyons, with M. de Chabrol de Crousol as Prefect. I was acquainted with the latter, with whom I had had a long conversation in the month of June, on his return from the Illyrian Provinces, where he was Director General of Finance.

We were at that time quite of the same opinion ; but now I found that he had modified some of his ideas ; still, we were agreed on all essential points, thanks to his good sense and experience of affairs. As for the Count, it was quite a different matter. As I was greatly influenced by the Mémoires of the Prince de Ligne, who had regarded him as the perfect type of French chivalry, I expected to find in him a man of the highest distinction. I found, however, nothing of the sort. Quite the reverse indeed ; for he possessed all the prejudices of the Émigrés, coupled with a complete ignorance of modern France and the worst petty weaknesses of the old régime ; he cherished no ambitions, entertained no theories, had not a notion of controlling public opinion, or any idea of loosening the ties that still bound so many to the cause of the Empire, by trying to reconcile them to the acceptance of a well-regulated liberty in the place of that glorious past which they were so prone to regret.

I could not help associating his conduct and language with the discourse of M. Ferrand and with what I had heard from the *entourage* of the Comte d'Artois and of Madame, and I perceived how chimerical were our hopes of national union. For that matter, I expressed my opinion very frankly on the subject. One morning that he was questioning me very seriously on the fidelity of the people of my Department to the King, I answered that I felt quite safe in guaranteeing it, even if Napoleon should return to France, provided, of course, that he did not come into the Department in person. He smiled, and said : "Monsieur, our prophecies as to the future are not of much account when we predict impossibilities." "Monsieur le Comte," I answered, "if I had the honour of governing the second city of France for the King, this impossibility would be for ever in my thoughts, and cause me unceasing anxiety both night and day."

In fact, the faults of the Government, the growing dis-affection everywhere, particularly in the army and among the middle classes, the imprudence of the Royalists, their passion for wounding the self-love and threatening the interests of the people, their reliance on the aid of foreigners, with which they were constantly menacing us (although the plainest dictates of prudence should have taught them to conceal their obligations in that direction), all heralded an impending rupture ; for the Emperor, from his observatory in the Isle of Elba, was far too shrewd not to have foreseen these errors and to turn them to account at the proper moment.

I resolved, then, to remain in my Department, not to go

I

to Paris—to fulfil my duty loyally, and to await events. I
kept a hospitable table, had frequent entertainments, and
was courteous to everybody. By these methods I succeeded in winning to my side a considerable number of
those who dissented from my views, and was in a fair way
to conciliate some of my more pronounced adversaries. I
banished all rancorous controversy, avoided all occasion of
reproach, refused to permit the dismissal of any of my
subordinates, and was as well obeyed and respected as any
functionary can hope to be, when I received the news
of the landing of the Emperor in a note from M. de
Bouthillier, Prefect of the Var.

I wrote immediately to the Abbé de Montesquiou :
" There is not a moment to be lost in such a crisis. You
will not find a single soldier in the whole French army
capable of firing a shot at Napoleon, who is well aware of
this, and indeed bases all his hopes and confidence on this
knowledge. Do not attempt to send any regiment against
him ; you would simply be sending recruits for his cause.
You should have foreseen the danger. Despatch the *Garde
du Corps*, and such of the National Guards as you can rely
on, by stage-coaches. It is the only means of escaping a
peril which no one seems to have known how to prevent.
My Department will remain faithful, but that is all that can
be expected from it ; I think I can answer for the troops, provided Napoleon does not appear among them." I then proceeded to adopt such measures as I deemed indispensable.

As the Emperor had himself authorised me to serve the
Government of the King, my line of conduct was quite
clear. I at once drew up a proclamation to the inhabitants,
convoked the Council General, in pursuance of orders
received from Paris, and wrote to Monsieur, who had just
arrived at Lyons, in terms similar to those in my letter to
the Minister. I offered to bring him the *élite* of the National
Guards, insisting that the 20th of the Line should be still
kept at Montbrison, because in that case I could rely on it.
It was decided otherwise, and the 20th, with the 24th of
Saint-Étienne, was ordered to Lyons.

I despatched one of the counsellors of the Prefecture to the Prince for the purpose of representing me, receiving his orders, and assuring him of my devotion ; but his mission was of short duration, for General Macdonald, not daring to answer for the soldiers, and having proposed that he and his officers should take the guns of the Grenadiers and advance, if the Princes would accompany them, the Comte d'Artois, whom this proposal did not please, left the city. As my envoy urged him to give at least some orders, he answered : " Tell M. de Rambuteau to do his best to save his Department ; as for us, we intend to leave France."

Such were the adieus of his Royal Highness. Still, I did not abandon either my cockade or my flag ; I persuaded the people to wait, instead of dividing themselves into two camps, and I succeeded in keeping not only them in this frame of mind, but also the battalions of the 20th and 24th of the Line.

Meanwhile, the Emperor ordered Bertrand to write to me. I answered that I should be as faithful to the established Government as I had been to his. With an object diametrically opposed to this, the younger Guizot [1] visited me ; he had been sent on a mission by the Minister of the Interior. The only burden of his song was : " Let us make civil war ! " " But," said I, " as you come in the name of the Minister, you ought surely to bring some instructions. What am I to do ? Should I muster the National Guards ? Can I dispose of the arms' factory ? and what military authority am I to recognise ? " To all these questions he had no answer. The Council General, which a royal decree had invested with extraordinary powers, was even more embarrassed than I was. Those who had so often denounced me were now trembling, and showed their prudence by decorating their hats with a cockade which I venerated, but would not tolerate so long as the King remained in France.

[1] The brother of the future Minister.

At this time the Council adopted three resolutions,[1] which they presented to me in a body, begging me to make my submission to the new Government in the name of the Department, and promising to support me in all that I believed should be done on this subject. The Marquis de Contenson, President of the Council, well known for his Legitimist sentiments, consented to act as my substitute in the Chamber des Répresentants, thus proving his fidelity to the solemn promise he had given me.

The King had already left France. In the opinion of every one, I had fulfilled my mission according to the severest rules of honour and duty. And so, feeling bound to reward the confidence and devotion which I had always enjoyed in the Department by giving them a last token of my appreciation, I now openly espoused the cause so dear to my heart by issuing a proclamation, in which I was careful to respect the misfortunes of those on the losing side. This proceeding on my part was, of course, highly displeasing to the Royalist agents. There was even a plot to kidnap me. A courier was robbed on his way to my residence ; whilst a still worse fate was reserved for me, one of the conspirators being a man who, for fifteen years, had pretended to be my friend.

Just at that moment the Duc d'Angoulême was advancing on Pont-Saint-Esprit. Many Royalist braggadocios boasted of the wondrous feats they might have performed if I had not purposely baffled their efforts, but truth to tell, those efforts were of such a very mild nature that they

[1] Resolution of the 22nd of March : " The Prefect believing that, in the present circumstances, it is his duty to leave the Department, the Council General has adopted unanimously the following resolution : 'M. de Rambuteau shall be requested and, if need be, required to retain the administration of the Department in any circumstances.'"
Resolution of the 24th of March : "The Council General, having taken cognisance of the events reported in the *Moniteur* of the 21st of March, declares the session terminated ; but, before separating, it has judged it of the highest importance, and for the good of the Department, that the Prefect be requested and required anew to remain at its head. The Council unanimously recognises that the Prefect has conducted himself with the utmost wisdom, and has shown in all his acts only the most rigorous principles of honour."

never gave me a moment's uneasiness. Had I not witnessed their flight from Lyons before the Prince, and seen how they came to ask me afterwards for a soldier's way-bill in order that they might hasten to his support when he was a good forty leagues behind them! At the same time, I am quite ready to do full justice to the personal courage of many of the Royalists, for whose cause I have the utmost respect, but I cannot deny that as a party they showed themselves utterly incapable of co-operation, neither understanding when they should agree to fight nor to what lengths it was safe to venture.

A few days afterwards I went to Lyons to meet Marshal Suchet and Comte Roederer, who had just arrived, the one as Commander of the army which was to be raised, the other as Commissary Extraordinary. Both were most anxious to have me as Prefect, having noted my conduct during the preceding year and the defence I had organised in the Loire against the Allies. They concealed neither their fears nor their anxieties from me, and, on learning my intentions of going to Paris, they charged me to tell the Emperor what they dared not write to his Ministers, namely : " Sire, there are certain persons who are only bent on making use of your person as a means to an end ; for another week they will cry : ' *Vive l'Empereur !* ' after that it will be : ' *Vive la République !* ' "

Just as I was about to start for Paris, I was appointed Prefect of the Allier.

CHAPTER V

PREFECT OF MOULINS AND MONTAUBAN

BEFORE starting for Paris, I considered it my duty to spend a few days in my new residence. In that I did wrong. I should have turned my undeserved removal to account by examining the situation before entering into any fresh engagements. This omission on my part was severely censured by Sémonville and several of my other friends. But my patriotic instincts quickened my apprehensions with regard to the alien invaders, and stimulated me to strain every nerve to defend my country. Everything combined to urge me to pursue the course upon which I had determined. Apart from my natural impulse to oppose the foe, and the keen sense of humiliation engendered by our reverses, along with my zeal for the honour of France, I could not forget the very slighting treatment I had received at the hands of the Bourbons, nor the poor appreciation they had shown for my services. I was still smarting under their behaviour to me at Lyons. I had served them loyally, although, to do so, I was compelled to stifle the memories and sentiments of my past ; yet they had fled without uttering a single word either of encouragement or gratitude ! And all this time the Emperor's extraordinary intrepidity was exciting the admiration of even those who were to perish in his fall.

After a short stay at Moulins, I adopted the necessary measures for raising recruits, recalling the old soldiers and arranging for the elections, all my plans being ably seconded by the Mayor, M. Desroys ; but at the end of a week I received my nomination to the Prefecture of Carcassonne. I felt deeply wounded. My services during 1814 certainly deserved a more important post. I now realised the mistake I had made in accepting Moulins. I set out at once for Paris.

After my arrival, I saw Bassano and Caulaincourt, both of whom shared my feelings, Caulaincourt especially, for he did not share the illusions of his colleague. I shall always remember my visit to Sémonville on the day when our worthy Maret,[1] who had always been his intimate friend, was appointed Minister of Foreign Affairs. Contrary to my expectations, he was seated on a little stool in his wife's boudoir, with his head in his hands. "Well," I exclaimed, "you look remarkably gloomy for a man whose best friend has just gained his heart's desire. Surely his good fortune has not already loosened your affection for him."

He handed me a note, in which Bassano offered him the post of Director of the Ministry, or any other he might prefer, and added : "Yes, I do feel gloomy, as any man might who sees his old comrade with a halter round his neck, and ourselves in pretty much the same situation." As this was evidently a riddle to me, he sprang up, and, taking hold of my arm, continued : "Don't you know what Maret is ? Are you not aware that of all the Emperor's devotees he is the most fanatical ? What is a Minister of Foreign Affairs ? He is a man who must be for ever shouting 'Look out' to the blind man in the game of blind-man's-buff. When the Emperor says to Maret : 'There's nothing that I can see even in broad daylight,' instead of opening his eyes, Maret will send for a score of candles. A man with that disposition will ruin us all, and, as far as I am concerned, I wash my hands of the whole business." I was no longer surprised to find that Caulaincourt did not share Maret's illusions, and failed to emulate him in seeing only the bright side of everything.

Nevertheless, they mentioned my name to the Emperor, who summoned me to the Élysée. "Had you joined me at Lyons," were his first words, "you would now be Prefect of the Seine." "Sire," I answered, "I was the last to

---

[1] Duc de Bassano.

leave you, and when your Majesty, of your own free will,
released me from my allegiance, I was bound to do for the
King what I had done for you ; besides, I know that your
Majesty did me ample justice yesterday in the presence of
Caulaincourt." "That is true !" he replied ; "if I had
had twenty-five Prefects like you, there would have been
no need of my abdication." "Sire," I answered, "your
Majesty can now dispose of my life ; you have more than
paid for it with these gracious words."

Then he referred to the different measures I had
employed for the defence of the Loire ; he informed me
that, owing to his satisfaction with my conduct, he had
commissioned me, by a decree of the 18th of March, to
organise the same methods of resistance in fourteen Departments, but that the decree was not in time to reach me. I
gave him an account of the message which Marshal Suchet
and M. Roederer had charged me to deliver : "What
does it matter ?" he answered. "The men to whom they
allude are the only men who can give me an army ! If I
fall, they must fall with me ; if I triumph, I shall soon
bring them to their senses. Let us speak of your National
Guards. You have succeeded remarkably well with them.
How did you manage it ?" I explained the matter fully.
He next questioned me on the Departments with which I
was acquainted, the regiments stationed in them, their
different positions, and then dismissed me with a few kind
words.

Our interview had only one witness—Corvisart—who,
with his elbow resting on the mantelpiece, had been listening to us with a smile. We left the room together. In
the first salon we found poor Labédoyère striving hard to
harangue two or three deputations, repeating the same
phrases incessantly : "Napoleon is much changed. He is
in favour of liberty, liberal institutions," &c., &c. Corvisart
drew me aside, and said : "Look at that idiot, who believes
that it is possible for a man to act in opposition to all his
inherent proclivities."

The words struck me. I compared my impressions

after this interview with those which I had carried away from my farewell audience with the Emperor, two years before. At that time, my faith in him was so strong that the possibility of his ever ordering anything unjust or unreasonable would never have entered my head. This absolute confidence had never forsaken me until his downfall. But now I realised that his colossal genius, although capable of the greatest deeds, might yet ruin everything ; and that, in his hands, the entire country was simply so much material upon which to try experiments. The Charter, by creating a well-balanced Government with guarantees, rights, and liberty to discuss national interests publicly, had afforded me much satisfaction. I was still devotedly fond of the Emperor, but my faith was shaken, and I dreaded to witness a revival of the past without even the victories that had given it its prestige. I was astonished, nay distressed, at this change in my ideas, which, however, did not influence my conduct in the slightest degree.

In a few days I saw how many were turning away from the Emperor—some because they had vainly tried to set limits to his will ; others, in order to keep an open door in the event of reverses. The small number of his true friends were well aware of their danger, and made no attempt to conceal it. One day, Las Cases (who was Equerry to Lucien, who had once more resumed the rank of an Imperial Prince), told me all the details of the plot which Foucher had hatched, and explained how the Emperor had discovered it by sending Fleury de Chaboulon, one of his private secretaries, to Bâle, where he had an interview with the envoy of M. de Metternich. He likewise told me that he had learned from Lucien himself that Napoleon was disposed to accept a place of retreat in Hungary, provided his son were recognised as Emperor under the regency of his mother, and that Montholon was about to carry these proposals to Vienna. But the Emperor changed his mind during the night, sent for Cambacérès, told him it would be time enough to adopt this extreme measure after a defeat, and so the matter ended.

Neither in word nor gesture did Foucher betray any embarrassment in openly receiving the almost official agents of the different parties. I had a plain proof of this one evening when I dined at his house in company with MM. Chabrol de Crousol and D'Arbaud de Jouques, Merlin de Thionville and Lanjuinais. The former were political agents from Ghent, the latter active ringleaders in the Republican conspiracy. "Well, Rambuteau," he said, after dinner, "so you don't care to go South—you prefer to remain in the Chamber! You're right. If the Emperor can save France, we ought to help and support him ; but if we have to choose between him and France, you are too good a Frenchman to hesitate."

Glancing at the faces of his other guests, I grasped that this speech was meant for a sort of challenge to them ; had I been alone, I should have thought he was anxious to take my measure. I answered quietly that the manner in which I had been chosen Representative by the unanimous vote of the Grand College of the Loire, made it especially binding on me to justify the confidence reposed in me. Then, as soon as I could withdraw, I flew to Caulaincourt. He threw up his hands, exclaiming : "I am convinced he is betraying us—and yet we are not strong enough to send him about his business ! " "Then, my dear Duke," I answered, "what you say amounts to this : the Emperor is very ill, and we are all very ill with him, and Heaven knows that France must take her chance."

All this gave me plenty of food for reflection. My position was a rather delicate one. Marshal Suchet, who was in command of the Army of the Alps, was very desirous that I should be appointed Prefect of Lyons, being certain of my loyal co-operation. But the Emperor refused his request. "Lyons is so devoted to me," said he, "that if I only sent one of my boots there, it would quite suffice ! You want Rambuteau because he is efficient. That is an additional reason for sending him to the South, upon which we cannot reckon securely, he must choose between Nîmes and Montauban ; later on, he can have Lyons ; but this is the time for services, not for rewards." There was no doubt that what I had done for the King lessened the value of what I had done for the Emperor. Perhaps he thought Lyons too near the Department from which he had removed me, and was afraid of my personal influence on the inhabitants, as evidenced by the flattering unanimity manifested by all parties in electing me to the Chamber.

On the other hand, Carnot, Minister of the Interior, had, without consulting me, proposed my nomination for Dijon, and that with a warmth which was ill received. I may as well state the reason which led him to think of me. I had called at his house after my arrival in Paris, and I had been rather coldly treated by him. Naturally, I felt hurt. The same evening I said to Foucher : " What is the matter with your colleague of the Interior ? Does he think I am so very keen on obtaining a prefecture ? I mean to tell him that not only shall I not go to Carcassonne, but that I shall go nowhere, and that I rendered quite enough services last year to command, at least, both esteem and consideration." Foucher burst out laughing : " Carnot has not been here long enough to know you ; all he has been able to see in you was the aristocrat and the chamberlain, and he has a dislike for both. Don't take any Department till I see him ; you'll find everything will turn out to your satisfaction."

The next morning I had a note from Carnot inviting me to breakfast. He began by offering apologies for the coolness of his reception, then he said : " I have sent for all the despatches in which your name appears, and, after reading your correspondence and your reports on the Simplon and the Loire, I cannot give you a higher proof of my confidence than by proposing you for Dijon, my own country. You may always rely upon my assistance, because I regard you as a good Frenchman, an able administrator, and an excellent citizen." After this we were reconciled ; I saw him frequently, and I still cherish a great respect for his sincere devotion, his unshaken courage, and his fidelity to the Emperor, as well as to his country. His was an old-world face, which was quite out of place in the modern frame of his surroundings.

Nevertheless, during a whole fortnight I refused to accept any mission ; then some words spoken by the Emperor decided me. I learned that he was saddened— more saddened even than annoyed—by the conduct of several of his old servants, and that I was among the number. I made up my mind at once, and wrote to him : " Sire, I know that your Majesty wishes me to accept a Department in the South. I am ready to start. For I will not follow the example of those who, after having received every imaginable favour from your hands in happier days, now either refuse their services or higgle as to their price. At the same time, however, I crave permission to lay at your Majesty's feet the irrevocable decision at which I have arrived, namely, that directly the present peril is overpast, I retire into private life, and never accept any public appointment in the future. I have resolved upon this step because, in spite of all the proofs which I have given your Majesty of my entire devotion to yourself, you have nevertheless seen fit to doubt my loyalty and good faith."

I preferred Montauban to Nîmes because Mme. de Rambuteau had relatives in the Tarn-et-Garonne, and I felt the need of whatever aid I could obtain. But I convinced the Ministry that a dependent position at a distance of two hundred leagues from Paris must be very embarrassing. It was therefore agreed, at a meeting held in the Ministry of the Interior, that I should be invested with the powers of Commissioner Extraordinary in addition to those of Prefect. Carnot encouraged me ; whilst Davoust said, if I succeeded in preventing civil war, I might consider that I had done well. Foucher inquired as to my plans. I answered : " I have none. It would be easy enough to invent all kinds of projects. But the probability is that, once on the spot, I should have to do the exact opposite of what I told you. You send me there because you have confidence in me ; you give me a clear field, because I decline to bear the blame of follies which I have not committed ; I understand that I am to prevent civil war ; and that for this purpose you will furnish me with men and money ; all else is secondary. I shall either succeed or I shall resign the position, so you have the whole matter in a nutshell." My outspokenness made a good impression, as I perceived from the Emperor's reception of me the same evening.

I did not like leaving Paris without visiting Sémonville at Fremigny, the place of his self-imposed exile. I was told that Louis XVIII. asked some one who had come from Paris : "What is Sémonville doing ?" "Sire, he has been exiled." "Then my affairs must be going on well, for, if they were not, he would be in high favour and in office." As for myself, I must say that during the thirty-five years I knew him, he showed the same kindness and affection to the young man, to whom he would have gladly given his daughter, as he afterwards evinced for his colleague, the Prefect of the Seine and Peer of France.

"My dear friend," he said to me, "if I had been near you, you would have resisted the very natural impulse to which you have yielded. You are dazzled by the Emperor's former glory, and you still believe in his fortune ; but you are under a delusion. It is not Napoleon who has returned, but a charlatan named Bonaparte. You are in the Chamber ; but, however honourable may have been the circumstances of your election, your position will not be the less difficult on that account. On the other hand, you are a Prefect, and a Deputy-Governor who saves a country may always expect gratitude ; such a reputation is worthy of envy. Of course revolutions live on reputations ; it is frightful to think what a number of them they devour. A reputation is also a sort of tontine ; and all you need is to live long enough to see your investment increase in value. So, be careful of yours ; confine yourself to your special functions ; do as much good and as little evil as you can ; when events take you by surprise, do what is needful, but no more ; then, no matter what pressure may be brought to bear upon you, retire, return to your home : that is the only way in which you can succeed in keeping whatever you may have acquired. Sooner or later you will find a post worthy of your acceptance. If you remain in the Chamber or return to it, you can neither become a Republican nor run any risk of attacking the Emperor, nor take part in ruining France beyond redemption. Therefore, set out for your Department ; prevent reactions of every kind ; submit yourself to the decrees of Fate, and then—I repeat it again —return to private life, so that the good you have done and the evil you have prevented may not be ascribed to any self-interested calculation on your part. You will be calumniated, possibly persecuted. The future will do you justice."

I followed these wise counsels, in spite of the attraction which the rôle of Representative had for me. I informed my colleagues that my mission, involving as it did extraordinary powers, was only temporary, and that, after restoring order and obedience, I should return to take my seat among them. The Emperor sent back my Chamberlain's key to me, saying that my election to the Chamber made it impossible for him to raise me to the Peerage like Sébastiani and others of his most intimate servants ; and therewith I departed.

I passed through Burgundy in order to see my wife and children, whom I did not care to expose to the dangers that might arise from the violent passions of the South. At Lyons I bade a last farewell to Henri de Vallin, then very ill, and whom I was never to see again. In him I lost my best friend. We had lived together for thirteen years like brothers, nor did the refusal of my sister's hand or our political differences (he was a Legitimist) ever raise the slightest cloud between us. I have always cherished his memory on account of his noble character and loftiness of mind. Even now the thought of him almost moves me to tears.

I stopped at Montbrison to arrange certain matters with my successor and to thank my friends, and then hastened to Montauban. My first visit was to Mme. de Balbi, sister of the Duc de La Force ; she was an old friend of the Comte de Provence, and I had often seen her in Paris.

When I accepted the Prefecture of Montauban, I said to her, " I reflected with joy that I should find you there, and that you would help me in conciliating the country. But I am bound to confess that though I could never be half-hearted in the service of any cause when I have once accepted it, I cannot blame those who act on the morrow in precisely the same way as I myself acted overnight. Consequently, you need have no uneasiness about the Royal Volunteers. You are too sensible not to understand that the future will be decided either by the armies in Belgium or by those on the banks of the Rhine, and that any attempt at a partial insurrection in the Departments would only gratify a few personal ambitions without having the slightest influence on general results. Here are the conditions which, through your intervention, I propose to your friends. I do not want to be told of any class that has been proscribed or persecuted for its past. I intend to ignore the existence of the Volunteers ; but neither do I wish on the other hand to have any persecuting party, and shall therefore not allow combinations or confederacies. What I do want is to secure respect and protection for Catholics as well as for Protestants, for ministers as well as for priests, for temples as well as for churches. But I shall require every assistance in providing for the departure of the conscripts and the National Guards that have been called out ; the taxes must be paid freely ; there must be no riots or plots, and you must await patiently the decisions of war and fortune."

Mme. de Balbi was a sensible woman, and the step I had taken appealed to her. She asked a delay of twenty-four hours, and, on the following day, sent M. de Preissac to me. This gentleman was afterwards my colleague at Bordeaux and in the Chamber of Peers, but had recently served as Major of the Volunteers and the Verdets [1] under

---

[1] Royalist companies secretly organised in the South of France after the 9th Thermidor, and so named because they wore a green uniform or a green ribbon on the arm, in memory of the uniform of the Swiss who died for the King on the 10th of August, in defence of the Tuileries.

the Duc d'Angoulême. He thanked me for my proposals,
promised to second me as far as lay in his power, and
guaranteed the tranquillity of the Department.

I also met the leaders of the patriot party—almost all
Protestants ; I had some trouble in getting them to chime
in with my ideas, but, thanks to the assistance of the
President of the Consistory and the Mayor, I succeeded
in repressing them. I had more difficulty with the extreme
Catholics, especially those belonging to the Faubourg of
Ville-Bourbon. These latter were in such an excited frame
of mind that no story was too preposterous to find credence
with them, so embittered were they by the memories of the
cruel past. For throughout our long Revolution, Montauban had always been the scene of intestine struggles, and
there was scarcely any one belonging to the various parties
whose hands showed no stains of bloodshed.

As for party songs, challenges, faction-cries, I did not
meddle with them, so long as they were not likely to entail
serious consequences. Luckily, I had four thousand
soldiers at my disposal, among them the 60th of the Line, in
garrison at Roanne the year before, and one battalion of
which had returned with me across the snows of Mont
Blanc from the Simplon. It had seen me at work, and at a
time when, owing to the perturbation of the minds of the
people, all leaders, civil and military, were suspected of
treason, and it vouched for my patriotism. Moreover, the
Abbé de Trélissac, Vicar General of the diocese, and a priest
whom Fénelon would have loved, rendered me the greatest
services, thanks to his influence over priests and laymen,
who were in a state of chronic excitement due to the anta-
gonism of the two creeds.

In fact, one day I received a deputation which betrayed
the greatest emotion, who had come to protest against the
cathedral being turned into a stable for the use of the
Reformers, a rumour having reached them that such a step
was in contemplation ! Now, the cathedral is built on a
rather steep elevation, and can only be approached by a
flight of a dozen steps, so I contented myself with replying

that, as I went every Sunday to the parish Mass, I should surely be the first to oppose a profanation that was as odious as it was improbable. But it did not take me long to realise the depth of the chasm that split the Department into two parts.

The Royalist party, consisting of nobles who, though very numerous, were not very wealthy, and were mostly Catholics, was closely allied with the common people through the bonds of those confraternities which are so powerful in the South; and its influence over this class was all the greater because it could dispose of the judicial authority, and therefore hold out promises of immunity to its adherents. The liberal party, made up principally of Protestants, consisted of landholders, mostly well-to-do, or manufacturers, who were the more circumspect because their wealth made them objects of envy. If I add that political hatreds were augmented by religious rancour, my position will be easily understood. Nevertheless, at the end of three weeks, I had succeeded in despatching seventeen hundred conscripts, and had assembled two thousand soldiers, some at Montauban and others at Toulouse.

Then the federates of Cahors and Toulouse, displeased at my opposition to every kind of federation in my Department, sent me a deputation, partly solicitous, partly threatening, and accompanied by some of their leaders. I answered that I would have no federation or anything else that was likely to interfere with the measures I had adopted; that I had already recruited nearly four thousand men; that the taxes were paid, and that peace prevailed everywhere. Further, I stated that I had not sent the Royal Volunteers to the frontier because those whose duty it was to serve had responded to the roll-call, and that I intended to leave useless individuals at home. Finally, I told them that they might bring any accusation against me they liked; but that I was their Prefect and Commissioner Extraordinary, a member of the Chamber, elected by a Department I had twice saved, and that no one should hinder me from doing at Montauban what I had done in the Loire. They were

K

furious, and wrote off to Paris. I received a very affectionate letter from Carnot, in which he assured me of his full confidence, at the same time advising me to be cautious about offending popular sentiment. I thanked him, and continued to follow the course I had sketched out for myself.

At this time certain Royalist agents who had been arrested in the neighbouring Departments were brought to Besançon.

Their wives came and threw themselves at my feet, beseeching me to save them. I answered that it was impossible for me to set them at liberty, but that I would have them conveyed to Montauban, on condition that they pledged their word not to try to escape or take part in any intrigue. I placed them in the custody of two gendarmes, and allowed them to select the best inn in the city as their prison, they paying all expenses.

Shortly after that I was awakened at five in the morning, and told that a stranger was below who wanted to speak to me immediately. I got up, and found myself face to face with M. de Marsillac, a gentleman I had known at Paris. He informed me that General Decaen, Commander of the Corps d'Armée of the South at Toulouse, was determined to have him arrested and brought before a military commission, and begged me to protect him. I was puzzled what to do. Finally, I proposed the same conditions to him that I had proposed to the others ; these he accepted, and when I had "incarcerated" him, I started for Toulouse to confer with the General.

The latter, who had been circumvented by the federates, and whose vanity was wounded by my having retained his prisoners, had written to me insisting on their being sent back to him, and authorising the formation of the federations which I had forbidden. I explained the matter to him with my usual frankness : "My motive in accepting the mission of the Government sprang solely from the belief that I could serve it effectively, not from any anxiety on my part to secure employment ; my powers as Commissioner Extraordinary made me independent of him ; I had now adopted successful measures for recruiting, assembling the troops, and collecting the taxes ; my methods were my own, and if he believed he had the authority to reduce me by force, I was ready to leave the Department that very moment. But it would be the beginning of civil war, for I should ascend the tribune of the Chamber and demonstrate that he was responsible for the French blood that would be shed by French hands ; and my statement would carry the more weight from the fact that I had made myself responsible for the obedience of the Department, if he were only willing to trust me." He looked steadily in my face ; then, gripping me by the hand, he complimented me in terms more soldierly than refined, adding : "I will do as you wish, for you are the only one of the great functionaries whom the troops do not accuse of treason." He was an honest man.

After this I was wholly absorbed with plans for promoting peace and concord ; I avoided everything like coercion, save in the case of a man named Jafard, whom I caused to be arrested ; he was, so to speak, the Trestaillons [1] of Montauban. He had been sentenced three or four times to death or the galleys for robbery and murder, but had always escaped owing to his influence with high political personages. He had afterward robbed a taxcollector, and the warrant for his arrest had never been executed. I discovered that he had found refuge in the house of a wealthy landowner, Comte O'Kelly, who, with his son-in-law, M. de Termes, had armed his servants, with the object of actually escorting the ruffian to the Garonne and baffling the pursuit of the gendarmes. I immediately requested these gentlemen to call at the Prefecture, and told them that, while I understood the position of those honourable men who held opinions different from mine and who might be expected to fight for them desperately, it had never entered my head that gentlemen of their birth and rank could become the bodyguards of an assassin ; that I

---

[1] A bandit who turned the White Terror to account in the South by committing all sorts of robberies and assassinations, under the pretext of political reprisals.

had given orders for Jafard to be captured, dead or alive, and for the arrest of those who had rendered themselves his accomplices by helping him to escape, and that, consequently, they would have only themselves to blame if any misfortune befell them. They were not slow in taking my words to heart.

My honest friend Decaen, in his new-born zeal, adopted measures of precaution for my personal safety, and every night a battalion bivouacked on the square in front of the Prefecture ; but, as my conscience was at peace, and being satisfied with my conduct, I had no fear, and used to slip out regularly through a little gate in the garden and enjoy a stroll by moonlight on the banks of the Tarn, in company with my secretary. I was often recognised, but never insulted, and the only hostile manifestation I encountered was from the little children who, when playing at war, used to cry " *Vive le Roi !* " after me. Thus calm was fully established at Montauban when, suddenly, the news of Waterloo and the Emperor's abdication reached us.

I was deeply afflicted, but not surprised. Feeling sure that now there was no other alternative for France but to return to Legitimacy, with the best conditions attainable, nothing was left me but to finish my task and rest contented with retiring into private life, having gained the good opinion of all parties.

The seventeen days that followed were, I believe, the most laborious and honourable in all my life. Placed between adversaries whom it was necessary to reconcile by moderating the impatience of one party and calming the irritation of another, which was the more hot-headed because it still controlled an armed force and could dispose of 4000 soldiers, I went perpetually from one camp to the other, in order to prevent ructions ; I was for ever occupied in stopping quarrels, and checking threats and challenges in the streets and squares. To the cries of " *Vive l'Empereur !* " I replied, " There is no longer an Emperor," and to the cries of " *Vive le Roi !* " I answered " There is no King as yet." To those who said, " Well, what shall we cry?" I answered, "Cry *Vive la France!* That is a cry that suits all times."

One Sunday some women fell on a number of officers in a public walk, and tried to tear off their Crosses of the Legion of Honour; whereupon the latter promptly joined forces, and flung the most violent into the river, the waters of which were, fortunately, low; I interfered in time to prevent further mischief. On another day, some of the garrison, exasperated by the provocations of the cadets, who were beginning to appear in their uniform, gave chase to them through the streets, as well as the women who had joined them. I rushed to the rescue, and, wresting a gun from the hands of a sub-lieutenant, I cried: "Would you dishonour your epaulets by charging women and children at the point of the bayonet!"

Nothing but the soldiers' respect and affection for me would have enabled me to appease their anger and restrain their burning desire to make reprisals, for they were beset by outsiders who flocked to the barracks, solely for the purpose of inciting them to violence: "In another fortnight," they said, "you will be leaving Montauban, so that if you sacked the town, you would, at any rate, secure a certain amount of plunder, and nothing would happen to you." Although these fomenters of disorder were, for the most part, strangers to the army, still, the Generals of the different corps, the leaders who were denounced daily, dared not to impose too strict a discipline, and I was frequently obliged to confine some of the soldiers to their quarters in order to prevent a disaster. I felt a particular dislike for the women of the lower classes. These harpies, blinded by their fanatical attachment to religion and the Royalists, braved every danger, jibed the men for their weakness, preached rioting, and blended their private with their public hatreds.

At length by dint of patience, kind words, and appeals to the Royalist chiefs, I at last reaped the fruit of my moderation. I let it be known that I should only retain my office during the time needed to secure the submission

of the troops, whose co-operation was indispensable for the
common safety ; and I am bound to acknowledge that the
principal inhabitants did everything that lay in their power
to aid me. On the other hand, I often assembled the most
influential soldiers, the most prominent Protestants and the
leaders of the liberal party, and showed them that any
attempt at resistance would have no other result than to
create a number of victims. In this way the minds of the
people were so well prepared that when the news reached
them of the arrival of Louis XVIII. in Paris on the 12th
of July, and when, as the Royalists desired me to proclaim
the return of the King, I called a meeting of the chief
military leaders, I was assured that I was the only person
who could bring about a general submission, and that I
might reckon on their support.

With regard to the cockade, it was agreed that, before
changing it, we should await the orders of the Minister of
War. The troops and the National Guard were drawn up
in a square. I took my station on horseback in the middle.
I then announced the events that had taken place in Paris,
and the return of Louis XVIII. ; I told them that, for the
sake of France, her repose and her safety, our submission
must be unanimous, and that I now asked for this final
proof of their devotion and patriotism. Then, at a given
signal, the National Guards and the Royal Volunteers joined
the soldiers, and, after directing them to form into a column,
I marched through the city at their head. It would be
impossible to paint the enthusiasm of the women or the
calm, resigned dignity of the soldiers. All was over at
eleven o'clock. Nevertheless, I thought it prudent to
confine the troops to their quarters.

Everything would have passed off successfully had not
a detachment of Chasseurs returned, a few minutes later,
from a tour of inspection in the Department. They were
surprised at all this merry-making and at the sight of the
white cockades, and, irritated by some insulting remarks,
they drew their swords and wounded a few of the inhabitants, both Volunteers and Verdets. I had them arrested

immediately, but this did not calm the public indignation. In the twinkling of an eye the military stores in the town-hall were pillaged, and the people marched on the gaol, determined to massacre the prisoners. I hurried at once to the building, and stood in front of the gate, using all the arguments I could think of to prevent them from forcing an entrance.

At the same time, I sent the commanders of the different divisions to the barracks to restrain the soldiers, who were exasperated by their comrades' danger ; and, for nearly six hours, I confronted a crowd of madmen, brandishing swords, levelling pistols, howling, " *To arms ! death to the assassins !* " At last I made myself heard : " What ! " I cried, " you have each of you a gun in one hand and a sword in the other, and yet you ask for arms, while my sword remains in its scabbard ! I am here in the midst of you for the sole purpose of preventing you and the prisoners from butchering one another ! " Towards evening peace was restored, and every one went home quietly. I believe that this was the only revolution since 1789 that terminated without bloodshed.

As soon as I had managed to have the change of Government proclaimed throughout the entire Department, and had received the assurance that order prevailed everywhere, I announced my departure. Nevertheless, the Commissioners of the Duc d'Angoulême declared, in the name of the Prince, that I might either keep the Prefecture of Montauban or take that of Toulouse, if I preferred it. I answered that my conduct had not been dictated by any personal interest ; that my sole chance of winning the esteem, if not the gratitude, of the inhabitants of the Tarn-et-Garonne was to retire now when my intervention was no longer necessary ; that with the establishment of the King's authority my mission ceased, and that I could not accept another. I added that it was my desire to withdraw from public life, and that their presence, joined to that of the inhabitants, at the moment of my departure, would prove I was free from peril and reproach, which was what my conscience desired.

Thereupon I entered a carriage in the midst of an immense crowd, among which were the leaders of the two parties, and hastened to join my wife and children once more. But I found my property in a wretched condition. It had been occupied, for the second time, by the Allies, and, what with forced contributions and requisitions of every kind, it was two years before I could reduce my estates to order or derive any profit from them.

A month after my departure, I received the most flattering expressions of sympathy and gratitude from the Prefect who succeeded me, the Conseil Général, the Mayor of Montauban, the Royal Volunteers, the Grand Vicar of the diocese, and Mme. de Balbi. The Conseil Général of the Loire also considered it their duty to give me a proof of their regret and esteem. I reproduce these documents [1] here, because I found them of considerable value to me, when an attempt was made later to oblige all the higher officials of the Hundred Days to defray the expenses of the war, and when it was actually threatened to prosecute them personally. The proposal was of course rejected, and, in any case, it could not, apparently, have applied to me, as it referred only to those who had joined the Emperor before the 23rd of March. But, in a time of violent reaction, no one can feel sure of not falling a victim to arbitrary power ; consequently these documents were not only flattering tokens of esteem, but were valuable as a safeguard.

---

[1] We quote only the last :—

"MONSIEUR,—The members of the Conseil Général of the Loire, in session at Montbrison, have learned of your return to Rambuteau. This circumstance enables us to give expression to our regret that this Department is deprived of the advantage of seeing you again at the head of its administration, for you have left behind you many claims on the gratitude of the inhabitants. We, who have been especially the witnesses of your labours, desire to pay a legitimate tribute to the wisdom you displayed in difficult circumstances, and to your constant and zealous solicitude for the public good and that of the Department confided to your care.—Believe us, Monsieur," &c. (*Here follow ten signatures.*)

CHAPTER VI

TWELVE YEARS OF LEISURE

THUS, after seven years of a feverish existence in the midst of, perhaps, the most extraordinary events in our history, I was restored to what are commonly described as the delights of private life. And high time, too, so far as the welfare of my property was concerned. Our house had been for two months one of the headquarters of the Allies, whom we had to lodge and board. The grocer's bill alone amounted to 2700 francs. Out of forty-two head of cattle there remained one cow ; seventeen oxen had fallen victims to a requisition in a single day ; not to speak of the assessments in money, &c., &c. God save France from another invasion !

As if these calamities were not enough, we had to suffer the horrors of famine for two successive years. In 1816 and 1817, bread was sold at eight-pence a pound, even in our mountains ; and but for the potatoes, half the population must have died of hunger. What was the best method of relieving such misery ? In my opinion, the most charitable plan that could be adopted was to give employment. I had all my woods enclosed with ditches, had two ponds cleaned out, and ornamental paths made through my park ; in short, I employed as many hands as I could, a proceeding that did not exactly improve my impaired exchequer.

Owing to the death of my grandmother de Laviefville, I was obliged to go to Paris at the beginning of 1816. I wore mourning, a very suitable garb, for all those who had held high places during the Hundred Days were treated as pariahs. Even the closest ties of relationship, as well as those of friendship, were shattered by this sudden outburst of party feeling. Thus, my cousin, Mme. de Lavillegontier, requested me not to visit her. I was well received, however, by the Duchesse de Narbonne, the Abbé de Montesquiou, Mme. de Fézensac, the Sémonvilles, and by the Jaucourts, who, after their return to France, had written to my wife : "We cannot forget the children of our friend ; tell us how we can serve M. de Rambuteau." I should say the same of Mme. de Balbi, to whose unaltered friendliness I feel sure I owed the gracious reception which the Abbé de Montesquiou bestowed on me.

I saw a good many of my old friends besides, who were pretty much in the same situation as myself—Marshal Suchet and his wife, who never proved false to their opinions ; General Belliard, General Andréossi, &c. It was now that I formed my close friendship with General Foy.

I had known his wife in 1812 and 1813, a charming woman, whose popularity in fashionable society by no means interfered with her duties as the mother of a family: the manner in which she brought up her five children made them in every respect worthy of being adopted by France.[1] They were living at the time in a little *entresol* in the Rue de Verney, where I used to eat my leg of mutton in company with Sismondi. One morning they invited me to a late breakfast, given to celebrate the deliverance of General Drouot, who had just been acquitted and was leaving the Abbaye. You may imagine our joy at this act of justice— an act of justice indeed, for, during the Hundred Days, he had refused to accept his salary for the past year spent in the Isle of Elba, saying he had no right to take it, as he was not then in the service of France. After our excitement had calmed down a little, we noticed, with considerable astonishment, his fine new frock-coat, for he had always been careless in the matter of dress. "Well," he said,

---

[1] The national subscription opened in their favour exceeded a million francs in a few weeks. Mme. Foy was the daughter of General Baraguay-d'Hilliers. She had married General Foy in 1807.

Héliog Dujardin Paris.

The Duchesse de Narbonne-Lara.

"you know I am very ugly, and a three weeks' imprisonment did not improve my appearance. But as I wished to look my best on the day of my execution, I had this coat made for me."

My stay in Paris gave me an opportunity of looking into the affairs of the Duchesse de Narbonne, who had no income except the little pension which we allowed her. For the Restoration had suppressed all pensions granted by the Emperor. I had hoped that the favour which the Abbé de Montesquiou enjoyed at Court would insure the restitution of her annuity ; he was her nephew,[1] and, having been brought up by the Duchess, the latter had strong claims on his gratitude. He assured me that he had made every possible effort, had used all the influence he could bring to bear on the King and the Comte d'Artois, but that, owing to the remembrance in which the Comte de Narbonne's devotion to Napoleon was still held, all his labours had been in vain. This reminded me of what my father-in-law once said to me : " Rambuteau, you are my adopted son ; but you will find that, during your whole life, this adoption will bring you more plague than profit. For remember, that hatreds which are born of political differences die hard." But the Abbé was mistaken. Louis XVIII. sent a note for *a thousand francs* to the Duchess. She returned it, with the remark that his Majesty had undoubtedly sent it to the wrong address, as he had evidently intended to bestow the money on the poor of his parish.

The Emperor was more magnanimous, as I have already remarked, for he sent Bertrand, the Grand Marshal, on the 23rd of March 1815, to inquire into the situation of Mme. de Narbonne, because, though hostile to the Empire and faithful to royalty, she was the mother of an aide-de-camp who had died in his service.

I did not, however, consider myself beaten. It struck me that the pension of the Duchess might be included

[1] He was the son of a sister of the Duc de Narbonne, who had married the Marquis de Montesquiou-Fézensac.

under the head of the debts of the Princes, for which the Chambers had just voted 25,000,000 francs. Fortunately, I found a supporter in the secretary of the Commission of Liquidation, who was a particular friend of M. de Mesgrigny. I reminded him how she had spent fifteen years during the Émigration with Mesdames at Rome and Trieste, during which time she had neither received her allowance as Lady-in-waiting nor the money she had advanced, nor did she even receive the legacy bequeathed to her by Madame Adélaïde ; and I asked why should not her claims be considered as among the debts due from members of the Royal Family. The Abbé de Montesquiou despaired of any result. But, for all that, I obtained a reimbursement of 180,000 francs, and her name was inscribed on the public ledger for a pension of 9000 francs. And so the future of the woman who had been *bequeathed* to me by M. de Narbonne was assured.

I will not mention my own troubles except to pay a well-deserved tribute to the strength of character, business capacity, and foresight of Mme. de Rambuteau. No one ever grew rich in the service of the King, and, certainly, no one ever grew rich in the service of the Emperor ; my emoluments as Chamberlain and Prefect never in any way equalled my expenses ; the Revolution, Emigration, and Invasion did the rest. It was only by selling a part of my estates, besides making other necessary sacrifices, and by exercising a rigid economy with regard to what was left, that I at last found myself in the possession of independent but greatly straitened means.

I devoted all my energies to the improvement of my property, and planted my first larches in 1817. Whilst I was Prefect of the Simplon, in pursuance of the Emperor's orders, and with special reference to the naval constructions at the port of Toulon, I had carefully studied the eighty thousand hectares of forest land in the Valais. I had been struck with the beauty of these trees, several of which were a hundred and twenty feet high and fourteen feet in circumcumference. As the soil seemed very similar to that of the mountains and moors of Rambuteau, I had often thought of acclimatising these larches on my own estates. Never did any experiment succeed better. In thirty years, my nurseries supplied me with thirty thousand larches, sixty thousand pines, firs, cedars, and other coniferæ, besides fifty thousand fruit, forest, and ornamental trees. In this way I planted magnificent woods, which are still the delight of my eyes.

My third daughter, Amable, was born the same year. I have good reason to thank God for her birth, since she is the only one of my daughters who has left me grand-children. But for her, my old age would have been gloomy and hopeless, for, alas! I had the misfortune to survive her ; but I thank God for not having suffered my family to die out.

During the winter, Marshal Suchet called on me one morning to ask my advice on an important matter. "The Duke of Wellington," said he, "is urging me to go to the Tuileries. I have confidence in your friendship and judgment. What do you think I ought to do ? " "Monsieur le Maréchal," I replied, "you are the only one left of our colleagues who occupies an important and independent position. All the débris of the Empire has gathered round you ; your betrothal to the Court would end in a marriage of reason, not of inclination. Learn to wait. Your temperate language and your prudent conduct have won you universal esteem ; the day will come when you will be sought after ; and then your co-operation will be all the more valuable, because you will have gained the confidence of all parties." He took my advice, and it was well for him that he did so.[1]

I also met during the same winter, Sebastiani, Caulaincourt, and Stanislas de Girardin,[2] who were glad enough to

---

[1] He was, in fact, soon afterwards restored to the Peerage, and was designated by the King as one of the witnesses to be present at the accouchement of the Duchesse de Berry.

[2] Son of the Marquis de Girardin, who had offered to Rousseau his last asylum at Ermonville. He himself took lessons in music from the illustrious philosopher, and owed his escape from prison during the Terror to this circumstance, which was pleaded in his favour by Mlle. Contat.

visit me in the country, but never went into society. My intimacy with Sainte-Aulaire still continued, and I believe that, both with regard to his mental and moral qualities, he was one of the most remarkable men of the time. I shall never forget how he tried to serve me on the occasion of his daughter's marriage with the Duc Decazes, when he proposed my nomination to the Prefecture of Nîmes. It was at the time when Stanislas de Girardin accepted that of Dijon, and when Marshal Suchet, Mollien, and others entered the Chamber of Peers. I refused it all the same, for I was convinced that my success in dealing with the Catholics and Protestants of Montauban was due to the absolute confidence reposed in me by the Government, but which I should not enjoy at Nîmes. There the leaders and members of different parties would exact undertakings from me which it would be either weak or base on my part to give ; and consequently I should forfeit the confidence of some and the esteem of others. It was therefore better to remain in seclusion.

I gave somewhat the same answer to the Abbé de Montesquiou, when, on two several occasions, he offered to present me at the Tuileries. "No. I served you faithfully until the 25th of March, when you expressed your approbation of my conduct ; but though you are still kind enough to extend your approval to me, I feel that we should never really understand each other, because we do not belong to the same school." "I suspect that you consider that Royalty is in a bad way ?" the Abbé said to me on one occasion. "By no means : if your fears were as few as our hopes, you would sleep more peacefully than you do now. I have no wish to serve you, but I will never conspire against you. I intend returning to the Chamber when I am forty. On that day I will go to the Tuileries to prove my loyalty."

I did more than keep my word, for I never visited the Palais Royal before the 3rd of August 1830, although my friends had for a long time belonged to the party of the Duc d'Orléans.

In 1819, M. Descazes nominated me member of the Conseil Général of the Saône-et-Loire and corresponding member of the Department to the Conseil Central d'Agriculture. I passed the winter of 1820 at Paris. The exiles of 1815 had just been permitted to return. I was delighted to meet Lobau, Bassano, and all the faithful once more, and a ball was given to celebrate the event at Marshal Suchet's on the 13th of February, and in the midst of it M. de Roche-Dragon announced the assassination of the Duc de Berry. There was a cry of horror and indignation. We begged the Marshal, who rushed off at once to join the King at the Opera, to convey to his Majesty the expression of our respect and sympathy ; the surest effect of crime is to draw antagonistic parties together.

The strong friendship I had for Sainte-Aulaire increased my indignation at the violence of the *ultras* and their odious calumnies against M. Decazes.[1] The King himself was deeply afflicted by the accusations, and even feared for the Duke's life. One day that I was speaking on the subject to Mme. de Balbi, she said : " That's just like the King ! His fears are for his friends, never for himself. In 1790 he entreated us to go away : ' *Monseigneur,*' I said, ' *women are not generally killed, they are whipped sometimes ; and perhaps they cry the first time, but they don't mind it the second, and I am too devoted to you not to run the risk.*' Repeat what I have said to M. Decazes, and tell him not to abandon the King." But the tempest was stronger than the affection of the one and the devotion of the other. M. Decazes was compelled to resign from the Ministry. Our intimacy dated from that moment.

I saw a good deal of Victor de Broglie in 1822, as well as of his brother-in-law, Auguste de Staël, with whom I soon made friends. This was about the time when the Doctrinaire school was coming into prominence. I had

---

[1] The *ultras*, who had been long trying to ruin him, accused him of complicity in the assassination of the Duc de Berry, and one of them, Clausel de Coussergues, demanded that he should be arrested and tried. Every one knows the odious words uttered on the occasion : " *Your feet have slid in blood!* "

much veneration for the Royer-Collards and the Guizots, but very little for their young adepts. "I have never governed the State," I used to say to them; "but I have managed several Departments in rather troublesome times. And it was only by advancing from the known to the unknown, by taking care not to ruffle prejudices, by weighing every circumstance, that I managed to attain certain results. Hence my reason for feeling some hesitation in sharing your sublime confidence in the absolutism of your Constitutional theories."

A characteristic trait of the Doctrinaires was their contempt for all who did not indorse their views. I have lived among them for nearly thirty years, but they have never adopted me, and I certainly never desired that they should. Such blind submission was repugnant to my freedom of thought and action; though I found them often just towards me, they were never kindly; whilst the younger disciples, when they realised that I was never likely to join their number, treated me as a person of no account, in spite of my friendship with their leader.

Broglie was the head of the school. He was a favourite with my father-in-law, and accompanied him on his different missions to Illyria and Poland, as well as to Vienna, where he was attaché to the Embassy. He was distinguished at an early age for his eminent abilities, his political integrity, his liberal opinions, his wide knowledge, nor did his maturer years belie the promises of his youth. I had every reason to feel proud of his friendship, although I cannot say that I was ever intimate with him. He had married Mlle. de Staël in 1816, and it was the happiest union I have ever known during the twenty-five years it lasted. It fully realised the dream of Mme. de Staël, who declared: "I wish my daughter to make a love-match, provided it be with a duke or a peer."

M. de Broglie was very friendly towards me during the whole course of his life, and gave me a special proof of his good-will by asking the hand of one of my daughters in

1832, for his younger brother, Comte de Rocca.[1] Still, I always felt rather ill at my ease in his salon when the Doctrinaires happened to be assembled there, for all the talk and laughter was confined to the adepts. They used to form into two or three groups from which the uninitiated —commonplace mortals like myself—were excluded, and so, in spite of the affability of the masters, particularly of my excellent friend, Auguste de Staël, I could not help feeling somewhat uncomfortable. So I fell back upon one of the most amiable of the friends of the family, Mlle. Arondal, and was delighted when I could prevail on her to relate all the particulars of Mme. de Staël's private life.

In 1822 General Foy was at the full height of his glorious parliamentary career. I remember a dinner at which I was present with Casimir Périer, Laffitte, Sebastiani, Chauvelin, Girardin, Dupont de l'Eure, and Caulaincourt. There was a long discussion on the Bourbons, and on the chances of their being able to hold their own, and as to the duration of the Constitutional régime. The General summed up his convictions as follows : " If the Bourbons accept the Charter unreservedly with all its obligations, our duty as Frenchmen is not only to welcome them but to serve them. No doubt they dislike us and feel reluctant to employ us. But of what account are our sacrifices ? Not for a moment must we allow them to weigh in the balance against the advantage of re-establishing our prestige in the eyes of Europe. For if we can once more restore our *locus standi* as a nation, the future is ours, and we shall need no more revolutions. The world at large will be grateful to us for overcoming our antipathies, and for sacrificing our individual interests for the attainment of this object."

Everybody applauded. Such was, at that time, as it was subsequently in 1828, the almost unanimous trend of public opinion : the people would have accepted the Bourbons, if the Bourbons had accepted the Charter. But

---

[1] Madame de Staël had married secretly, in 1810, a young Italian officer in the French service, Comte de Rocca.

from 1815 to 1830, the Royalist party thought much more of securing the privileges which would accrue to itself if the Bourbons returned to power, than of recovering the Crown for the latter.   Hitherto they had been powerless to re-install a sovereign and equally powerless to safeguard his throne, and many of their number declared openly that they preferred to witness the downfall of Royalty to being sup-ported by those who were at heart disloyal to the cause. The year 1822 nearly proved fatal to me.   I underwent an operation for a hydrocele, due to a fall in 1814, when I was riding in great haste from Montbrison to Sainte-Étienne to take measures against the invasion.   A tumour was formed, accompanied by high fever.   Forbin, who attended me, considered that Mme. de Rambuteau should be told of my condition.   She immediately hastened to my bedside.   I was very ill, but I felt convinced that if she arrived in time she would save me.   She called in Larrey, who operated on me, assisted by the senior doctor of the Invalides.   While he was tying up two or three of the ligatures, he was so sur-prised at my silence that he exclaimed : " Why don't you scream ?   You should just hear some of the old soldiers ! they simply deafen me with their yells ! "   " But," I answered, " what is the use of screaming ?   That would not relieve me, for I should have to suffer all the same."

Shortly afterwards I was attacked by a very dangerous fever.   Larrey passed fourteen hours at my bedside and treated me as if I had the plague.   He had me covered with hot oil, and then rubbed with warming-pans.   As soon as I perspired freely, he wrapped my head in ice.   The con-sequence was that whenever they removed the silk bag which held the ice, in order to drain off the water, I always lost consciousness, just as if it were actually attached to this queer kind of head-gear.   Notwithstanding the sweat, which streamed from my body, he made me swallow quantities of iced drinks in order to stop the black vomiting.   At last, after a week, he administered large doses of quinine, so as to prevent a return of the malady, and I owed my life to his treatment, for the

Duc de Richelieu, who was attacked precisely in the same way and at the same time, succumbed in thirty-six hours.

General Foy called almost daily to inquire for me, after quitting the Chamber, and he was sure to find Caulaincourt at my bedside. The pleasure I took in their conversation promoted my convalescence. Singular to say, never has my mind been clearer, my perception quicker, and my powers of expression readier. But it was ten months before I was completely restored to health.

After that it was my daughters' turn to fall ill. All three were attacked by brain fever during the autumn of 1823. I still shudder at the recollection of that time, for no sooner was one out of danger than I had to tremble for another. God preserved them to me ; but no one knows the torturing anxiety which we long endured on account of their health.

In the following year, however, happiness was restored to our hearth. But I had my disappointments, nevertheless. Thanks to the Royalist zeal of M. le Prefet, I lost my election to the College at Mâcon, for he saw fit to cancel more than sixty votes given in my favour. This set-back, by prolonging my enforced inoccupation, enabled me to build Rambuteau. The first stone was laid on the 4th of May 1824, and two years afterwards I was living in my new residence. Just about this time, the Société de l'Encouragement à l'Agriculture commissioned M. Boscq to inspect my larch plantations, and, on his report, the Society awarded me their grand medal of gold as recognition of my labours.

I spent the winter of 1826 at Paris, always with the same friends : Bassano and Caulaincourt, who showed me the contents of their portfolios stuffed with curious documents, interesting for the different points of view with regard to the events of 1813, 1814, and 1815 ; as well as with Montholon (who was squandering the generous legacies of the Emperor and trying to indemnify himself for his six years' seclusion at St. Helena), Sémonville, Royer-Collard, the Dupins, Laffitte, Girardin, &c. Subsequently I returned to the country, where I received Anselme de Braamcamp,[1] very much excited by the political events that had just caused his exile from Portugal. He refused to recognise the institution of the peerage.

"My dear fellow," I said, after I had exhausted all the reasons I could adduce for the necessity of a balance of power, "apart from other considerations there is much wisdom in knowing how to turn prejudices to account. This knowledge is a most useful factor in governing, as the Emperor (who knew something about the matter) always declared. Those very men who pride themselves on their exemption from prejudices are always those who are most subject to their influence. Certain tales told us by our nurses are those that remain the longest in our memories. The only distinction that survived during the Revolution was that enjoyed by a member of the Institute ; the possession of this privilege was deemed an honour by Bonaparte. The Monges, Laplaces, and Berthelots were not the last to take pride in a blue or red order or in the title of Count and Baron. You are really far less advanced than we are. Remember that it is not an easy matter to attach certain forces to the shafts of the governmental car, which might otherwise pull in an opposite direction. Did I succeed in convincing him ? I doubt it. All discussions, especially on political matters, always work round to the same spot. ' I am right, and you are wrong.' "

I spent a part of the autumn at Coppet with Auguste de Staël, who was at the head of a vast agricultural enterprise, and who held a great festival annually at which the leading agriculturists of Switzerland and of foreign countries were present. I returned the following year. His sister was anxious that he should marry ; I did my best to second her, for he was too religious and moral to lead the life of a bachelor. "My mother," he said to me, "wished me to marry an Englishwoman ; but as the Englishwoman had also to be a Protestant, I found it impossible to comply with her desire. The great obstacle in my way was the character

---

[1] His brother had married the eldest daughter of Comte de Narbonne.

of the women I met. Those who were pious and virtuous were generally straight-laced prudes whose temper would drive a husband crazy. Others had taken leave of all decency, and left a would-be husband in no doubt of what he might expect from them."

An unforeseen incident threw him at length in the way of the charming woman who ultimately became his wife. Their happiness, alas ! was short-lived, for, at the end of a year, he became the victim of brain fever, a terrible and hereditary disease that had attacked the mother and which subsequently overtook his brother and sister, thus uniting them all in one and the same melancholy fate. His friend, M. Lullin de Châteauvieu, author of the *Lettres de Saint-James*, conveyed the sad tidings to me at the very moment of my election to the Chamber, and when the voters of the Department of the Ain were ready to give me for colleague one who was my brother in arms and always ready to fight at my side.

In fact, I was elected in the month of November, in spite of the opposition of the Prefect, M. de Villeneuve, who, however, waged war against me in quite honourable fashion. My opponent was M. Doria, the Ministerial candidate and the President of the College, who had held the seat for twelve years. We had been intimate friends ; he was a man of honour, to whose fine qualities I rendered full justice, but politics rupture all ties, and we may congratulate ourselves when it does not shatter all reciprocal esteem as well ! As for myself, I was the candidate of the liberal and constitutional cause which I had served after the fall of the Emperor, and I had announced, as early as 1824, that I would sit between M. Royer-Collard and General Foy. Alas ! I had little time to rejoice over my success : a cruel sorrow was awaiting me. I lost my sister, Mme. de Mesgrigny, who was the victim of an accident. One night when she was going up stairs to her bed-chamber, the taper in her hand set the ribbons in her cap on fire ; the flames caught her hair, and, although immediate help was at hand, she was seriously burned in the neck. It seems the wound contracted the jugular vein, causing an attack of apoplexy to supervene. I can still feel her arms about my neck as she cried, "Save me, brother!" All remedies were useless. In vain did Larrey (who loved her as his own child) lavish the most devoted care on her : she expired at the end of two days. I have often spoken of our childhood and of our great affection for each other. So there is no need to dilate on my sorrow at her loss.

CHAPTER VII

IN THE CHAMBER

THE elections of 1827 were a decided victory for liberal opinion, thanks to Chateaubriand, who, by countenancing the opposition led by C. Périer and Sebastiani, hastened the downfall of M. de Villèle. Right glad was I to find myself again among my old colleagues, many of them, too, my old friends ; they formed the gallant little cohort which had been fighting for twelve years under the command of General Foy, and which had triumphed at last. They were but seventeen to start with ; now recruits were flocking to them from all quarters ; although they were still not strong enough to become a solid majority. But, with the aid of Chateaubriand's party, called the " Réunion d'Agier " (after President Agier, at whose house it used to meet), the two Centres, with a part of the Left, were powerful enough to insist on the formation of a liberal Ministry and on the election of Royer-Collard to the Presidency of the Chamber.

The Left also had its meetings at the Hôtel d'Ogny, under the direction of Casimir Périer and Sebastiani, supported by Laffitte, Dupont de l'Heure, Royer-Collard, and Bertin de Vaux, all devoted to a constitutional monarchy. As for myself, I took my seat next the lobby which separated the Centre from the Left, on the same bench with Augustin Périer, Pelet de la Lozère, and Dupin.

The opposition numbered several of the King's most faithful friends, disgusted with an intriguing, onesided administration, which was bent on excluding from its ranks every man of any capacity. They found no lack of courageous and able individuals amongst us ready to rally to any Government that would give liberty and prosperity to France at home, and honour and independence abroad. As a result of this closer connection and of our uniting together for one common end, many prejudices were removed, and, such is the power of disinterested loyalty, that at the end of a few months MM. de La Ferronnays and Hyde de Neuville had managed to convince Casimir Périer and Sebastiani that their intentions were as upright as their own.

Whatever might have been our starting-point—no matter whether it were Empire or Revolution, Emigration or Restoration—we were all ready to accept the Bourbons, some because we were satisfied with the Charter, others because we wanted to keep the Bourbons, and saw that the surest way of doing so was to comply unreservedly with the provisions of the Charter, and thus preserve the conquests of '89. Doubtless the task was made more difficult by the traditions which each side still retained. But, by extending a hand to such Vendeans as Hyde de Neuville and La Ferronnays, who grasped it with a confidence of which they had no reason to repent as long as they remained in power, we hoped that our devotion would be understood and appreciated by the King.

Unfortunately, his mind was entirely warped by prejudices. He distrusted his best servants, who had dared to tell him the truth, and his only prevailing idea was to conspire against the form of Government created by his brother—against that Charter of emancipation which was intended to span the gulf between the past and future, and to compensate France for her vanished glories by establishing her liberty. I am convinced that ninety-nine per cent. of the Chamber would have been inclined to give a favourable hearing to those wise utterances of General Foy, which I have already recorded, and the sincerity of our sentiments (which we fully intended to carry out in our actions) was enough to explain the existence of our union, which even the Address of the 221 could not succeed in destroying. It only needed the "Ordonnances" to drive us into the background and to restore our distinctive colours to each one of us.

One of the most important points in our programme was our alliance with the *Réunion d'Agier;* nevertheless this alliance was vehemently opposed by the Abbé de Pradt, who hoped to play a great part among us. "How," he exclaimed, "can you speak of an alliance and of negotiating with people who only yesterday were our opponents, and who have been brought to join us merely by their regrets and disappointments. How can you, I say, when you have justice for your fulcrum and France for your lever?" This indignant declamation found little echo, and Mauguin, bantering the Abbé on his revolutionary inflexibility, reminded him of Jupiter Scapin. He had been publishing works for ten years, all intended to promote his candidateship for the Chamber and to enhance the glory of his début in the tribune, which, however, he never ventured to ascend, not having enough courage to make that first appearance.

On this matter Stanislas de Girardin gave me some sterling advice. "When you enter the Chamber," said he, "be sure you are not afraid of the tribune. Such fear is something like the involuntary terror of the soldier when he is first exposed to the enemy's fire ; you must surmount it at all costs. If you remain a fortnight without speaking, you'll never speak. Begin as soon as the question of the verification of powers is discussed ; do not attempt to be eloquent ; test your capacity by letting yourself he heard on questions that have no special importance. The power of making long speeches will come later."

I took his advice, and found it to my advantage ; for it is most important not to break down in a first attempt ; which create prejudices that die hard. Consequently, whenever I have ascended the tribune, during the ten years of my parliamentary career, I have always been more anxious to descend from it with honour than to win applause. Moreover, I was too conscious of my limitations to anticipate anything approaching an oratorical triumph. I was amply satisfied when, as a business man and as an administrator, I could make myself useful by scrupulously studying my subject and by availing myself of the counsels of those superior men in the Chamber who were willing to enlighten me by their experience. I took less part, therefore, in the debates than in the functions and commissions for which my past experience had prepared me. My colleagues were good enough to credit me with a certain measure of ability in my management of such matters as came before me. I remember a meeting at Chalon in 1828, after our election to the Grand College, when M. Thiard, who was annoyed by the counsels and recommendations of certain personages, exclaimed, with some show of temper : " Ah, gentlemen, let me alone ! Every one to his trade ! When you want to speak of laws, talk to Rambuteau ; he has all that sort of thing at his fingers' ends, when you want to talk scandal, come to me ; no one can beat me at that ! "

In fact, the sessions of the Council of State, at which I had been present during three years when in attendance on the Emperor, besides the office of Prefect, which I had held in times of storm and stress, my wide acquaintance with men and things, my ten years' retirement, during which I had devoted my leisure to the study of political economy, and my connection with the most distinguished leaders of the opposition parties during the winters I spent in Paris, reinforced by a certain facility in delivery and a capacity for grasping the essentials of a subject, had all contributed to fit me for my rôle as a deputy. But before taking part in a great concert one should have a clear conception of the compass and pitch of one's voice, and I was not at all inclined to tax the patience of my friends. It was enough for me that my moderation, well-known devotion to constitutional principles, and respect for illustrious memories had secured me the approval of men like Royer-Collard and Casimir Périer.

The first thing I did was to fulfil my promise to the Abbé de Montesquiou by going to pay my respects, as deputy, to the King and Royal Family ; but I also visited the Bertins, whose house was the daily rendezvous of a part of the Ministry. It was at the club which met in the offices of the *Débats*, a sort of constitutional sanctuary, that M. Hyde de Neuville, ex-Minister to Portugal, and a friend of my brother-in-law, M. Braamcamp de Soral, introduced me to the Marquis de la Ferronnays, of whom I became the intimate friend.

He was the typical "perfect *gentilhomme*," as faithful as he was brave and disinterested. It was his deep sense of loyalty which led him to promote a reconciliation between the King and the Charter, between the Revolution and the Bourbons, and he reckoned on the co-operation of all well-disposed people, judging their hearts by his own. Périer and Sebastiani had more confidence in him than even in M. de Martignac, who, fearing to give any cause to the King to doubt his fidelity, often kept unpleasant truths to himself, while M. de La Ferronnays was always outspoken, whatever his frankness might cost him. Thus, on one occasion, when I was awaiting him at Hyde de Neuville's house, he entered, quite beside himself with anger : "What am I to do with a man who has just said to me, with the utmost seriousness, and almost without listening to me, '*My dear Marquis, you wish to save my Crown, and you will, perhaps, succeed in doing so ; but you will not help me to save my soul, and that is the important point !*'" I have always regretted that the state of his health forced him to retire in 1828, for he alone could have prevented the rise of Polignac, which from that moment was assured, to the imminent peril of the country.

During the course of this session, I was nominated member of a Commission charged with the duty of studying the organisation of the Council of State. For a long time the Opposition had demanded that the Judges presiding over the Courts of Equity (in which all lawsuits and matters of litigation were heard) should share in the privilege of irremovability from office enjoyed by all magistrates, seeing that the former had to pronounce judicial sentences ; there were even some who recommended the extension of this same privilege to all the other Judges. I had always admired the old State Council, composed as it was of the illustrious men to whom we owed the Civil Code ; for it might, in some respects, be regarded as the very keystone of the Imperial Government. As there was no danger of publicity, the utmost freedom of speech was permitted ; nay, more, encouraged by the Emperor, who sometimes advanced false arguments himself in order to get at the truth ; no one on these occasions made any pretence to eloquence, and I confess the recollection of these sessions somewhat lessened my appreciation of the finest discussions in the Chamber, where I found that most of the speeches were made for the gallery and seemed to come from the lips of brilliant lawyers rather than of grave judges.

I understood, of course, that representative government and the action of the Chambers and of the tribune would deprive the Council of State of a good deal of its authority, but, nevertheless, I felt that it was a necessary measure, both for the forming of laws, the regulation of public administration, and the maintenance of order and discipline in the great administrative body, whose co-operation must constitute the strength and security of the throne. The Council of State, as the guardian of Royal institutions, ought therefore to remain always under the control of Royalty, and have nothing in common with Parliaments. For one of the greatest benefits conferred by the Con-stituent Assembly was the entire separation of the Depart-ment of Justice from that of Administration, thereby providing an absolute guarantee for judicial independence, which had been insured by their measure for the irremov-ability of Judges.

The Court of Cassation was the crowning of the department of Justice, the Council of State that of the department of Administration, and the section of the " Contentieux " (Equity Courts) maintained the division of powers by removing to its tribunal all acts of litigation which could not very well be dealt with in either depart-ment. The wisdom of this arrangement has been justified by time. But if in judicial matters eventualities can be foreseen and prejudged with all the impassiveness of the law, the same thing does not apply to questions belonging to the department of Administration, which cannot forecast the results of all cases or anticipate their delicate circumstances. It must be satisfied with laying down general principles, always allowing sufficient latitude to the administrative *personnel* to insure their execution. For this purpose we have Ministers, Prefects, Mayors, &c.—legislators on a small scale, and it is their decisions, rules, regulations, &c., whose limitations are ultimately fixed by the Council of State. Consequently, a permanent Council of State would be more powerful than any Ministry, and would thus constitute a danger for the country as well as for the Government. Such were the views I put forward in the Commission, and I was very much surprised at the silence of M. de Cormenin, who read two or three memoranda ; for this gentleman, eloquent as he was when wielding his pen, had never been known to speak either in the Chamber or in the Council.

M. de Portalis succeeded M. de la Ferronnays ; unfortunately his devotion to Royalty was of too recent a date to permit him to venture on speaking unreservedly to the King. So we began to feel that M. de Polignac's hour had struck ; in fact he was already on the way to Paris. But our leaders, whom we all hastened to join, raised such a cry of alarm, and the attitude of the Chamber was so threatening, that he quickly made his way back to London.[1] Portalis was not the sort of man to inspire M. de Martignac with energy : we soon perceived the fact on the introduction of the Municipal and Departmental Bill, which was to be a pledge of union, but was really a second edition of the double vote. Its aim was to supply a fulcrum to the aristocratic party, aided by the General Councils, which were henceforth to act as a counterpoise to the influence of a popular Chamber. The law, in fact, would reduce the number of electors by nearly a third, and this result, having been represented to the King in its most advantageous light,

---

[1] Where he was Ambassador.

decided him to consent to a measure which he had hitherto
regarded as a dangerous concession.

It had been almost settled that the scheme should be
submitted to Sainte-Aulaire, Le Pelletier d'Aunay, Pelet de
la Lozère, Meschain, and myself, all of us ex-Prefects and
familiar with everything connected with the Departments.
But we were disappointed, and not a little surprised, when
we heard the Bill read in the Chamber by M. de Martignac.
After descending from the tribune, he was kind enough to
ask me what I thought of it. "You have tried," I said
"to please the Left and the Right, and you will satisfy
neither. The very principle that you have just asserted
will furnish me with arguments against you, and I shall
warn every one of the consequences which this Bill will
have in his own individual Department. I don't believe,
by the time I have finished, that you will find a single
member of the majority inclined to support you."

After that I shut myself up for three weeks with my
cousin, Choppin d'Arnouville ; we drew up comparative
tables of the electoral lists of the several departments and
arrondissements, and, after the debate on the bureaus, I
was elected a member of the Commission. I would have
been nominated reporter, had not Sebastiani been most
anxious for the position ; when I realised this, I retired,
having always preferred a friend to a success ; moreover,
the high position he held in the Chamber made up for his
lack of special knowledge on the subject. I was chosen
Secretary, and Dupont de l'Eure President. Guizot drew
up a brief statement of the principles at stake, and the
report concluded with a demand for the suppression of the
Conseils d'Arrondissement and the election of the General
Councils by all the electors.

The discussion was very animated. Royer-Collard
said to me : "You are not strong enough for a hand-to-
hand struggle with Martignac, but I will make Vatimesnil
and his party over to you." Before entering upon the
separate clauses, an attempt was made to negotiate with
the Commission, and Dupont de l'Eure and I were

chosen to confer with the Government. But the Ministry refused almost every concession, and Dupont de l'Eure broke off the conference, saying : " I have been accused of hostility to the Bourbons ; if I were their enemy, I should rejoice at your obstinacy, for it will alienate the majority from the Ministers and the King. But, in very truth, all our efforts have been directed to the maintenance of the institutions and the Government to which you claim we are opposed." And nothing could be more sincere than were his words. Although Dupont was not a man of superior ability, he was thoroughly high-principled, an upright magistrate and a moderate liberal. Provided that France regained her independence, he cared very little at whose hands it was received. In dismissing Dupont from office,[1] M. de Villèle committed a grave fault. Having failed to secure a seat for him in the Court of Cassation, for which we had asked, and which M. de Ferronnays had promised, if he went to the Tuileries, we had elected him Vice-President of the Chamber.

At this period I often met M. Portal, ex-Minister of the Navy ; he was then in high favour with the Duc d'Angoulême, who could not have confided in a better man. He persuaded me to visit the Prince. I was honoured with an audience, well received, and listened to with attention ; but I retired more grateful for my reception than hopeful of the result of my frankness.

On Shrove Thursday, 1829, there was a fête at the Tuileries to which we were all invited. The *Muette de Portici* was performed. This selection seemed to me odd, to say the least of it, for the representation of a riot, the tocsin, red-capped Revolutionists, in such a place and under the very eyes of the Duchesse d'Angoulême, was distinctly out of place. " What do you think of it ? " Mme. de Balbi asked me. " Upon my word, Madame, I can almost fancy myself at the feast of Balthazar, with the three fateful words writ large on the wall ! " My forebodings were so strong that I took M. de Martignac aside, and said to him :

[1] That of First President of the Court of Rouen.

" Monsieur le Ministre, there are circumstances in which the
most trivial incidents affect us deeply. Two things divide
us, the Conseils d'Arrondissement and the electoral lists.
Make this concession to us : allow the members of the
Councils General to be elected in the same way in which
the deputies are elected, and I promise to obtain from the
Commission the maintenance of the Conseils d'Arrondissement." "You are a good citizen," he answered, pressing
my hand, "but we have got to such a pass that, if you
asked me for a pin I could not give it to you." Some
days after, the Bill was withdrawn.

I was on the Budget Commission for the War and
Home Ministries, and here again, thanks to the conciliatory
spirit I displayed, I was able to render more than one service
to M. de Martignac, and specially to M. de Caux. Indispensable reforms had to be introduced into the War
Budget, notably for the Swiss Guard and the Staff of the
Princes. M. de Caux confessed as much, but he hoped to
obtain them from the King, and therefore begged us to
let him take the initiative in these painful concessions, and
thus save his Majesty's *amour propre* from being wounded.
He even pledged himself to bring them forward at the next
session, and to resign if they were not accepted. We agreed
to this delay ; the Budget was discussed quietly ; another
proof of our desire for concord.

I will not speak of the Commission of Customs, of
which I was Secretary, nor of the tedious discussions on
iron and sugar manufactures. Other events were hastening
to their fulfilment which were to render our peaceful
labours of no avail. The accession to power of the
Polignac Ministry had deeply wounded the majority. The
Right Centre, flanked by the Chateaubriand group, vied
with the Left in violence. Hyde de Neuville and Bertin
led the attack in the *Débats*, while Royer-Collard and
Guizot made use of the columns of the *Globe*, a journal
founded by the *Aide-toi, le Ciel t'aidera* Society.[1] It was the

---

[1] A club founded in 1826 by Guizot, Odilon Barrot, and Barthe ; it soon
included all the members of the liberal opposition. The manifesto said :

organ of the Doctrinaires, almost republican in sentiment, deriving from Constitutional principles all that could diminish the royal authority, and (resembling in this the old Protestant party after the League) it sought to establish a system which should be almost independent of Royalty. A third paper, the *Temps*, steered a middle course between the *Débats* and the *National*, and interpreted the sentiments of a large portion of the Left ; its managers were three deputies, MM. Gautier de Bordeaux, Augustin Périer, and myself.

The Opposition was therefore very powerful, having rallied all its strength in defence of that Charter which had restored to some the liberties won by the Revolution, to others the ancient race of our Kings, and it will always redound to the honour of Louis XVIII. that for ten years he succeeded in revivifying and maintaining a monarchy which had been restored under the most unfavourable conditions, but to which France undoubtedly was indebted for her subsequent peace and prosperity. The fact that he died peacefully in the Tuileries was sufficient testimony to the value of compromise and moderation. But, unfortunately, Charles X. had very different political views. As soon as the Chambers opened in 1830, I was unfavourably impressed by M. de Polignac's attitude. He was well aware that he was the object of legitimate suspicions ; all the same, he affected a self-assurance, or rather a self-asserting arrogance, which may have testified to his courage, but certainly not to his parliamentary ability. No one could have staked his own fortune as well as his master's with greater recklessness and more ill-placed devotion.

The address of the 221 was our answer. I attended the different meetings held for the purpose of deciding upon the terms in which it should be presented. The Chateaubriand group astonished us by its impetuosity : beneath which the sullen rumble of the disgraced Minister

---

" We can rely only on ourselves. If, then, we wish to preserve the remnants of the rights so gloriously conquered forty years ago, let us remember : *Heaven helps those who help themselves.*" Hence its name.

M

was plainly audible. On the other hand, Guizot and Royer-Collard displayed the ordinary gravity at the deliberation which distinguished the manner of the Doctrinaire, mingled (no doubt unconsciously) with a certain degree of pleasurable excitement, due to the thought that they were giving a lesson to the Mamurras of loyalty.[1] The address was the work of the most ardent Monarchists ; Casimir Périer and Sebastiani took no part in it, in order not to interfere with its success, for it was intended to be simply a salutary warning, its aim being to point out the danger to the King and prevent a catastrophe. And now, after thirty years, I do not shrink from asserting what I then thought and said, that, among the 221, who were afterwards so misunderstood and calumniated, there were not three who desired to overthrow the Throne.

Some days after the dissolution of the Chamber, I happened to meet M. de Talleyrand at Mme. Gaucourt's. He asked me what I thought of the situation. I told him that, as far as I could judge, every one of the 221 would be re-elected ; they would return irritated, and, reinforced by other malcontents, would be very hostile towards the Crown ; and, being convinced of the ill-will of the King, would not leave him prestige enough to enable him to govern. I went on to say that it would be very difficult to steer clear of the mistakes made by the Constituent and Legislative Assemblies, which, though they wanted to retain the King, distrusted him, and only thought of tying his hands, forgetting that his *raison d'être* was to reign, and that by their own actions they were preparing the way for a new Revolution. It was therefore our duty, I urged, to support Legitimacy. " Very fine sentiments, truly," answered M. de Talleyrand, " but very futile. I do not know who will bury the Bourbons, but I do know, and that very well, that they are already dead at the present moment, and will never come to life again."

---

[1] Mamurra, a Roman knight, commissary and favourite of Cæsar during the expedition to Gaul, where he grew rich in the service of his master. The epigrams of Catullus on his robberies, luxury, and fawning adulation have rendered him famous among courtiers.

And, when I asked him to explain what he meant, he employed the same language as Corvisart had used on another occasion, when his words made a deep impression on me : "'*A man cannot act in opposition to his inherent nature.*' In the case of Charles X., he is guided by a conscientious principle which will involve him in the most momentous consequences. I foresee these consequences ; but that is my secret." What wonderful sagacity this man always displayed l It is easy to comprehend how, so far from suffering from revolutions, he turned every one of them to his personal advantage. One day Louis XVIII. expressed his surprise at his continual good fortune in this respect. "Sire," said he, with a smile, "Providence undoubtedly protects me, and has ordained that misfortune shall always pursue those who are antagonistic to me."

I was not mistaken as to my election ; I had more votes than in 1827, thanks to the ill-advised proclamation of the King, in which the 221 were declared to be enemies of the Crown. On the evening after the election, two hundred voters came to the drawing-room of M. Tondu to congratulate me, and to ask for an account of the present situation. I told them my colleagues would have the same success that I had, and that, if the King kept his Polignac Ministry, they would struggle to the last extremity ; but that a Constitutional Ministry would certainly save the situation. M. de Talleyrand, however, had made no mistake either. At the very moment I was speaking, everything was lost : the King was signing the Ordinances.

When they appeared, I was at the waters of Saint-Alban with my wife and children. I anticipated trouble, and therefore hurried back to Mâcon, where I heard of "the days of July." I was electrified by the news. When the mail-coach arrived on the 30th, flying the Tricolor, the fall of the Monarchy was proclaimed, and the Prefect was replaced by an administrative commission. I persuaded my friends to take the initiative in the movement, so as to prevent disorder. I then started at once for Paris, stopping at Chalon, where I also persuaded the Sub-prefect to adopt the measures best adapted to restrain a population holding such advanced opinions, and assured him of my support. His courage and coolness were afterwards rewarded with the Prefectship of the Landes.

I met the Duke de Chartres [1] in the forest of Lieursaint ; he had left Joigny with his regiment. I gave him news of our Department, and he decided to remain that night in Villeneuve-Saint-Georges.

It was rather late when I reached Paris. I found persons at the barriers making collections for the wounded. The populace were returning from Rambouillet, and I heard Pajol,[2] who commanded the expedition, say that, with five or six squadrons, he could have scattered the mob like sheep, and not a single one of them would have been left to return to Paris.

My first visit was to Casimir Périer, who met me with the words, " You must go to the Palais-Royal." Now for ten years I had constantly refused to do so—not that I entertained the slightest dislike for the Prince and his family ; quite the contrary. The kindness shown by the Duchesse d'Orléans and Mme. Adélaïde to my sister[3] had touched me keenly. But I had always remained sincerely attached to the house of the Emperor ; moreover, I did not care to take part in any intrigue, and certainly not in any conspiracy. So I always endeavoured to preserve my independence, and, if I went to the Tuileries, it was merely in my capacity as deputy, and then only once or twice a year. In my opposition to the Ministry, I pursued the path traced out for me by General Foy, and was faithful to Legitimacy as long as it was faithful to the Charter. In vain had Périer, Sebastiani, Dupin, and Auguste de Staël, an intimate friend of the Orléans family, urged me to visit

---

[1] Eldest son of Louis-Philippe, colonel of the 1st Regiment of Hussars.

[2] An ex-general of the Empire, very hostile to the Bourbons. He had at one time served under Comte de Narbonne. We know that this march on Rambouillet forced Charles X. to depart for Cherbourg.

[3] They had repeatedly tried to persuade her to become a member of their household, and Mme. de Mesgrigny would have consented but for her widowhood and the education of her son.

the Palais-Royal; I had rejected all their appeals. Now, however, the case was different. In a quarter of an hour, Périer convinced me of my duty. I also had a talk on the subject with Sebastiani. Both of them informed the Prince of my intention, and I was notified that I should be received early the next day.

I was punctual. On the way, I encountered Gautier de la Gironde, one of the most notable members of the Réunion Agier, and an old friend of the Duchesse d'Angoulême. "Where are you going?" "To the Palais-Royal." We chatted. "Well," said he, "when you pledge your fealty to the Duc d'Orléans, you can speak for two; for I am half with you; in fact, we have no other resource." At the Palace I expressed a wish to see Mme. de Montjoie, who had been very fond of my poor sister; she said she would be pleased to receive me. I was then introduced to her.

I found the Duke alone with the Duchess: he was in a long frock-coat, an ordinary pair of trousers, and wore no neck-tie; she was wearing a cambric wrapper, and was sitting at a small table pen in hand. His Highness embraced me. He told me how glad he was to see me, and how he had long wished to have me for a friend, having always set the highest value on my character. "Monseigneur," I answered, "I never do things by halves; when I devote myself to a cause, I devote myself entirely, and always with the object of serving France; I would have served the late King with all my heart, if he had let me. Now, however, you are the only person who can save her; and so I bring you the same unconditional and boundless devotion which formerly I dedicated to the Emperor." He embraced me again. "The only way in which a person can show his confidence in a man like you is to speak to him frankly and from the heart. I have no cause for uneasiness with respect to England and Russia; but I have to think of Vienna—my natural enemy is there!" "Monseigneur," I returned, "you may be quite certain that if there were any hope for the Emperor's son,

1 should not be here. But we were taught in his father's school that the welfare of France takes precedence of everything. So that now that you alone can save the monarchy, and avert the direst misfortunes—namely, the Republic and civil war—all the Bonapartists will rally round you."

He then begged me to see Bassano and write to General Drouot, both of which I promised to do immediately. He also questioned me as to the feeling of the Chamber ; I repeated the words of Gautier, which were an important indication of the disposition of his party. Finally, he added : " Still, I cannot accept the crown as long as the King remains in France ! " At these words the Duchess raised her head, and broke the silence she had maintained until then. " No, M. de Rambuteau," she exclaimed, " that is impossible ! " I was much impressed by her emotion and tears. " Madame," I said, " revolutions neither recede nor stand still. You will be a Queen before Sunday, or you will never be one. To return to the shades of Neuilly is no longer in your power : either the throne or exile is your destiny and that of your eight children." She sighed and made no answer. I dwelt at length on the needs and expectations of France. Then I took my leave of their Highnesses, and paid another visit to Mme. de Montjoie. She would not let me go without having been introduced to Madame Adélaïde, who requested me to repeat the conversation I had just had with her brother. I rehearsed all I had said, but with even more warmth, entreating her at the same time to use her influence with the Prince. " If he fails us, we are certainly on the high road to a Republic under the Presidency of M. de Lafayette. Therefore he must come to a decision at once. He cannot, of course, afford France the luxury of victories and conquests ; neither can he rely on the ancient traditions and the time-hallowed claims of Legitimacy ; but he can be a new King, a citizen King, chosen by the Chambers, acclaimed by the country, strong in the principles of '89, sheltered and protected by that Tricolor flag which he has served and carried. And so, profiting by the lessons which he has learnt in exile, let the Prince resolve to depend solely on the support of the *people*. For however worthy of respect and consideration the clergy might be, no clerical party could form a fitting basis for the Government, whilst if, on the other hand, the nobility strove to revive its prestige and privileges, it would soon discover that it had lost all its influence on the country in losing its substantial property. Thus unquestionably the day has come for the middle classes to reign supreme, provided they be careful to ameliorate the condition of their poorer brethren."

Madame Adélaïde requested me to write down a brief summary of my ideas, as it would help her to make an impression on her brother. Then I hurried to see Bassano, and discovered that he held exactly the same opinions as myself. He recognised the fact that nothing could be done for the King of Rome, and that a Republic was inevitable, if we did not do our best to prevent such a calamity ; he assured me that all the friends of the Emperor—Drouot, Lobau, Durosnel, Corbineau, Exelmans, &c.—would be on our side. In fact, the letter which Drouot wrote in reply to mine was a model of disinterestedness, patriotism, and wisdom.[1]

From there I went to breakfast with the Duc de Broglie, and met Prince Adrien de Laval-Montmorency, who had arrived from Rambouillet on a mission to propose the abdication of Charles X. and the accession of the Duc de Bordeaux under the Regency of the Duc d'Orléans. "It is too late," answered M. de Broglie ; "it might have been possible three days ago ; now the game is played, and only a dynastic sacrifice can save the country. We are bringing about an English revolution ; France will have her 1688 with the nearest heir in the Constitutional line, as England had, at that period, the nearest heir in the Protestant line. The whole matter will be settled by the Chambers, and that, too, without any further change in the Constitution. What strength could a Regency have? Supposing that

---

[1] We have not been able to find this letter among the papers of Comte de Rambuteau.

Henri V. were put on the throne, what could be done with Charles X. and the Duchesse de Berry, and the Duc and Duchesse d'Angoulême ? Every day would witness the renewal of the same conflicts and the same difficulties."

Even M. de Sémonville, who had exerted all his efforts to save the crown of the Duc de Bordeaux, could not gainsay these arguments. He assured me that, if he had been listened to at Saint-Cloud on the 29th and 30th of July, and if the young Prince had been sent to the Palais-Royal or to the Hôtel de Ville, he would have been immediately proclaimed. As for myself, I am convinced that the Duchesse Marie-Amélie would have received him as an eldest son, and I knew the meaning of the tears I had seen her shed on that morning.

During the day, I paid a visit to M. de Lafayette, who was holding a sort of quasi-revolutionary court at the Hôtel de Ville. I saw M. de Talleyrand in the evening, after the session at which the Chamber had selected the members of the Commission of the Charter, which was to present its report on the following day. He was very favourable to the movement which he had so accurately forecast. "But," said he, "would it not be better to create a Provisional Government for four or five weeks, and thus allow the Chambers to effect the necessary changes, calm the public excitement and prevent the usual tumult that follow insurrections ?" "No," I replied, "that is not my opinion. The revolution has taken everybody by surprise, and everybody is already seeking to turn it to his own advantage. The Chambers have only a semblance of power. If a head is not given to the State immediately, in two days' time we shall have to choose between the Republic at Paris and Charles X. at Rambouillet. So far, the people have been as generous as brave. To wait would be to supply fuel to their passions. Moreover, do you feel competent to control the storm, and have you the *quos ego* of Neptune wherewith to still the waves ?"

And, indeed, the agitation on the following day was extreme. As the National Guard had not yet been organised, volunteers in rags mounted guard at the Palais-Royal, and the entire populace of the quarter, which was devoted to the Duc d'Orléans, rallied round his residence to protect it from pillage. For more than three months these tatterdemalions were to be seen everywhere, in the yards, on the staircases, in the ante-chambers ; and it was only with great trouble, and at the expense of much diplomacy, that they were at last prevailed upon to make way for the National Guards.

The day was spent in cabals, where the policy to be adopted in the evening was discussed. The Republican party proposed to put the Chamber to flight or to compel it to elect Lafayette President ; the success of the skirmish at Rambouillet had elated the people, and everything was to be feared. There is one man for whom I must express my profound respect, having proved by his conduct on this occasion that he was as good a Frenchman as he was a clear-sighted politician, and this was M. Odilon Barrot. More than any one else, he helped to enlighten M. de Lafayette, and to persuade him to refuse the Presidency of the Chamber or to proclaim the Republic, assuring him that Louis-Philippe, with his own liberal institutions, would personify the best of Republics : wise words which he remembered, and declaimed when he presented the Prince to the people at a window in the Hôtel de Ville.

It was to Odilon Barrot that the France of 1830 was indebted for her good fortune in escaping the scenes of 1848. We have long lived in hostile camps, but I have always valued his noble character. In 1850, we met at the Vichy waters. He was sad ; and, referring to the revolutionary part he had played in recent events, he added : " If I devoted all the remaining years of my life to repentance, that would not be enough to atone for the error of a day : I wanted the Monarchy to be reformed, not overthrown."

And now the dangerous moment for the Chamber had arrived. The mob, in a state of extreme excitement, filled all the approaches to the Assembly, and no one could cross the bridge through the menacing crowds without using the password, " *One of the* 221." Nevertheless, I heard the following answer five or six times : " That's all very fine, but you'll be thrown into the water if you vote for a King." The manœuvre of the Republicans was palpable : cheers for Lafayette were heard in all directions ; why should he not profit by so fine an opportunity ? Under the peristyle I found Benjamin Constant, Augustin Périer, and Alexandre Laborde, who were trying, with small success, to pacify the crowds. I entered the hall. M. Bérard had just finished the reading of his report ; M. de Salverte was in the tribune, insisting that the debate should be adjourned to the following Wednesday. The deputies seemed uneasy at the clamour and threats which reached them from out-side. When he had finished, M. Laffitte, the President, asked whether any one desired to speak on the question of adjournment. Every one was silent. Happening to be at the foot of the tribune, I ran rapidly up the steps and made an address, which was practically as follows : " Gentle-men, Paris has saved France from despotism ; now it is for the Chamber to save her from the anarchy that is howling at our gates ; it assumes the right of dictating how we shall act, and threatens to throw us into the river if we demur. I now demand that the abdication of Charles X., who has violated the fundamental compact of the Constitution, be officially recorded ; that the Duc d'Orléans be called to the throne ; that the report on the modifications of the Charter be discussed in the present session ; and that the Chamber shall not adjourn until it has accomplished this important step. Recollect that in England the Parliament prevented the civil war which was on the point of breaking out by voting in a single night the Bill of Rights, at the same time calling the Prince of Orange to the throne, and that this fortunate precipitation insured to that country a hundred and forty years of liberty and prosperity."

The debate on these proposals was very spirited. Sal-verte opposed them ; they were about to be put to the vote, when M. Guizot, who had been appointed that morning Commissary to the Department of the Interior, made a speech, in which he said : " The Chamber may feel reassured as to the dangers with which it is menaced unless it is frightened into holding a night session ; the Provisional Government declares that it is strong enough to protect it and guarantee its safety ; its deliberations will be as free to-morrow as they are to-day." This ended the discussion, which was adjourned. How often have I deplored the action of the Chamber ! It was on that very night, too, that Louis-Philippe was persuaded to reserve the question of an hereditary peerage, a reservation which foreshadowed its suppression, and which led the way to the fatal measure from the effects of which the Crown suffered during eighteen years.

The principle of heredity would have been the strength of the Monarchy ; it would have attached the old nobility to the new dynasty. Already more than fifty peers, who ranked among the greatest personages of the Court and of Legitimacy, had left Charles X. at Rambouillet, had made their submission to Louis - Philippe, had shared in the deliberations of the Chamber, and voted the deposition of Charles X. What followed ? Wounded by the withdrawal of the fundamental principle of hereditary descent, forty-four of these resigned ; the conservative forces were divided into two camps ; many of the great families that would have rallied to the new régime in hope of gaining a peerage remained hostile to it, the more so as the King possessed none of those powerful attractions which had stood Napoleon in such good stead. He had nothing he could restore, for the Revolution of 1830 had been attended with no confiscations ; he had nothing to give, for hereditary rights were all that had made a peerage worth accepting, and a prize which had hitherto been much sought after.

" How is it," I said one day to Beugnot, with whom I was on very intimate terms, " that you could make such sacrifices for such a useless trifle ? " " *Sacrifices*, my dear fellow ? Say, rather, how I could stoop to such *meannesses !* But—how could I help it ? You have no idea how valuable a title is when you want to use it to make a fool of a woman and marry your son ! " In fact, an heredi- tary peerage was quoted at *a million* in every notary's office in the country, and although the price fell down to *half a million*, after the batch of peers made by M. de Villèle, still, half a million was not to be despised.

To fill up the vacancies caused by these resignations, which deprived the Chamber of some of its most dis- tinguished members, all belonging to ancient families, it was necessary to have recourse to notabilities of the Empire, then to the members of Parliament, who did not always care for the honour, and passed it on to their relatives ; as Sebastiani, Duchatel, and Dupin did. At last it was offered as a sort of compensation to the deputies who had been rejected by their constituents, so that the peerage lost all its prestige, and ceased to be the dis- tinguished circle which was intended by the Charter to fill a place between the Chamber of Deputies and the Crown. I am speaking quite impartially on this matter, seeing that, having only daughters, I could not have any personal interest in an hereditary peerage. My feelings and utter- ances on the subject were dictated by mere political instinct ; for I was convinced that we should retain all that we possibly could of the old government in order to make the new more acceptable to Europe.

I return to this session, which culminated in a great display of emotion. I was joined in the Salle des Pas- Perdus by Mauguin, who said, angrily : " Rambuteau, after your speech this evening you deserve to be shot ! " " Oh, nonsense ! " I retorted. " I could certainly count many friends amongst my audience, but not a single murderer ! " The fact was that congratulations rained on me on all sides. Later on I asked him (for we had always been on excellent terms until then) why he made such an insulting remark to me. He answered : " I was furious, because we wished to prolong the session at all costs ; we had prepared a movement in favour of the Duc de Reich- stadt ; we were waiting for the arrival of the federates of

Rouen and other cities. All we wanted was to gain time, and we thought we could count on you, because of your devotion to the Emperor—and you turned out to be the very man to ruin all our hopes!" I proved to him how vain these hopes were, as even Bassano and Drouot were forced to own. I assured him that neither Lafayette nor the Doctrinaires would have acknowledged the King of Rome, and that, if we had acted in accordance with his wishes, we should have incurred the risk of having a Republic. Though he understood my point of view well enough, I could not convince him.

During the night news came that mobs had assembled at L'Estrapade and other places, and were to march next morning on the Legislature and prevent it from holding a debate. Consequently we all received messages after four o'clock, summoning us to meet at six in the chamber, which would be protected by about twelve hundred well-disposed defenders, for the National Guard had not yet been organised. Lafayette had promised to support us, and so did Benjamin Constant and Laffitte ; the latter was anxious that the triumph of Royalty should be regarded as his work, and he employed his best endeavours in getting Louis-Philippe proclaimed King. He was proclaimed almost unanimously. The Charter was rapidly revised. I took no part in the discussion, except incidentally, when the question of the Israelitish cult came up. I proposed, from a sense of justice, that it should be placed on the same footing as the other religious denominations which were salaried by the State ; all that was necessary to achieve this was to incorporate a single clause in the Budget, and then all citizens would be on a footing of equality.

On the 7th of August, the Chamber brought the new Charter to the Duc d'Orléans, who had already been invested with power. I took the arm of General Clausel. The popular excitement had ceased. For that matter, it was open to doubt if the people really knew what they wanted. We were spoken to several times on the way, being assaulted by various questions such as, " You are going to make a

King ; why not make an Emperor ? We'd as soon cry
' *Vive l'Empereur !* ' as ' *Vive le Roi !* ' " That is the kind of
thing one generally experiences in revolution.

As soon as the National Guard was organised, I at once
enrolled myself in the 2nd battalion of the 1st Legion. I
was present at all the important engagements, and was on
duty at the Luxemberg the night of the trial of the late
Ministers. I still seem to hear the shouts of the rioters, for
the exasperation of the riot was then at its height ; no
one amongst them apparently understood the motives that
inspired the generous intervention of the Government,
for the Ministers were only bent on preventing bloodshed.
The very severity of the season served to increase the
people's violence. The same cry was re-echoed from camp
to camp : " Why can't they be thrown down to us ? that
we may shoot them, and then go to bed ! " We expected
to be attacked at every moment. It needed all the coolness
and energy of M. de Montalivet to secure the safe return of
the Ministers to Vincennes ; and indeed the first debates
in the Chamber so often gave rise to heated outbursts, that it
was clear that the influence of the recent violent scenes still
made itself felt on the minds of some of the members.

We had not yet learned the value of discipline, and our
leaders had some difficulty in wheeling us into line. On
one occasion, indeed, Sebastiani used such strong language
with regard to myself that, being deeply wounded, I thought
fit to write to him. I have kept his reply ; it is the best
evidence I can produce of our friendship—a friendship that
was only ended by death.[1] But what self-control and
moderation do political differences exact ! I really believe,
that it was to the exercising of conciliation and courtesy,
which I made the absolute rule of my life, that I owed the

---

[1] This is the letter :—

" MY DEAR COUNT,—I pledge you my word of honour that no one heard
us, and you know I am too truly your friend to deceive you. *I beg your
pardon* for an expression which I really regarded as a joke between intimate
friends. I hope this will satisfy you. You know that friendship alone can
make me speak thus. I am doing what M. de Narbonne would have done."

popularity I enjoyed with all parties, during the whole of my parliamentary career.

I was a member of several Commissions ; first of the Commission for revising the Liquor Laws, which was violently opposed, and not less violently defended by M. Boursy, Director-General of indirect taxes, who preferred to have the duties reduced by a third rather than allow the institution itself to be touched. We were equally anxious to husband it and preserve it by improving the resources of the Treasury.

We had proposed, in order to make up the deficit, to increase the tax on personal property, the taxable items of which had been greatly extended since the Revolution, and two Bills were introduced with this object in view. I was appointed to report on them, and was thus frequently brought into contact with M. Thiers, Financial Under-Secretary of State. Every morning MM. Saurimont and Vitalis spent some time in initiating him into technical details, and such was his wonderful facility of assimilation that often, after listening to the first part of the discussion, he handled the second *ex professo*. It was from that period that our friendship dated, of which I have had frequent proofs.

The two Bills were passed. Such laws have taught me a useful lesson : namely, that we should always retain those taxes which, so to speak, have been hallowed by custom, and to which the taxpayers have grown used. The thirty-six millions of reductions effected by these measures, at the close of the year, were a benefit, for which no one felt grateful. On the contrary, the collection of the new taxes that were needed to counterbalance the old ones met with such opposition that, either from weariness or necessity, we were forced to reduce them by one half. This experience, however, did not interfere with the suppression of the tax on salt, which, in spite of some self-interested complaints, had always been easily collected. Agriculture derived no advantage from its removal, and the country-people showed no appreciation of the so-called boon.

But the most important Commission of all was that of the Constitution. I belonged to it, along with MM. de Broglie, de Barante, Benjamin Constant, Augustin Périer, Guizot, Rémusat, and others. My first proposal was to submit the revision of the Charter and the election of Louis-Philippe to the sanction of the Primary Assemblies, as had been done in the case of the Consulate for life and the Empire. In my opinion, such a ratification would be more effectual than any other. Guizot opposed this proposal with great warmth.

"You are," said he to me, "a child of the Empire, and your memories lead you to disapprove of Constitutional principles. Did not the Act of its Parliament, in 1688, suffice the English nation, and did not that Parliament pursue its task in the name of the nation? The case will be identical in France, and there will be no need to recur to revolutionary methods." "But," I answered, "the English Parliament had an existence of several centuries; it was a legal authority, recognised and respected by all. From the moment it had overthrown Charles I. and restored Charles II. precedents gave it the right to dispose of the crown, while no such power is lodged in us. The return of the Bourbons was the work of foreigners; the conceded Charter, although it instituted representative government, did not establish it on an immovable foundation, as was proved by the events of July. Does not all this fall far short of the three million votes that elected the Emperor? At the present moment we need have no doubt as to how the nation will exercise its suffrage; why should we deprive ourselves of such a force?" And I concluded with a repetition of the words I spoke at Saint-Etienne to the Comte d'Artois in reference to the Tricolor flag: "You should keep it, Monseigneur, if only to prevent it from falling into the hands of your enemies. For the latter would certainly hoist it as a rallying signal directly they thought that the right moment had come for turning against you."

I failed, however, to carry my point.

Another question with which the Committee had to deal was that of the Civil List.   One evening that I happened to be with the King, he approached the subject.   "Sire," I said, "since your Majesty has deigned to consult me, I think you should address the Chamber directly in a message declaring that, so far as you were personally concerned, 'a horse and sword' were all you needed in order to serve France, but that the honour and dignity of the nation demanded more, namely, that its sovereign should be suitably equipped to fill his place among the princes of Europe, among whom the ruler of France has always occupied the first rank."

He interrupted me : "What amount would you give me ?"   "Sixteen millions."   "I want eighteen.   Laffitte promises them to me."   "Then, Sire, he has undertaken more than he can fulfil, for your best friends think, as I do, that sixteen millions will make your Majesty richer than Charles X. was.   You are no longer under the obligations which formerly hampered the crown : the great offices of the Court, with the subsidies to the royal theatres, cost more than a million, and these your Majesty has abolished. The Gardes-du-Corps cost three millions ; the Garde-Royale and the Staffs, two ; there were five millions spent on pensions, which the Chamber has decided to continue as life-annuities.   On the other hand, your Majesty has reserved for yourself the revenue of the entire appanage of Orléans, the income from which is three millions a year.   It is only politic to let the people see that there is a notable difference between the old and the new Civil List.   An allowance of a million a year will be entered immediately on the Budget for the Prince Royal, to be doubled when he marries ; the Chamber further intends to provide for your children. What more do you wish ?"

He was obstinate, with the result that, five or six months afterwards, we had great trouble in getting a grant of twelve millions for him.   With the four additional millions that would have been voted for him in the beginning, he could have finished the Louvre and won the hearts of the

N

Parisians ; while the neglected condition in which he left the palace of our kings, hoping, no doubt, that the excess of the evil would bring its own remedy, created a bad feeling both in the Chamber and the city. I warned him more than once, at the risk of offending him, that when a new Civil List was mooted the Chamber would, on the demand of the city of Paris, take away the Louvre and its dependencies from his control, so that the nation might have the right to complete that grand building, and that thus, through his own fault, the Crown would lose the patronage of the Fine Arts, its noblest prerogative.

The reform of the electoral law was the most important work of the Commission—I might almost say that it was my own work, for I was entrusted, along with M. de Barante, with the task of drawing up the Bill, his business being with the text, mine with the formation of the colleges. In order to accomplish this, I sought information from all quarters, and listened attentively to all local deputations, for I wished the several interests in the arrondissements to receive fair treatment. In those that were to have two representatives, I endeavoured to keep the industrial and city interests entirely distinct from the agricultural interests, so that each class might have its own supporters.

With regard to the territorial divisions, I grouped the electors together, rather than the inhabitants, in numbers that were pretty nearly equal. The lowering of the qualification for voters favoured this system, which, by getting rid of the *scrutin de liste*, insured a more honest selection and supported the most estimable and capable candidates. Finally, I discovered that I had increased the number of deputies by 39, so that there would be 459 instead of 420 in the next Chamber. Of course I had to defend my work before the Commission, which proposed a score of modifications ; but I succeeded in having them all rejected, and the scheme was adopted in its integrity. So also was the lowering of the suffrage. We had proposed a plan for adding a number of eligible men to the electoral colleges ; M. Dupin would not hear of it, but events have proved how wise and far-seeing our proposal was.

In the midst of my labours I was often cross-questioned. by M. de Lafayette. One day he took my hands, and, clasping them in his, said, "These hands are full of privileges, open them very widely, then, so as to satisfy all our wants." "General," I replied, "I am ready to grant privileges wherever I find the two conditions which I consider indispensable for their use—these are independence and capability. That is why I have never wished that the law regulating elections should be restricted by Parliament ; on the contrary, it should be free to advance with the times and to extend its scope as circumstances may require. At the present moment we are clamouring for the lowering of the voting qualification to two hundred francs and capacity in the voter. This appears to us to meet the present necessities, but the future will do more, if it can. But to bestow rights on those who do not know how to make an intelligent use of them is like imitating those Indian statues which have a hundred arms and no head."

The reins should never be slackened except for a good reason, and I had occasion to give expression to my views on this subject with reference to the Popular Societies. The latter had been revived after the days of July. In the Commission, opinions were divided as to the proper way of dealing with them. M. Guizot, who strongly advocated the right of free discussion, and was still under the influence of the *Globe* and the *Aide-toi, le Ciel t'aidera* Society, spoke of introducing a law to regulate their existence and modify their present abuses. Alarmed by a measure which would give them a legal sanction, I imparted my fears to several of my colleagues, and also thought it my duty to communicate them to the King. He had, in fact, exacted a promise from me that I would undertake no serious step in the Chamber without notifying him previously. I therefore went to see him : "Sire," said I, "it is impossible to govern by methods that are inconsistent ; the Chamber and the clubs naturally exclude each other ; if your Majesty wishes to place his reliance in the Popular Societies, the Chamber is useless ; if you do not, the clubs must be closed ; to-morrow I intend to submit a proposal to this effect in the shape of an address to the King, and I am certain of a great number of adherents." He begged me to do nothing of the sort, assuring me, with all that seductive grace and ability which he possessed in so eminent a degree, that, though he shared my feelings and saw the danger, he desired to think the matter out for himself without being invited to do so by the Chamber. A fortnight afterwards the National Guard closed all the clubs in Paris, whereupon the King sent for me in all haste. "Well," he exclaimed, "haven't I kept my word with you ? Are you satisfied ? " "Not quite, Sire, for, if the National Guard can close the clubs to-day, it can open them to-morrow, and I do not know whether I ought to congratulate or pity your Majesty for being guarded once more on every step of your grand staircase by the ragged rabble who once saved the Palais-Royal from pillage."

The close of the year 1830 was marked by a public mourning. Benjamin Constant died on the 10th of December. The crowds were so great at his funeral that the members of the Chamber, not having a distinctive costume, which would have enabled them to recognise one another, and keep together in a body, were soon scattered among the throng, in spite of the ushers and police. I was with Dupin, who said, peevishly : "Let us get out of this, for it is quite clear that, though we are all present, the Chamber does not count for much ! "

Benjamin Constant was a very clever and distinguished man, but he was of a litigious and eccentric turn of mind ; and, in fact, so *blasé* that everything palled on him. His writings were superior to his discourses, the effect of which was spoiled by a monotonous delivery, added to a conspicuous lack of conviction. He had, moreover, an unfortunate trick of always swaying himself to and fro. He was asked one day what he liked best in the world : "*Ma foi*," he answered, "to win at a game of cards ; it is the only

pleasure left me in which I can find any amusement."
"But surely with all your talents, and after so many
successes, you must be interested in other things ? " " No,
except, perhaps, in losing at a game of cards." For thirty
years his political principles have been the guide-book of
our younger generation. It was thus that he defined Constitutional Royalty : " *The power which passes judgment on
other powers, of which it should be the arbiter and the providence.*
If the Chamber went wrong, the King should dissolve it and
appeal to the country ; if the Chamber of Peers showed too
great a spirit of resistance, he should create a sufficient
number of Peers to give him a majority ; finally, it rested
in his hands to change the executive power by changing
the Ministry." All this is very far removed from the
tenets of the " Doctrinaires " : " *The King reigns and does not
govern.*" How can the supreme power be exercised, if it
remains impervious to every influence, in every direction ?
The fall both of Charles X. and of Louis-Philippe proved
that ministerial responsibility has never saved either King
or Crown.

At the beginning of January 1831 the attitude of the
Ministry became a source of serious uneasiness to the Réunion de la Rue Rivoli, to which I belonged. After an
animated discussion, M. Etienne and I were sent as a
deputation to M. Laffitte. We requested a private
audience. He was surrounded by some of his friends,
amongst whom was Béranger, and he assured us that he
had no secret they did not share, and that, in any case, our
society was too numerous to render secrecy possible ; that,
if we were there to accuse him of negligence, his answer
must be that this negligence was the inevitable consequence
of the embarrassed condition of his private affairs, but that
in three months they would be reduced to order, and then
he would devote all his time to the service of the King.
My answer was that we had come to tell him that, if he
severed himself from Casimir Périer, 160 deputies, whose
spokesmen we were, would be found in opposition to him
on the very next morning after the rupture. He made

us many promises, which were but scantily fulfilled, as was shown by the riot of the 13th of February. No doubt the demonstration made by the Legitimists, under cover of the anniversary service held in memory of the Duc de Berry, was the pretext if not the actual cause of the disturbance ; but the absence of all protection, of all surveillance, allowed a free vent to revolutionary passions.

One of the greatest faults of the King at that time was the weakness that led him to sacrifice his friends. Ah, we were far removed from that English Revolution which had served as a model for the days of the 7th, 8th, and 9th of August ! In 1688 the English Parliament had disposed of the Crown with, at any rate, the tacit consent of the nation. Instead of a Government deriving its strength from its origin, we insisted on a Royalty supported by Republican institutions from which every vestige of the old régime, and even of the Empire, was to be banished, so that, when the time came, a President might the more easily be substituted for a King.

The abandonment of the *fleurs-de-lis*, effaced from the royal armorial bearings, was a concession to Republican sentiment which was as inexcusable as it was unnecessary. For the preceding ten months, no protest had been raised against them. France had chosen a Bourbon for King, and nobody would have been surprised if he had used his own arms, just as Napoleon had had his eagle. Louis-Philippe was undoubtedly popular ; the cry of " *Vive le Roi !* " which greeted him whenever he appeared was sincere ; at the review of sixty thousand soldiers on the 30th of August in the Champ-de-Mars, he was acclaimed as enthusiastically as Napoleon had ever been in the midst of his triumphs. The tendency to rally round his person was so general that I congratulated him on having received in succession three irreconcilable adversaries of the Emperor : Lainé, the Abbé de Montesquiou, and Royer-Collard. He ought therefore to have made his arms inseparable from his name. These kind of concessions were displeasing to foreign nations. They imparted a revolutionary colour to the new régime, which, otherwise, would have been accepted by European Courts as simply a change of individuals incidental to an abdication. In consideration of the distrust felt toward us by our neighbours, an alliance with England was not only expedient but obligatory, and so, when the throne of Belgium was offered to France, this fruit of a revolution that was the daughter of our own had to be declined in favour of an English prince.[1]

The days that elapsed between the 13th of February and the 13th of March were about the worst that had been encountered so far. To financial troubles were added street disturbances. Laffitte, in great dismay, was constantly assembling some twenty of our number at his house in order to discuss what measures should be adopted. The last time I was with him, he and I had a bitter quarrel, and I left his study in high indignation. At the door I met Admiral de Rigny, and said to him : "My dear friend, if you want to see France thrown out of the window, you need only stand here on the balcony ; she'll soon be taking the leap." Luckily, Laffitte, having no longer either money or credit, was forced to resign.

The King immediately sent for Casimir Périer. On that day I happened to be dining with M. Coste, the editor of the *Temps*. In the middle of the dinner a message was delivered to me from Admiral de Rigny, asking me to go with him and Casimir Périer to M. Louis's house, and there use our best endeavours to persuade the latter to accept the portfolio of the Finances, as Périer was resolved not to attempt to form a Ministry without Louis's co-operation. After a time, M. Louis yielded his consent. Périer then said to me : "Rambuteau, you will belong to the Commission of the Finances ; you will make an inventory of the Treasury ; you will have our reputation in your hands. Everything must be made public. If anything be concealed, our measures are useless and our fall is certain."

---

[1] Leopold I. was, in reality, a German Prince of Saxe-Coburg, but he had been naturalised in England after Waterloo, and, on his marriage with Princess Charlotte, he had been created Duke of Kendal.

As soon as the Ministry was formed, the Chamber named a Commission of Finance, of which I was elected a member. To Humann and me fell the task of making the inventory. We spent two days and two nights on end over it. We found hardly two millions in specie in the public coffers ; there were five millions in paper, the bills of exchange for March and April had been discounted ; two hundred and ninety-eight millions of Treasury bonds were circulating at more than 6 per cent. interest. It was necessary to provide for the half-year one hundred and twenty millions to meet the expenses of the Ministry, which were everywhere in arrears. We furnished an account of this sad state of affairs to the Commission, and Humann was named reporter. I said to him : " My dear friend, be sure you keep back nothing ; if you do, I'll cross-question you myself in the Chamber. I have signed all the documents, and made up all the totals, and my papers are all in the hands of Périer and Louis. There can, therefore, be no escape." He complied with my wishes fully and freely, and so the three millions of Hayti,[1] with sundry other matters which certain persons would have liked to suppress, were made public.

The financial system brought forward by M. Louis consisted in creating credit by rigorously fulfilling all previous obligations. A loan of a hundred millions at par was voted, a good part of which was subscribed for by the members of the Legislature, each subscribing according to his means, and the public, seeing that the Chamber gave such guarantees, became imbued with sufficient confidence to seek a similar investment for their capital.

In the month of April 1831, I was recalled to Mâcon by the elections. I was received with great kindness and affection. The entire National Guard was waiting for me at the pier where the vessel landed me, and it

---

[1] In 1825, Charles X. recognised the independence of Cuba, on condition that an indemnity of 159 millions should be granted to the former colonists. This indemnity was afterwards reduced to 60 millions, then to an annual payment of 4,000,000, by virtue of an agreement that doubtless concealed some irregularities.

escorted me to Champgrenon. The next day, I was en-rolled in the first company of grenadiers, and mounted guard for the first time a few days afterwards. I spent the night in patrolling. In the morning, after we had been relieved, my comrades offered me a splendid break-fast, to celebrate my admission into their ranks, after which, headed by a band of music, they escorted me back to Champgrenon through the faubourg La Barre, at the same time calling my attention to the fact that its name had been changed to that of Rambuteau.[1] Then, during a grand review, my wife fastened a knot of ribbons sent at my request by Mme. de Lafayette, to the flag of the legion.

I was elected by an enormous majority. But, after my return to Paris, I did not conceal from Casimir Périer the impressions I had brought back from the department : a trend of wild excitement had taken possession of men's minds, the so-called *liberal* ideas were making such progress that constitutional institutions were already beginning to be considered as superannuated. The heredity of the Peerage was condemned. Its abolition was an error, a very grave error, as I have already said ; Périer held the same opinion, and the mistake would not have been committed but for that untoward adjournment of which I have spoken, and during which Lafayette and his friends brought their influence to bear on the King.

Louis-Philippe believed that a life-peerage would increase personal authority, while, on the other hand, being hampered by the Law of Categories,[2] he never was able, during his whole reign, to get his best friend, Baron de Montmorency, admitted to the Peerage. The latter could not succeed his father, and, on account of his very loyalty, was made the victim of wretched formalities. The King could not

---

[1] This name was given to it definitely by the city of Mâcon after the death of the Comte de Rambuteau.

[2] According to the Law of Categories (December 29th, 1831), the King was forced to choose the peers from *certain categories :*—Presidents of the Chamber of Deputies ; Deputies who had served in three Legislatures ; Marshals and Admirals ; Lieutenant-Generals and Vice-Admirals, after two years' service ; Ambassadors after three years' service ; Councillors of State after ten years' service.

forget, although it would have been to his advantage if he had done so, the offences, and even insults, which had been directed against him by a number of peers during the reign of the Legitimists, so he was not unwilling that a blow should be dealt to the entire institution, which had been so steadily defended by Benjamin Constant in 1815, and which had been maintained in the Additional Act.

Now, it would have been easy enough to save it in 1830; all that public opinion demanded was the abolition of the peerages created by Charles X.; nay, a step further might have been taken, and the whole Peerage renovated from beginning to end, as M. de Talleyrand recommended. But the suppression of hereditary rights was the worst solution of all. It divided the Royalists into two camps, at a time when they were not numerous enough in France to support two royal candidates, and, as party-feelings always induce men to sacrifice even their own interests, their political rancour led them to become the allies of the Republicans, simply that they might the more successfully attack the Government. They advocated universal suffrage, did not repudiate the license of the press, and, in short, behaved in such a way, that if '48 disappointed their hopes, they had only themselves in a great measure to thank for it.

As for myself, all I could do was to strenuously support the maintenance of the pensions granted to a certain number of Peers, in the name of the union existing between the two Chambers, and of their joint complicity, if I may so speak, with recent events. Had not several of the Peers who were closely connected with the immediate associates of Charles X. voted in favour of the accession of the Duc d'Orléans to the throne? People do not usually repudiate obligations in the hour of their success which they have contracted in their day of trouble.

The meeting of the new Chamber imposed many duties on the re-elected deputies; they had, in the first place, to make the situation and the matters under discussion known to more than two hundred colleagues whose zeal equalled their ignorance, as well as to overcome their distrust and secure their co-operation ; in addition to this, by way of supporting the Ministry, they had to discourage the hopes of some and soothe the regrets of others. Consequently, things did not always work smoothly ; now and then, irritating words were exchanged. Thus, one day I had to reply to certain consequential individuals who thought to win distinction by vilifying my past career. "Learn, gentlemen," I said, "that I have never betrayed any confidence, have never sold myself to any party, and that, if I have served under three Governments, I have never cringed, and have always acted with integrity and rectitude."

We had, besides, to work very hard : we spent more than a month in discussing the different sections of the Budget in the bureaus. In my department, we had to study those of the Ministry of the Interior and of Public Works. I personally filled the breach during sixteen sessions, so, as a reward, I was appointed to the Commission of Finances, and, later on, reporter.

I had still to examine the secret funds, made specially interesting by the chapter on the "Black Cabinet." Since the days of Louis XIV. this institution had been within the jurisdiction of the Ministry of Foreign Affairs, and was concerned only with the correspondence of foreign diplomatic agents. Its organisation was a sort of State secret ; it was composed of a number of trustworthy employés, liberally paid, recruited, for the most part, from the same families, son following father, and endowed with a sort of cautious circumspection which had become a kind of hereditary virtue, for I have known a family that could reckon four generations in this service. The most ingenious ciphers did not escape their penetration. All they needed were three or four letters in order to interpret the most delicate keys. They had, indeed, complete collections. An impression was taken of every new seal in soft plaster, which hardened rapidly. Only the rapid transmission of the mail by the couriers to the Ambassadors caused them some difficulty, but they generally succeeded in learning all that was required from the correspondence of secondary agents, who had recourse to the post. The Black Cabinet was doubtless sometimes employed as a factor in domestic politics, but much less frequently than was believed.

These various labours were, certainly, sufficient to fill up my time. My secretary entered my study at six in the morning. With his assistance I prepared my reports, after a careful examination of all the official documents that were likely to shed light on the subject upon which we were working. I have sometimes read, pen in hand, seventy columns of the *Moniteur*, in search of information on a single point. No wonder, then, that I was nicknamed *le piocheur* (the digger), and was sometimes met with the question : " Where the mischief did you get all you have just been telling us ? "   " Why, in the technical works, and the reports which are sent to each one of you, and which not one of you ever read." At ten, I gave audience to a string of petitioners for office, that thumb-screw of deputies and governments, particularly after revolutions. After a hasty breakfast I made my appearance at the several Commissions of which I was a member ; then, at two exactly, I was in the Chamber, ready for my conference with Casimir Périer.

During the sitting I took my place behind him, when he would often whisper to me : " Pay close attention to such or such a point ; always keep yourself well prepared ; you will have to answer in my stead from the tribune." But, as soon as the critical moment came, his impetuous activity got the better of him, and he failed entirely to call to mind that he had intended to have recourse to others ; so, all my preparations went for nothing ; my regret was more for his sake than for my own, because I clearly saw that he was exhausting himself in these incessant struggles, instituted by Mauguin, Lamarque, and Jaubert, for the express purpose of harassing him and driving him to act quite inconsistently with his own character.

In 1829, when he would have saved the Crown if only Charles X. had trusted him, he was considered too radical. In 1831 he was considered too conservative. Nevertheless, he was the same man, with the same inflexible will and the same rectitude. He had a horror of disorder and anarchy; he was incapable of weakness or compromise. Truly there was something grand in loving him and fighting at his side, because not a grain of personal vanity or self-interest was to be discovered in the most hidden recesses of his soul. He loved France passionately; to serve her was his sole ambition, and his sincerity was so obvious that he was fully justified in declaring one day from the tribune : " I entered public life as a man of courage ; my sole aspiration is to leave it as a man of honour." At the time of the debate on the secret funds, he said to me : " My friend, I have no secrets from you. I have, therefore, ordered that all the documents you may wish for should be communicated to you ; you will study them and then judge for yourself." I did so, and my inspection of these documents convinced me of the soundness of all the departments ; the half of the supplies granted were enough to pay the debts of the past as well as those incurred by preceding régimes—nay, even those incurred by the Committee of Public Safety !

But in the winter of 1832 his strength began to fail. He was discouraged, worn out by an opposition which his irritability only rendered the more exhausting. I saw him every day at Mme. Foy's residence, where he used to go for a few moments' repose. He would accuse his friends of weakness, indifference, desertion. " They are cowards," he used to say, " who abandon me in presence of the enemy. No one thinks of anything but his personal interests, his personal ambition. They will not see that I am reduced to the last extremity, that I am spending my life for a cause that is not only the cause of duty, but the salvation of the country."

Hurt by hearing him make no exceptions in his reproaches, I could not help exclaiming sadly : " And yet, for the last ten months I have sat behind you, and have laid my hand on your shoulder a score of times at every session, and begged you to spare yourself. I have begged you, over and over again, during the same period : ' Be calm ;

don't get excited ; keep silent ; don't play their game ; surely you must see that they are turning your feverish impetuosity into a weapon against yourself, and that they want to bury you under your very victories ! ' And, with all your quick temper, you have never shown that I annoyed you, you have never evinced the least impatience when I expressed my disapproval at some of your actions. And why not ? but because, in your heart, you did me justice. Ah, you were juster to me then than you are now ! " He threw himself into my arms. Alas ! in a few days he was dead.[1]

No doubt Louis-Philippe appreciated his value and his devotion, but he was afraid of his imperious temperament and the stubborn tenacity of his opinions ; he did not feel at ease with so masterful a servant, and his death, whilst occasioning him some regret, was undoubtedly a great relief to him. As I sometimes acted the part of a prudent intermediary between them, I may be allowed to know something of the matter. Perhaps the King was thinking of these good offices of mine when he said to me some time afterward : " I am sorry I have not been able to do anything for you, considering that you have rendered me such important services ! " " Sire," I answered, " my services to your Majesty have been as disinterested as were those which I formerly rendered to the Emperor ; sooner or later I shall find what suits me, but, if we are ever to fall, we shall fall together, and it is all the same to me whether I fall from the *entresol* or from the fourth story."

The next year I was Prefect of Paris.

[1] The day after this premature death, Comte Mollien wrote the following letter to M. de Rambuteau : " The day (the 16th) upon which you wrote to me will be memorable in our history. On that day we lost a man whom the ablest of our politicians will surely permit me to call a pre-eminently *necessary man*, even when compared to them. If he did not succeed in correcting in many of our public men the modern tendency to mingle in public affairs only for the purpose of advancing their personal ambitions, he at least set them an example of an entirely opposite principle. He also taught them what we all need to learn, that respect for conventional usages and social proprieties plays a part in the affairs of this world ; he had a keen sense of all their different values. Foreign diplomatists were especially struck by this characteristic, which contributed not a little to our peaceful relations with other powers," &c.

Héliog Dujardin Paris.

The Comte de Rambuteau.

CHAPTER VIII

PREFECT OF THE SEINE

ON the 24th of June 1833 I took the oath of fidelity to the King.[1] I asked permission to add a few words to the customary ceremonial, and said : "Sire, your Majesty knows that I have never solicited the post which you have deigned to confide to me to-day. The cholera,[2] my friendship for Casimir Périer, my devotion to your august person, have alone decided me to abandon the Chamber where I have had the good fortune to do some service. I beg your Majesty to consider my presence in the Hôtel de Ville as that of a commander in a citadel. My resignation shall always rest with you, and I will never seek support from either individuals or measures in opposition to your desire and will."

I had long enjoyed the friendship of the Royal Family, particularly that of Madame Adélaïde, who allowed me to

[1] Long before this it had been intended that Comte de Rambuteau should be appointed to the office so soon as it became vacant. Comte d'Argout wrote to him some months previously : "You know that there is a certain post which I am most anxious that you should fill. But as its present occupant, Monsieur Bondy, is fairly popular, it will be necessary first to find some other suitable appointment for him. At the same time, I can assure you that every one with whom I have discussed the possibility of your coming here eventually has expressed unfeigned satisfaction at the prospect of having some one at the head of affairs who will be capable of restoring order and setting to rights much that has been neglected.

"The Prefecture of the Seine is almost as important a position as a post in the Ministry. But it will need much patience and courage to re-establish it on a firm basis. I have no doubt that sooner or later we shall be able to accomplish it. Meanwhile, I am doing all I can."

[2] The terrible epidemic which had devastated Asia and Europe broke out in Paris on the 26th of March 1832; it lasted for 190 days, and had nearly 20,000 victims. Casimir Périer was stricken two days after visiting the Hôtel-Dieu with the Duc d'Orléans.

visit her in the morning, whenever I had leisure, and continued this favour as long as she lived. "Whenever you wish to warn or advise my brother," she said, "but feel any awkwardness in doing so, only come to me. By taking me into your confidence you will not forfeit his, and you will be all the surer of securing a hearing."

At no time did her affectionate protection fail me. Before I had been Prefect of the Seine for a year, she took me aside one day, and said: "My brother is very pleased with your conduct, but he is quite sensible of the difficulties of your situation—a situation rendered still more delicate by your personal attachment to him. He has charged me to extract a promise from you that, whatever happens, and whatever annoyances you may have to endure, you will not resign. He is strong enough to refuse to dismiss you, but not strong enough to decline to receive your resignation during a Ministerial crisis." She repeatedly reminded me of this promise whenever circumstances occurred that involved my administration in difficulties.

The first time my duties obliged me to address the King officially was on the occasion of laying the foundation-stone of the Pont des Saints-Pères: "Sire," said I, "the mission with which you have honoured me implies a great obligation, which may be summarised in a few words: *To give the Parisians water, air, and shade.*" Such, in fact, was my programme, my constant thought, the goal of all my labours. These labours I mean to speak of elsewhere, for the benefit of those who, instead of being scared by statistics, are in quest of figures and documents; and, should the account of them fill only a single page of the history of our Paris, that page will repay me for fifteen years of toil.

The Parisians are like children; their minds must be incessantly occupied, and, when it is impossible to present them with the bulletin of a battle every month, or with a new Constitution, one must amuse them by letting them have some new public works that are worth a visit, or by the display of various plans for the beautifying of the city. Such entertainments serve as a safety-valve for their continual craving for novelty, and their inherent love of finding fault with the powers that be.

The National Guards had replaced the *grognards* of the Empire. Napoleon had always taken care to ascertain the feelings and hear the remarks of these old grumblers, and it was equally necessary to feel the pulse of the National Guards, for during the interval of 1815 to 1848 they constantly troubled the repose of both Ministers and Sovereigns. To teach a lesson to the authorities was apparently one of the rights which they had acquired in 1830, and only considered it an exercise of their proper functions; and such good use did they make of this supposed privilege that one fine day they discovered they had brought about a revolution when they had only intended to reform a Monarchy, and, to their intense shame and astonishment, found that they had created a Republic of their own making.

I sought, then, both to amuse Paris and to improve it as well, by constructing monuments, opening streets, making plantations and gardens, giving balls and *fêtes;* in short, I undertook whatever might prove beneficial as well as entertaining to the public, as will appear further on. My task was by no means an easy one, owing to the jealousy and rivalry which I encountered from different quarters. To enable me to see my way clearer in every transaction, I included in the Municipal Council the most substantial and capable citizens to be found among the interested parties, so that every cause might be represented and receive fair consideration. I had learned, in the school of Casimir Périer, how it proves one's goodwill and creates confidence in one's motives. In fact, it was Périer's custom to submit all the great measures he intended to introduce during his Ministry to Commissions of twenty or thirty members chosen from the *élite* of the two Chambers, without distinction of party. I followed his example in my humble sphere, and it would be impossible to over-rate the immense help I received from all those to whom I addressed myself, no matter whether they were artists or literary men, or magistrates or manufacturers, &c.

It is to them, it is to their strong and faithful co-operation, that I am indebted for whatever good I was able to achieve; I am also bound to pay a tribute of heart-felt gratitude to my dear and worthy companion. There were no cases of distress which she did not succour, no misfortunes which she did not console: all the benevolent institutions benefited by her inexhaustible charity; but what contributed most of all to the prosperity of my administration was her sympathy, her affability, her charming simplicity, her fascinating courtesy. I have seen her receive three hundred lady visitors on a Tuesday, for each of whom she had a smile, a kindly word, and a cordial greeting. She had wonderful tact in making every one feel at home, always addressing some remark to each lady, which made her feel that she had a personal interest in each individual.

How many prejudices were entirely disarmed by her delicate *savoir-faire*, and how often she succeeded in captivating those whose over-weening opinion of themselves made them ready to take offence on the most trifling provocation. Even the most exacting of her visitors yielded to the power of her charms. Sometimes, when I have seen her ready to drop from fatigue after a six-hours " At Home," she would still find strength to say to me, " I do hope, my dear, they have gone away satisfied, for when the wives are pleased, it is easier to manage the husbands. In that case, my drawing-room will be of some use to your cabinet." A Municipal Councillor once said to her, " You have really educated us, Madame la Comtesse, and made us capable of taking our place in the best society." [1] And it was true, for

[1] No one will be surprised that the daughter of the Comte de Narbonne should possess these fascinating manners; they came to her by inheritance. The particular affection which Queen Marie Amélie entertained for her was not lessened by misfortune and exile, as is shown by the following letter, written to the Count on learning the death of the Countess :—

" CLAREMONT, the 8*th* of *January* 1857.

" MY DEAR COUNT,—Neither age, time, nor absence can make me forget my old friend, and it is from the depths of my heart that I add my regrets to yours for the loss of your excellent wife, who was so good, so charitable, and who always cherished so much affection for me. God alone can console you, but you will also derive a very sweet comfort from the

the Parisians are especially sensible of the attraction of superiority. They have always wished to have persons of distinction in authority. The National Guard was commanded by Comte d'Artois; among its colonels were the most illustrious marshals, and even the Ministers, men who would have regarded obedience to a commander of lower rank distasteful and painful.

In 1834, the King informed me of his intention to summon me to the Chamber of Peers. I was undecided whether I should accept this flattering offer or not. I had not left the Chamber of Deputies without feeling a certain pang of regret, shared by my colleagues, who wanted to retain me. M. Dupin, the President, had even offered to introduce a measure excepting the Prefect of the Seine from that provision of the law which excluded public functionaries from the Legislature; but I objected, and for two good reasons. In the first place, no one can be of sufficient importance as to justify an exception to the law in his favour; in the second, I had taken my new duties very seriously, and I was convinced that they would occupy all my time, especially as the Municipal Council was about to be elected, and the authority with which it would be invested would most probably increase the difficulties of my administration. Nevertheless, the memories associated with my parliamentary career were so gratifying that I hoped, if circumstances permitted, to return to the Chamber at some time or other. As regarded my elevation to the Chamber of Peers, I thought it advisable to consult M. Thiers, Minister of the Interior, with whom I had become more and more intimate, although we occasionally had our little quarrels, originating in those professional jealousies that sometimes raise a cloud between Minister and Prefect.[1]

sympathy of your two dear daughters. Tell them that I share their sorrow. My children have also asked me to convey to you their regrets for the loss you have sustained.—Your very affectionate friend,
"MARIE AMÉLIE."

[1] M. Thiers was very quick-tempered, and M. Rambuteau sometimes acted the part of mediator between the ruffled statesman and those who had offended him. The following letter was occasioned by an unfortunate

"If I were certain," I said to him, "to remain in the
Hôtel de Ville, nothing would be more natural than for me
to accept the peerage; but, if you consider that I am not
likely to continue Prefect of the Seine for any length of
time, then I should prefer returning to the Chamber and
resuming the honourable place I have already achieved
there. I should be a new-comer among the Peers, and
have at least thirty competitors all older, abler, and more
experienced than myself. Do not expose me to the risk
of being obliged to send in my resignation as a Peer,
because, having failed to make any mark in my new
position, I find myself thankful to return to my former
seat in the Chamber with all the advantages it offers."

"My dear friend," answered Thiers, "you are a faithful
and discreet lieutenant, although I must confess you have
sometimes enough determination to be troublesome; hence
the occasional skirmishes which occur between the Ministry
and the Prefecture, but which do not alter my confidence
in you, or lessen my esteem and affection for you in the
slightest degree. You will succeed in the Hôtel de Ville
because you so thoroughly understand your mission—that
I feel convinced you will achieve a triumph. Limit your
ambition to that; you will have a long and splendid
career; and will see the downfall of more than one
Minister without sharing in it. Doubtless, with all your

expression used by Delassert during a debate on the Sunday Labour question :—

"MY DEAR RAMBUTEAU,—I will answer M. François Delessert directly
when he addresses me directly; he has already done so often enough, not
to shrink from doing so again; he will always find me ready to answer
courteously questions that are asked me courteously. *If he is deputy of
Paris, I am deputy of Aix.* I am also Minister of the King, and always
prepared to reply to every appeal, provided it be made in suitable terms.
The word *scandal* hurts me, and I say so. Twice you have accepted the
rôle of intermediary. You will be good enough to transmit my answer to
him whether it pleases him or not. The Administration of Public Works
is not the source of scandal; it presents a spectacle of activity that is quite as
moral and useful as that of indolence; it does not fix the days of labour,
&c., it neither prohibits nor permits Sunday employment. The workmen
are paid by the piece, and may choose their own time for doing the work.

" *November* the 13*th*, 1833."

Adélaïde de Narbonne - Lara,
Comtesse de Rambuteau.

talents and intelligence, and your special aptitude for reporting on the Budget, you might make a good Secretary of State. But you have neither the gifts nor the eloquence needed in a member of the Council. If you were a Guizot, a Broglie, or a Molé, I should say to you: 'Stay in the Chamber, risk the vicissitude of political life, and you may yet have your day of power!' But to be a Minister always subordinate to another Minister, no matter how excellent may be your work in your own department; to see your future at the mercy of the reverses or the faults of your chief; to fall at last while engaged in noble enterprises and laborious toils that merit the highest approval—that is to be simply a journeyman Minister, nothing more. You deserve a better fate. You may repeatedly make one of a Ministry, and yet leave no results to show that you ever belonged to it; whilst, on the other hand, you can continue Prefect of Paris some fifteen or twenty years, do good service to the city, and then retire, either voluntarily or in consequence of a revolution, leaving behind you a name that will be remembered." He was right: I accepted the peerage.[1]

As I have spoken of M. Thiers, I may mention that it was to him I owed my acquaintance with M. Mignet, his most intimate friend, and his loyal and faithful comrade, who did me the honour one day to request my assistance in a matter of singular delicacy. It had to do with M. Thiers' approaching marriage.

M. Mignet spoke of his anxiety and regret at seeing him reject several alliances which, beside bringing him great advantages in the way of fortune, would insure him strong political support. He also took General Garraube, a deputy into his confidence, and it was agreed that we three should have an interview with M. Thiers.

[1] It had long been intended to give the peerage to Comte de Rambuteau, and Comte d'Argout wrote the following note to him in October 1832 :—

"You are already aware of my desire to see your name figure in the first list of Peers, but, after due consideration had been given to the subject, we came to the conclusion that it would be unwise to deprive the Chamber of Deputies of influential and able men like you, until there was a majority in favour of the system of 18th of March."

He listened to us very complacently, at a little dinner given in the home of the Minister of Foreign Affairs, thanked us for the affectionate interest we felt in his future welfare, and added: "When I came to Paris (you remember it, Mignet) he and I were two poor comrades without money and without protection. Both of these I found in the Dosne family, which received me hospitably, loved and adopted me. To the Dosnes I owe my first successes, and now that fortune smiles upon me, and that I have attained an influential position, . I should be ungrateful indeed if I did not share my honours with those who protected me then. Such a debt of gratitude must be repaid, and I shall never regret the decision I have adopted."

I was also well acquainted with M. Pasquier for more than thirty years, and used to visit him frequently, particularly after Sémonville resigned the office of Grand Refendary, in 1834. His great mental powers, his vast experience, his almost infallible insight into men and things, his calmness of judgment, often led me to seek his advice. What long conversations I have had with him, and what a pleasure it was to listen whilst he related the important events in which he had taken part, and gave a correct version of incidents that had been entirely misrepresented, as well as of details that had hitherto been unknown! He wrote them down in the last years of his life, and he regretted that my failing sight did not allow me to read his memoirs in manuscript. But he was good enough to read them to me himself, and the charm of his voice lent an additional attraction to his words. I remember his description of the taking of the Bastille, at which he had been present in Mlle. Contat's carriage, and of the wedding dinner given on the occasion of the marriage of Mlle. Cabarrus,[1] and M. de Fontenay, which he related while we were dining in the very same dining-room in which the banquet was held, in the palace of the Archbishop of Paris!

I remember, after the establishment of the Second

[1] Afterward Mme. Tallien.

Empire, which seemed more or less the result of the indelible memories left by the First, and sought to emphasise my arguments by reminding him of the thrill that shook Paris in 1833, when the Emperor's statue reappeared on the Column, and again in 1840, on the "Retour des Cendres," when even the extreme severity of the cold could not chill the heat of their enthusiasm, and which had now sprung into life once more and given five million votes to his nephew. "What you say is perfectly true," he replied, "so true that after the Strasbourg affair, I said to the King: 'Sire, the memory of the Emperor is so deeply rooted in the heart of France, that had his son, and not his nephew, returned, your Majesty would have been dethroned on the spot.'" On another occasion, when we were speaking of 1814, he told me that, on receiving information, as Prefect of Police, of a plot to assassinate the Emperor, he wrote to warn him: "I had left his service," he added, "but could not forget his kindness to me when I held office under him." I expect he referred to the plot of Maubreuil, although he did not mention the name, but I am not quite sure.[1]

I have no more intention of giving an exhaustive account of Louis-Philippe's reign than I had of fully describing that of Napoleon. I shall only speak of the events I witnessed, and the impressions they made on me. Besides, I was too much occupied to have time to waste on watching the doings of others. It is all I can do to recall my own, having reached that time of life when one lives more in the past than either in the present or future. Certainly, I have forgotten much; but there are certain words which still linger in my memory—certain scenes engraved, as it were, on my mental vision which I could never forget were I to live for another hundred years. One of these was Fieschi's crime. We all felt very uneasy on the morning of the 28th of July 1835, when the King was to review the National Guard in person. We had

[1] No doubt he was thinking of Maubreuil. Chancellor Pasquier has detailed the affair at full length in his *Mémoires*, c. iii. p. 365, *seq.*

heard disquieting rumours from different directions, just the sort of reports that herald riots and criminal attempts. I mentioned them to Marshal Lobau, and, when we entered the King's cabinet to inform him that everything was in order for the review, I entreated his Majesty to let the aide-de-camp receive petitions presented to him instead of allowing the petitioners to break through the ranks and approach himself, paper in hand : "I have no objection to your proposal," he replied ; "but, my dear Prefect, you need feel no uneasiness ; if there is any danger it will come from the windows and not from the streets." We went down stairs ; I gave my arm to the Duc de Trévise,[1] who had the gout, and found walking painful.

During the review groups of "gallows-birds" and such like scoundrels were to be seen congregated together at the corner of the Place Vendôme, and in front of the Pavillon de Hanovre and at the Porte Saint-Denis—the sort of bad characters who never come together unless some disturbance is at hand. At the entrance to the Boulevard du Temple we found the Eighth Legion, whose lieutenant-colonel, M. de Rieussec, took his place between General Aymès, aide-de-camp on service, and myself. I said to him : "You had better go back and remain at the head of your legion, for I see that your colonel is not there, but with the King." Marshal Lobau was on his Majesty's right, M. de la Rue on his left, and I was immediately behind him. The Prince de Joinville was next to the Marshal, and the Duc d'Orléans next to M. de la Rue. M. de Rieussec answered me : "Allow me to remain for a moment among you, as I want to say a word to the Duc d'Orléans about the races at Chantilly."

We were packed so close that my knee was pressed down under that of M. de Trévise, who had stayed beside me since the beginning of the review. I was about to apologise when this incident saved my life, for that very moment a loud detonation was heard, which I imagined to be a misplaced discharge of fireworks. Our horses reared ;

---

[1] Marshal Mortier.

and, seeing that the Marshal swayed in the saddle, I put out my hand to steady him, saying : "Take care, Marshal, or you'll fall." Suddenly, however, his huge body leaned over on my horse's neck, and M. de Rieussec dropped in front of me.

Then I understood the truth. I vaulted over the body of M. de Rieussec, and shouted to the King : "Forward, Sire, and get out of the range of the firing ! " At the same time, I pointed out the window from which a thick smoke was escaping to the National Guards stationed on my left, crying : "Seize that house and everybody in it ! " But Major Flahaut had been before me, and was looking into the matter. "Gentlemen," cried the King quite calmly, "resume your places, and let the review go on." He told me afterwards that, on turning round, I was the only one he had perceived behind him. General Lachase and Colonel Raffé of the Gendarmerie had been mortally wounded ; one bullet had gone clean through the nose of General Mathieu Aymès ; General Dumas had received another in his hat, and the Duc de Broglie one in his cravat. He never discovered its presence till we called his attention to it at the Chancellerie, and then as he untied the necktie the bullet dropped to the ground. The King's horse had been struck with buckshot on the neck and the crupper ; his Majesty himself having received a bullet in his coat, but he would not allow any mention of this.

The order to carry on the review prevented us at first from realising the extent of the disaster ; indeed, I had barely time to order Barrière (one of the two Staff officers in attendance on me) to gallop to the Chancellerie and reassure the Queen and the Royal Family as to the King's safety, and then to proceed to my wife and inform her that nothing had happened to myself. The National Guard, in the course of the review, marched as far as the Jardin de Beaumarchais, returning to the Place Vendôme ; and it was only when we crossed the spot where the catastrophe occurred, and which was spattered with blood, that we understood all its horror. The wall of the Jardin Turc was riddled with bullets; besides those victims who had fallen in the royal procession, twenty-five or thirty of the spectators and National Guards had also been injured. I gave orders for their removal to the Hôpital Saint-Louis, where, alas, in spite of every care, very few survived their wounds. Finally, the review was brought to an end by the last eight legions, in the midst of a heart-rending silence, on the Place Vendôme.

There we experienced a poignant emotion, the Queen, her daughters, the young Princes, and Madame Adélaïde were awaiting the arrival of the King with an anxiety easy to conceive. They all threw themselves, weeping, on his neck; whilst on their side the ladies of their suites sprang toward us and looked eagerly in every direction, one for a brother, another for a husband, another for a father who had escaped from this butchery; as for myself, I had the happiness of clasping in my arms my wife and daughters, to whom Providence had so recently preserved me. But the ceremony was not over yet. In spite of the burning heat, the King again mounted his horse, and we had to resume our places and remain for the march past, which lasted more than two hours.

The news spread as fast as a train of gunpowder. It would be impossible to do justice to the enthusiasm of our good National Guards, which found expression in their cheers and hurrahs; not content with manifesting their attachment to their sovereign by their cries, they broke their ranks, and, pressing forward, tried to touch his boots, as they could not reach his hand. Extraordinary creatures! whose hearts move faster than their heads, whose enthusiasm of to-day does not efface the prejudices of the night before, or save them from the illusions of the morrow! Thus, in 1847,[1] I happened to be reviewing the Second Legion, also on the Place Vendôme, when the report of the attempted assassination of Lecomte reached us. Thereupon a cry rose at once from six thousand breasts: "*To the Tuileries!*

---

[1] A slip of the memory; the attempt to assassinate Lecomte occurred on the 16th of April 1846.

to the Tuileries! lead us to the King!" I put myself at the head of the legion, together with the colonel, and led it into the courtyard of the château. The King came down, holding the Comte de Paris by the hand. He was received with as hearty cheers as when he had appeared before them a dozen years or so before. The next day the Sixth and Seventh Legions begged me to allow them to make a similar demonstration, and if I had been authorised to do so they would doubtless have evinced the same wild enthusiasm. But only a few months later all this was forgotten; it was the National Guard that brought about the Revolution of February.

The obsequies of Fieschi's victims were on a magnificent scale. There was a procession of seventeen hearses, the first containing the body of a Marshal of France, the last that of a young girl, escorted by twenty-four of her companions, and this spectacle made a deep impression on the people. The whole *cortége* vividly emphasised the horrors of civil strife, which strikes blindly, without any regard for age, sex, or rank. When the King sprinkled the coffins, one after another, with holy water, a visible shudder ran through the crowd; many eyes were wet with tears; then the mortal remains of these innocent people, united alike in a common death and a common burial, were interred in the Invalides in one and the same vault.

When I first entered the Hôtel de Ville I kept myself to some extent in touch with the Chamber and with politics, for when a man has once taken part in parliamentary life he is generally beset with a craving to retain a share in all its thrilling experiences and its exciting intrigues.

But my duties as administrator soon monopolised all my attention, and forced me to sever these bonds. I felt that I could not do better than devote my time exclusively to that Paris whose very name spells Glory. Gradually everything else became indifferent to me, or rather dropped out of my life entirely; and, indeed, if it had been possible to double my hours of labour, these hours would not have sufficed for my task. I paid little heed to the words and

deeds of Ministers.   All I asked of them was to let me
accomplish my work, but I was inflexible directly I saw that
they were trying to hamper it.

I had, for instance, a very serious quarrel in 1838 with
M. Humann, the Minister of Finance, when he insisted on
remodelling the tax on licenses, so that he might get larger
returns from it.   He had addressed circulars to the Prefects
and Directors of Taxes, calling their attention to the large
numbers of omissions on the registers and instructing them
to see to it that all those engaged in any industry whatever,
and who were not in the pay of employers, should henceforth figure on these registers.   This question was one
of paramount importance to Paris, where so many little
industries have been created by assiduous labour, combined
with skill and ingenuity, and where so many artisans earn
their modest livelihood by working at home.   Until now
they had been exempted from the tax.   Moreover, from a
desire to show their sympathy with the indigent classes,
the Municipal Council had also remitted the tax on personal
property to all those who paid less than 200 francs in rent,
and to balance the loss incurred thereby by the Department,
it set aside 3,200,000 francs, raised by the returns from
the town-tolls.

The circular and the demands made by the Minister
aroused a very bitter feeling in the Municipal Council,
which had met to discuss the Municipal Budget.   A
strongly-worded and well-reasoned motion, in which the
project was condemned, was introduced by M. Lafaulotte,
one of the most influential and moderate members of the
body.   I had no difficulty in persuading them to adjourn
for a sufficiently long time to give me a chance of mediating
between them and the Minister.   " My dear friend," I said
to the latter, "your officials have placed you in an awkward
position, at any rate as regards Paris. You are quite justified in trying to get the largest possible returns from the
taxes, but in doing so you should act with prudence. I
have been only five years in office, and yet the number of
licenses has increased from fifty-two thousand to seventy

thousand; and the returns, from four millions and a half to seven millions. Where I found a deficit of sixty-five francs, I have created a surplus of nearly four hundred thousand. And it is this increase which your officials wish to appropriate, by driving me to place certain taxes on the registers which will never be recovered, as, for example, this one which you want to levy on twenty-five thousand workmen, who are absolutely unable to pay their personal quota. You are on the wrong tack. If I have increased the revenue from licenses sixty per cent., it is because I recommended the Tax Commission to make a note of all those who can pay taxes, and erase from the register the names of those who cannot. You know the resolution that has been laid before the Council. If it is carried, as it undoubtedly will be, it will be certain to make a great sensation, and no doubt five hundred communes will follow the example of Paris. But if, on the other hand, you let me manage the affair, I shall continue to act as I have done ever since this question was raised—that is, as far as possible in harmony with the Council; and though I may have a little skirmish with you now and then, I will act with moderation, a course dictated by my own interests. It is of course in your power to defeat me, but the consciousness of having rendered an important service to the King and to the Government by preventing serious troubles will console me." He showed considerable annoyance, and even a little anger, but he surrendered. We were never such good friends again as we had been, but the city and the State were none the worse off for that.

It was also in the interests of the city that I had a conversation with the King, in 1840, relative to the Eastern Question. I was taking a few days' holiday at Champgrenon, when the warlike reports I received from Paris obliged me to hurry back to the city. I went at once to Saint Cloud. The King spoke to me with considerable warmth of the sacrifices that the present complications might entail on France; men's minds were terribly excited;

there was a suggestion of war in the Treaty of London, and it might be necessary to go to that length.

"Sire," I answered, "with your permission, I shall confine myself to the effect which a war may produce on my own Department. To my mind the most obvious result of the present state of affairs has been to put a drag on business for the last six months. On the 17th of February the octroi duties showed a considerable increase over the preceding returns; to-day, the 15th of September, there is a reduction of 1,800,000 francs; so we can calculate the loss at more than two millions and a half for the half year; this means that the consumption of provisions in Paris during that lapse of time has been diminished by some forty-four millions. If the mere dread of war has produced such consequences, your Majesty can understand what the reality would do. You will have to send the garrison to the frontiers, whilst only the National Guard will remain to defend the Crown and society. Now, it is composed of tradesmen, manufacturers, and persons who have a fixed income of some sort or other. The manufactured products exported by Paris every year gives bread to a hundred and sixty thousand workmen; in addition to this, there are always at least fifty thousand foreigners in Paris, on whom fifty thousand Parisians depend for their subsistence; a war will paralyse the one class and banish the other, and drive the rentiers and the saving-bank depositors crazy. Sire, I will perform my duty, just as I did in 1814 and 1815; but to insure a display of equal zeal on the part of the Municipal Council and people, I must be able to show them that I have done my best to set before your eyes the sacrifices they will have to make, and also prove to them that the hour has struck 'when honour and necessity demand such sacrifices."

The King took my observations in good part, and was more pacifically inclined toward the close of the conversation than he had been at the beginning.

I will relate another conversation with Louis-Philippe, which was of a wholly political character. It occurred at the time when M. de Salvandy replaced M. Villemain,[1] in the Ministry of Public Instruction. The King said to me: "Well, my dear Prefect, you see I have got another of the fanatical votaries of your friend, Molé, to join my Ministry. You ought to be satisfied now!" "Oh, not at all, Sire; your Majesty is well aware of my opinion; a Constitutional King ought always to have a body of men (un ministère en cas) outside the Ministry and close to his hand, just as it is advisable to keep a spare carriage; so that if one carriage breaks down, the occupant can get into the other and use it while the first (which he may find serviceable later) undergoes repair. Now, when you deprive M. Molé of all his friends, one by one, you reduce him to impotence, and, for the sake of prolonging the life of the Ministry for a few days, you deprive yourself of useful auxiliaries in the future. Should you ever ask M. Molé to form a Ministry, he will have to beg MM. Thiers and Barrot to give him some of their lieutenants, who will certainly retort: 'As you are willing to play our game, you must hold the cards.' What is likely to happen in such a case I have sometimes heard your Majesty say: 'That little dare-devil of a Thiers will get me out of this scrape.' And so he did both as regards the Regency of the Duc de Nemours and the fortifications of Paris, but your Majesty is too well advised not to distinguish between the claims that may be made on you by a Ministry you have yourself chosen and those made by a Ministry which has been forced upon you."

I had a similar conversation some time afterward—I think about the first of August—with Madame Adélaïde, who was then very ill, but not confined to bed. She had sent for me to discuss the state of affairs, which she did not find at all as satisfactory as her brother imagined them to be. She always encouraged me to speak frankly, and I did so on the present occasion. I told her how imprudent

---

[1] On the 1st of February 1845. Villemain, whose health was impaired by his four years' service in the Ministry, resigned on the 30th of December 1844.

it was of the King to place all his friends in the same
Ministry, reserving none of them for critical circumstances,
and thus making himself liable to the necessity of framing
an entire Ministry from the Opposition ; and how the omnipotence of the majority placed the Prefects under the
control of the Ministerial deputies, and not of the King,
so that there was no longer a real Prefect, properly speaking,
except in those Departments which were influenced by the
Opposition.   Moreover, Paris was hostile, and this hostility
was not confined to the so-called advanced liberals, but
extended to the middle classes generally.   I cited the
support given to the candidature of M. Berger in the
Second Arrondissement, and told her the most influential
conservatives in the district had confessed to me that
more than three hundred of their friends had voted for
M. Berger, solely from a wish to convince the Government
of their dissatisfaction with the present condition of affairs ;
and that Colonel Talbot had voted for Berger with the
same object : I also told her that the National Guard was
untrustworthy, as was implied by the fact that for the past
five years the Government had not dared to hold a general
review of its legions ; moreover that the union between
Guizot and Duchâtel was anything but solid, and that it
would be wise to satisfy public opinion in certain directions,
by making some sacrifices, like those effected in 1840, with
a view to dissolving sundry threatening alliances and gaining
a hold on certain individuals in the event of probable
difficulties.

Madame Adélaïde listened with close attention; but
she maintained that Guizot was a man upon whom one
could safely depend.   I returned : "Your Royal Highness
will permit me to remind you that here, in this very place
where I have the honour to be sitting beside you, I saw the
King shed bitter tears because he had to surrender to the
Coalition and accept Guizot, who had been its mainspring,
as his Minister.   Have you not yourself, Madame, frequently expressed your dislike for the Doctrinaire school
and the finality of its theories?"

"True," she replied, "but my brother removed my prejudices by showing that none of his Ministers had been so submissive to his will, none so ready to accept his views in matters relating to the administration of Foreign Affairs, and that Guizot had been the first, if not the only one, who understood him and devoted his great abilities exclusively to his service. Have you not often told me yourself that Guizot defended you from the ambitious intrigues of the Duchâtel family?"

"Certainly, and that is why I have not said one word in his disfavour; on the contrary, I am thinking of his welfare as much as of the King's. He would return to power all the stronger for the errors of his enemies, all the better enlightened as to the state of the public mind and the dangers of a majority composed of those whose interests are purely selfish. Both his Majesty's age and that of the Comte de Paris make it most desirable to avoid any conflict with public opinion. We should unite all the well-disposed in a policy that will insure the transmission of the Crown. Our party-divisions must not lead us to surrender the helm of State to the common enemy."

She promised to give careful consideration to our conversation, but death did not allow her time to do so. It was a great misfortune: she was the only person in the country to whom the King would listen, or who could shake his confidence in Guizot, or the National Guard, or the majority. For some time he had been growing more and more irritable; he was easily put out of temper, and would fire up at the least contradiction, and after all, however anxious one may be to serve others, one can't be perpetually enraging them. Consequently it was always to Madame Adélaïde that the true friends of the King had recourse; she was always accessible, always a willing mediator, and Montalivet, Gérard, and Dupin, who, without being supporters of the Ministry, were devoted and loyal, found her a most useful go-between in bringing their views before her brother.

I can't say that the King was never dissatisfied with

my freedom of speech, which, however, I exercised but
seldom at this period : I was now simply an administrator,
in no way connected with politics, and so I was not often
consulted.   And yet, thanks to my continual contact with
the lower classes, I was often in a position to communicate
very useful information.   When the insurrection of '48
first broke out, many who, in the exercise of their duties,
ought to have gathered some hints of coming events, were
taken far more by surprise than I was.

I had, in fact, been very uneasy for a long time.   I
was conscious of vague threatenings in the air.   The same
strong feeling that had agitated the Chamber and France
in 1839 and 1840, at the time of the Coalition, were again
disturbing the people.   A spirit of disaffection was spreading
almost everywhere.   We were the victims of that malady
which is especially prevalent among the French : lassitude,
the disease that springs from a surfeit of prosperity; and
which we often detect in women who live in great affluence.
These latter grow tired of domestic happiness, of the
commonplace pleasures of home, of the respect and consideration that surround them, and so abandon themselves
to some passion or other, without calculation, without love,
without the heart being really affected, but from mere
thoughtlessness, because they crave for change and novelty,
anything, in short, to break the monotony of their daily
life.   All they desire is a new experience, no matter
whether it be pleasurable or the reverse; what they want is
something that will disturb the absolute serenity which is
boring them to death.

And it is the same with every prosperous nation, but
more especially with the Parisians.   They cannot grow
accustomed to the smooth uniformity of a settled government; it becomes too wearisome, and, after a time, they
want *something different*, and, as I said to the King, at the
beginning of my administration, you must always keep their
minds employed as you would in the case of children,
otherwise they will be for ever in mischief.   When you
cannot give them a war, you must at any rate provide in

its place such substitutes as the erection of monuments, public works, and all sorts of projects with which they can glut their natural taste for criticism and their short-lived curiosity. Such was the system I adopted to hinder the elective Municipal Council from rushing headlong into reforms, solely for the pleasure it took in innovations and in winning popularity by demolishing the budget and the Government. I kept it constantly occupied with works of importance, proportioned to the resources of the city, never attempting anything which might involve her future, and never ceasing to defend her from responsibilities that might sooner or later prove burdensome.

The fact is that in matters of administration one must always anticipate the unforeseen, if I may so express myself. I saw this clearly in 1847, when the high price of cereals proved a strong endorsement of all my previsions. I had renounced the system of storing great supplies of provisions and thus interfering with the freedom of commerce, a system that, during the rise in the price of food in 1816 and 1817, had cost the city thirty-eight millions. Doubtless the State had taken more than the half of the burden on its shoulders (about twenty-one millions), but I could not expect similar assistance in my department, so great was the idiotic jealousy which the provinces felt for Paris; and the Chamber (where this unworthy feeling found only too ready an echo) would never have voted such subsidies, even had the Government dared to propose them.

I arranged matters, then, in such a way that I was able to do without them; and, by scrupulously paying the old debts, by respecting all engagements, and by never encroaching on the incoming revenues, I had nearly twenty-five millions in the Treasury. In three days everything was ready for circulating, regulating, and distributing systematically the bread-checks to be bestowed among those who could not afford to pay more than eighty centimes for the loaf of four kilograms. Thirty-four millions of checks were dealt out in this fashion, and four hundred and fifty thousand persons succoured; so that even if we had had another bad harvest, the city would have been able to continue these benefits.

As the last municipal elections had increased the ranks of the opposition, by adding to the quantity and diminishing the quality, it appeared necessary to find some guarantees for the execution of my works. In support of the financial measures, ratified by the Chamber in July 1848, I laid before the Council a vast scheme for the expenditure of Eighty millions to be realised in five years. It embraced the Halles Centrales, the town-halls of the 3rd, 11th, and 12th arrondissements, the church of Sainte-Clotilde; the completion of quays and bridges, the lengthening of the Rue de Rivoli, regulations for the proper management of drainage, sewers, street-paving, &c. All this was to be finished in 1853: it was, in some sort, my last will and testament, and it was time for me to sign it.

Every day the elections were sending persons to the Council who were far more disposed to play the game of politics than attend to the business of the administration, and serve their own or their party's interest rather than that of the city's. The spirit of sophistry and systematic revolt which had invaded the Council and which, in the Chamber, led thirteen out of every fourteen deputies to join the opposition, penetrated also into the National Guard. We had lost some of its most reliable chiefs, Ganneron, Hérard, &c. The latitude allowed to the non-commissioned men to select officers and delegates outside the company had enabled the secret societies to group their members in certain companies, nineteen of which were noted as being altogether hostile to the dynasty. Several officers actually refused invitations to dine at the Tuileries, and those who did not go quite to this length showed a studied indifference to the matter.

Members of the upper classes all joined together to form very select companies composed exclusively of the *élite*, thus depriving all the less distinguished ones of their salutary influence. Then, little attention was paid to the election of the non-commissioned officers, and thus the opposition was allowed to organise its supporters wherever it took the trouble to do so. As for the rest of the citizens, very little reliance could be placed on any of them. The Parisian is a caviller by nature; he fancies that he makes himself important by his criticisms, and shows his refined taste by adopting that *nil admirari* without rhyme or reason. He seems to have retained faithfully in his memory d'Alembert's advice to his son : "If you want to pass for a highly intellectual person, always say, on every occasion, that such or such a thing is bad, but carefully refrain from saying why it is so l" Always the *tarte à la crème* of Molière.

But there was something, still more grave and alarming, which I had already|brought to the notice of the King and of the Ministers. A movement was spreading among the working classes, directed against the bourgeoisie, analogous to the movement in the Tiers-état of 1789 against the privileged orders. Every means was adopted to excite the jealousy and hatred of the people ; their credulity was imposed upon by the dream of a new social organisation, by baseless theories, by verbose systems whose surest effect was not to ensure their happiness and prosperity, but to lash them on to fury against present conditions. The very education and the acquisition of useful knowledge which we were trying to place within their reach became an evil, on account of the pernicious use to which they turned it.

Since 1832, the Polytechnic Association had organised evening courses for workmen, and, although most of the professors, and even the president himself, had been compromised in the insurrection at the Cloître Saint-Merry, I did not reject their petition when, after my accession to office, they begged me to patronise their work. The language they used on the occasion, though somewhat highflown, was not objectionable. I severely reproved them for their past conduct ; but I soon discovered that reflection, age, and experience had modified their views, and I never had occasion to reproach them afterwards. Well, strange to say, it was M. Perducet himself who, two months

after those February days, came to entreat me to disallow the
opening of new courses on constitutional government, because he feared that they might serve to mislead the class of
persons for whom this constitution was designed, by giving
them false ideas as to the rights of citizens and political
economy.

" These lectures," he declared, " will undo all the useful
and practical teaching given to the workmen ; they will be
stuffed with false ideas and badly digested opinions.   Instruction of that nature is not an advantage, but a danger
to themselves and society."

I discovered also that there were five journals, exclusively
intended for workmen (I knew the individuals who managed
them), not to speak of the propaganda carried on by pam-
phlets.   Indeed, the very presence of M. Considérant in the
Council was a sufficient proof of the danger.   It was a queer
and curious circumstance that he actually owed his election
to the co-operation of the legitimist party !   Yet he never,
then or later, concealed his ambitions and hopes.   Thus
when, after a prolonged discussion in the session held on
the 18th, there was a conversation in which the most advanced members of the opposition took part ; the language
of himself and Delorme became so violent and aggressive
that at length I said, " I am going, for although this is
supposed to be a confidential conversation, I am bound to
remember that I am prefect."

I was followed into my cabinet by M. Seguin, who said,
" My dear Prefect, you know that my position as a manufacturer places me in daily relations with all classes of the
population.   Don't deceive yourself; the situation is far
greater than any one supposes.   People are getting tired of
the King and want a change.   Should the movement come
to a head, our only chance will be in the abdication of
Louis-Philippe and the regency of the Duchesse d'Orléans,
for Nemours is detested, and they won't have him at any
price."   Besson, colonel of the 3rd legion, told me he could
place no reliance on it.   Lariboissière, Husson, Lavocat,
Chapuis, and Boutarel said the same.   The 1st and 2nd legions

were, perhaps, not quite so bad, but they were decidedly lukewarm. The mayors and the most loyal members of the Council made no secret of their fears : there was no doubt that, at the first collision, we should find indifference and listlessness on one side, opposed to audacity and activity on the other, and I felt certain we should see the uniform of the National Guard in the ranks of the rioters and on the barricades. Now it was an understood thing that the regular army could only act against the people after the National Guard had had its turn. Upon what force, then, could we count?

I thought it my duty to communicate this information at once to Guizot and Duchâtel. I was received as coldly as a man who wakens another at an unwelcome moment. Nevertheless, I returned to the charge in the evening, when I met Guizot at the residence of Mme. N———. He exclaimed impatiently: "If you had as much work on your hands as I have, you would not worry over this trash about Paris."

As for Duchâtel, he trusted the reports of Delessert, the Prefect of Police, who, although he did not deny I had some foundation for my alarm, assured me that the secret societies would give no trouble at present. They would need three or four months to make the necessary preparations, and the struggle would be adjourned until spring. On the other hand, the negotiations of the Ministry, represented by Velet and Morny, with the two delegates of the opposition, Duvergier and Massenisse, with regard to the banquet of the 5th of February, forbidden by the Government, as well as the repugnance of Odilon, Barrot, and Thiers to stake their all in the quarrel, the good disposition of the troops guaranteed by Sebastiani, the support of that part of the National Guard controlled by Jacqueminot, all fostered a feeling of false security in the minds of the Ministry who felt sure of a majority in the Chambers.

Nevertheless, on Friday evening I went to the Tuileries. I made several attempts to converse with the King, and tell him of my anxiety. But it was hard to get him to listen to anything he did not like. Some minister or other has said, " The King speaks to me, but I do not speak to the King." To obtain the attention of Louis-Philippe, you had to push persistence beyond the verge of importunity. In spite of his confidence and his kindness, I found him so testy, not to use a stronger term, that I avoided putting myself forward and speaking of even what concerned my own sphere. I had not the same difficulties with the Duc de Nemours, who was much more affable. So, when I saw that all my efforts failed with the King, I had recourse that same evening to the Prince. I told him all I had heard of the threats of the Republicans, the rumoured possibility of an abdication, the disloyalty of the National Guard, the risk of incurring a struggle which could be averted by wise concessions, not to speak of the folly of prohibiting a banquet of a hundred deputies [1] (who had thirty or forty thousand supporters at their back) on the mere injunction of a Commissary of Police. It seemed to me like tempting Providence! The Prince listened attentively and promised to conceal nothing from the King.

On Saturday I had a grand dinner of sixty covers; among those who attended were diplomats, a few foreigners interested in our affairs, mayors, deputies, municipal councillors, and commandants of the National Guard. At night there was a reception, which was crowded. All were in a state of alarm, and all were agreed on the extreme gravity of the situation. On that day, too, there was a banquet at the Chamber of Commerce, to which the ex-presidents had been invited. About eleven o'clock they all came to me in a body. Their dean, M. Aubé, who acted as their representative, informed me, in consequence of the general excitement and commotion, and the anxiety existing among merchants and men of property, they appealed to me, as the chief of the city and as a vigilant

[1] Eighty-seven deputies had promised to be present at the banquet, in spite of the prohibition of the Government. Fearing there might be a collision, they changed their minds. Only Lamartine declared that, " even if the Place de la Concorde (place of meeting) were deserted, and all the deputies failed in their duty, he would still go alone to the banquet, with his shadow behind him."

friend of fifteen years' standing, to enlighten the King and his Ministers on the situation. There were twenty-seven of them. The step they had taken and the language of their address produced considerable feeling in my salons, but no surprise. The general opinion may be gathered by what M. Séguin said to his wife: "We must attend the Prefect's reception; it will probably be the last one held in the Hôtel de Ville!" Ah, how keenly, at these critical moments, did I regret the loss of Madame Adélaïde! She would have listened to me, and would have forced the King to listen too.

I had seen M. Montalivet twice; he shared my sentiments with regard to the National Guard and the banquet; he believed that only a change of Ministry could prevent a crisis; but how convince the King, now more impatient than ever of any contradiction? Marshal Gérard was still more outspoken; and yet all this foresight and perspicacity were to be in vain!

On Sunday, the 20th, I made my official visit to the Public Savings Bank, for I was scrupulous in fulfilling my duties as an administrator every year; such visits evinced my interest in one of my most useful institutions, and also afforded me an opportunity of becoming thoroughly acquainted with its machinery. I had the accounts transmitted to me at the end of each month, and they furnished me with valuable hints on the moral and financial condition of the population. Now, on this morning there were deposits of 315,000 francs, and withdrawals of 1,280,000 francs, while, on the preceding Sunday, there had been 800,000 deposited and 487,000 paid out. This symptom appeared to me to be so grave that I at once wrote to Duchâtel to notify him of it. I have since learned from General Trézel, at that time Minister of War, that at the Ministerial Council, held on that very Sunday, he had called the King's attention to the fact that it was necessary to decide who should be Commander-in-Chief of Paris in the event of an insurrection, representing to him that Jacqueminot would not like to have to obey Sebastiani, because the National Guard ranked before the army, and that Sebastiani could not be subordinate to Jacqueminot, because this precedency did not extend as far as that.[1] It was agreed that the superior command should be entrusted to Marshal Bugeaud and not to a Prince, for collisions being possible, if not probable, it would not be advisable to render the Royal Family responsible for whatever blood might be shed.

After leaving the Council, Duchâtel informed Jacqueminot of this arrangement. Whereupon Jacqueminot flies into a passion, cries that he is dishonoured for ever if he is deprived of his command, and tenders his resignation! In reality, he had long been on the look-out for an excuse for resigning, believing that his resignation in such circumstances would favour his ambitions. But the confidence both of the King and his advisers in Jacqueminot was so extravagant that they actually believed he could cut his way through all difficulties, and save everything. Then Duchâtel declared that he could not remain in a Ministry from which his father-in-law had seceded, and he, too, tendered his resignation. For five or six months he also, in a roundabout way, had been trying to be freed from the responsibilities of office ; he was somewhat jealous of Guizot, and did not care to stake his last card on the game of his colleague ; besides, he was anxious about his health, and, as he was enormously rich and was possessed of real talent, he thought it well to reserve himself for the future, possibly for the chance of presiding over a new Ministry. His ambitions were, indeed, on a large scale ; he himself was to be President of the Council, his father-in-law Marshal and Commander-in-Chief of the National Guard,

---

[1] Sebastiani, brother of the Marshal, and formerly aide-de-camp to M. de Narbonne, had always occupied high posts in the active army : quartermaster-general in 1823, lieutenant-general in 1830 (eight years before Jacqueminot), he had commanded the division of Paris since 1842. Jacqueminot had left the army in 1815 for industrial pursuits, then for politics, and the Monarchy of July had rewarded him for his participation in the expedition to Rambouillet by nominating him general of brigade on the staff of the National Guard, and afterward commander.

his brother in the Hôtel de Ville—and all these dreams were to be realised, too, during the old age of the King, and under the regency of the Duc de Nemours!

But the King was not inclined to purchase the support of the masterful Marshal Bugeaud at the price of these two resignations.

He detested the Marshal, and did not conceal his dislike. "Bugeaud in the Ministry of War!" he said; "why, at that rate, my children could not dispose of a single nomination in the army, not even of a lieutenancy!" Accordingly on Sunday evening he said to General Trézel: "Keep back the decree I issued to-day, it is useless; I shall set matters right by sending Nemours to the staff." He did send him on the following Tuesday, but charged him to do nothing on his own responsibility, and to avoid a collision at all costs.

I called on Delessert on Monday morning before nine o'clock. I told him I had not come to pry into his secrets, for I was well aware of his reticence on subjects connected with the police, but that I felt it absolutely necessary to communicate to him what I had ascertained; I then entered fully into the particulars of the circumstances that alarmed me. I emphasised the extreme peril of the situation. I drew his attention to the blindness of the King, and I pointed out the mistake which he made in believing that they could command the support of the country because they had a majority in the Chamber. Finally, I entreated him to explain all this to the Court. He answered that he shared my fears without dreading their consequences. "The agitation was more superficial than deep; the insurgents had neither arms, ammunition, nor organisation; a very large proportion of the opposition, afraid of being carried to too great lengths, was resolved, as far as could be seen, either to withdraw or come to terms; the ringleaders of the secret societies were in favour of delay. No doubt the danger was only deferred, and the future looked threatening enough, but nothing serious was going to happen at present; the very panic which had originated among the citizens, and especially among the merchants, had, at any rate, this advantage, that those who had anything to lose felt that they must rally round those in power; in short, all the necessary measures had been taken; and the Hôtel de Ville, in particular, would be protected by considerable forces."

I went on to see Sebastiani. "My dear friend," I said, "you are quite satisfied with the spirit of your troops; you are willing to vouch for their fidelity; you have assured me that the Duc de Nemours is the idol of the army; it is all very well to say this sort of thing at the Tuileries, and, in case of a war with the English or the Russians, I should never think of doubting the loyalty of your soldiers and officers; but a war in the streets of Paris is quite another thing. Have you ever contemplated the possibility of seeing the National Guard drawn up against you and joining with the insurgents? That is a matter you would do well to consider, and, if need be, you should at once march your men against the rebels, without leaving them time for reflection nor their adversaries time to tamper with them." But apparently Sebastiani was as deluded an optimist as Delessert.

Next I saw Jacqueminot. He was apparently unwell. I found him at table, in his dressing-gown. I told him that the seventeen colonels and lieutenant-colonels of the seventeen legions, not to speak of mayors, municipal councillors, and thousands of others whose word might be depended upon, assured me the National Guard would not respond if they were called out. Some of them would be at the prohibited banquet, some would take part with the rioters; even the best affected companies would not resist the cry of "*Long live Reform! Down with the Ministry!*" It was therefore our duty to open the King's eyes to the truth, and consequently I wanted to take counsel with him as to the best way of doing so. Furiously brandishing a smelt at the end of his fork, Jacqueminot exclaimed: "If we were not friends of thirty years' standing, I should tell you that you calumniate the National Guard; that you do not know it as I know it; and that I have only to mount my horse to have fifty thousand men behind me. Those who have been telling you the stories which you are so ready to believe are nothing better than cowards and alarmists."

It was useless prolonging a conversation on these lines, so I left him, praying with all my heart that he might be right and the event might prove me wrong.

But I was by no means alone in my fears. When the Queen received me that evening she showed her uneasiness both by her words and the expression of her face. " My dear Prefect," she said, "we are in a bad way!" "Yes, madame," I answered, speaking as a good subject rather than as a courtier; "but it is in the King's hands to save the situation." "Speak to him frankly," said she. I approached the King. At last I could oblige him to listen to the truth!

The scene is still vividly present to my mind. We were between two windows, leaning against a console upon which rested a magnificent filigree casket. I told him all I knew, beginning with the plots of the Republicans, and ending with my conversation with M. Séguin on the abdication and on the regency of the Duchesse d'Orléans. I likewise told him of the defection or coldness of the National Guard; the proceedings taken by the Chamber of Commerce and its ex-presidents; of the withdrawal of deposits from the Savings Bank; and of the sluggishness of the Ministers, who, because they had a majority in the Chamber, believed they were masters of the situation. I spoke rapidly and impressively, for I was afraid of exhausting his patience and of not being allowed to finish all I had to say. In conclusion, I dwelt on the urgent necessity of taking immediate action in order to stifle the disturbance before it had time to break out.

At length the King interrupted me. "My dear Prefect," said he, "certain persons have been trying to frighten me for a whole year, and they have not succeeded. These same persons have adopted another plan to-day, that of frightening you, for they know how much I trust and like you. But rest assured that all your apprehensions are only a straw fire, which will burn out in a couple of hours. In a week's time, my dear Prefect, you will heartily regret your fears, and be very much ashamed of them, too." Therewith he left me, perfectly satisfied himself, and in high spirits.

I then fell back on the Duc de Nemours, and once more rehearsed my doleful anthem. I laid stress on all that I had told him on the preceding Friday, reinforcing my report with fresh particulars. I bitterly deplored the King's incredulity, and did my utmost to convince him that the crisis demanded not only courage, but prudence. But all in vain! He maintained that I was mistaken; that all the necessary measures had been adopted; that they were sure of the soldiers; that the National Guard was more faithful than I imagined; and that the Ministers knew from reliable sources that the banquet had been abandoned, &c. I left in despair. That evening I saw the Royal Family for the last time.

After my departure, the King said: "The Prefect is a worthy fellow, useful and devoted, but he is breaking down, and he is getting feeble-minded." I suspect, if matters had turned out differently, I should have found it rather difficult to keep my post. After Madame Adélaïde's death, his Majesty was my only support against the ambition of Duchâtel, who wanted to see his brother in my place. Guizot opposed him, at least I think so, as well as the rest of the Ministry. Had not this been the case, Duchâtel, by threatening the King, would perhaps have attained the object of his hopes. It was a saying of his, which I often heard him repeat: "If I am strong enough, the majority will not balk me; if I am too weak, I may as well be defeated on one question as on another."

After quitting the Tuileries, I went to a *fête* at the residence of the Prince de Ligne. All the leading members of the diplomatic corps were present, and were evidently uneasy as to the possible developments of the next day. I picked my words carefully in conversing with them, though I did not conceal my own impressions. I made one more attempt to convince Duchâtel; but he was still hopeful of coming to terms with the opposition. He was good enough to give me one piece of information. This was to the effect that after I had ceased to take part in the Parliamentary schemes, I had entirely lost all the political influence which I had ever enjoyed; that I was looked upon as a good ædile, and a useful chairman in the Municipal Council, efficient in preventing disorders (as in the affair of the supply of provisions), and in settling difficulties between different departments of the Government, as in the case of the law for licences. In short, he gave me to understand that I was a sagacious municipal steward, but totally incapable of managing elections or of rendering any Ministerial service, and as such should be restricted to my own limited sphere. At the same time I was kept in reserve as a sort of emergency man, because it was not desirable to raise an outcry in Paris, or irritate the Municipal Council; but so far as the Ministry went, I was neither liked nor even appreciated.

After these fruitless visits, I returned, for the last time, to the Hôtel de Ville, resolved, no matter what happened, to do my duty to the end. On Tuesday, I was informed that the troops were beginning to arrive. They were composed of the 7th light infantry, the 63rd of the line, six squadrons of cuirassiers, four pieces of artillery, a squadron of the National Guard, and detachments of the 7th and 9th legions. General Taillandier, who was in command, did not arrive until four in the evening; it was M. de Luzy, colonel of the 7th, who commanded as senior officer. I was very anxious for the general's presence, both on account of the rivalry between the National Guard and the army, and because Boutard, colonel of the 9th legion, was rather susceptible. His tendency to jealousy did not, however, detract from his merit. I had known him well since 1839, when I had good reason to appreciate his courage at the time of the insurrection of Barbès; I saw him march with one hundred and fifty grenadiers against the rioters of the Rue Baubourg, his men skirting the houses, and he in the gutter, calm and tranquil, his sword under his arm. For the last four or five years I had supported him against certain individuals who had succeeded during that time in preventing him from getting the command of his company.

He said to me: "I bring you a hundred and eighty men whom I believe safe and sure, but take care to feed them well, for if I allow them to go home for their meals, they will not return." I had a table laid, then, in the great antechamber of the ushers, with thirty covers, for the exclusive use of the National Guard; I had another set out for the officers of the line and staff; the general and colonels ate with us, and the troops received (as they had always done, for that matter, when on duty at the Hôtel de Ville), supplementary rations in bread, wine, cold meat, and wood for the bivouacs. I had made preparations for such a contingency long before. The bakery of the hospitals was my resource; it always had fifteen or sixteen thousand rations ready. The bread having been baked twenty-four hours in advance, nothing was easier than to procure a fresh supply. I could make certain, on Tuesdays and Wednesdays, of having from three to five thousand rations early in the morning.

It was fortunate that I took these precautions, for, on Thursday, the barricades cut off all means of communication; the troops did not receive any distribution of either victuals or forage, so that the horses of the artillery had to be fed on bread. On Thursday morning I had been obliged to make a clean sweep of the slaughter-house in the neighbourhood; so it was not surprising that the insurgents found twenty-six legs of mutton on the spits when they invaded the kitchens of the Hôtel de Ville.

Naturally, one of the first questions I put to the colonels of the line was to ask if they were quite sure of their regiments. "I would vouch for my soldiers even more confidently than my officers," replied M. de Luzy; "they will follow the National Guard courageously." I have already stated that for eighteen years it had been settled that the army should march behind the National Guard. Thus it was necessary that the latter should set the example and open fire; for that reason I lavished every attention on Colonel Boutarel's men, those belonging to the 7th legion having disappeared on Tuesday night.

On Wednesday morning, we had been obliged to send a very strong detachment to the Mairie of the 7th Arrondissement, for the purpose of taking away the arms stored there, which were insufficiently protected by the National Guard. General Taillandier had also ordered a body of soldiers to occupy the Place du Châtalet, where poor Major de H—— was shot in the back at nightfall by a street Arab.

During these two days of Tuesday and Wednesday, I had as much as I could do to defend myself against the entreaties and almost threats of the most advanced members of the Municipal Council, who insisted that I should immediately convoke that body. They told me I was incurring a grave responsibility by not consulting the Assembly in such circumstances. But I held my ground, for I was convinced that any rising of the Commune of Paris, in whatever form, would be the ruin of the Monarchy, and I declared that I should regard any unauthorised meeting as an act of rebellion and deal with it accordingly. Certain persons took up their residence in the Hôtel de Ville to act, I believe, as spies for the enemy, and to co-operate with some of the employees; I cared little, however, about any public reports that might be circulated concerning my conduct; I made no secret of my determination to do my duty and to make those around me do it also.

General Taillandier left us at five on Wednesday morning to fetch his daughter from the École Militaire; he did not return until four in the evening. Before starting, he had ordered the cavalry to remain on horseback. It was grievous to see these fine troops exposed to the heavy rain and drenched to the skin, yet refusing to go under the arches of the Hôtel de Ville, where they would have had

Q

shelter. I had sent a messenger to Delessert at eight in the morning to ask if I could go to the Tuileries. He assured me that there was no cause for alarm, that none of the secret societies had as yet invaded the streets, that he believed it would be an easy matter to maintain order, and that there would be no necessity to summon the suburban police, who, though useful on an emergency, became a nuisance at the end of twenty-four hours. All the same, he added, that though I should probably find no difficulty in reaching the Tuileries, he could not venture to guarantee me an equally safe return. Such being the case I determined to remain at my post, for how could I possibly desert it in such a unparalleled crisis, when there was no Minister in authority, no recognised head of the military! Everything combined to hurry on events, the retirement of the Ministry, the intervention of the Duc de Nemours, the resignation of Jacqueminot, the hesitation of Sebastiani, who, not caring to compromise himself, preferred to take his stand behind the Prince, expecting that the latter would be Regent and, possibly, King. So great was the mismanagement that nothing was provided for the troops, not even cartridges! At five in the evening, Colonel de Luzy entered my cabinet, saying: "Monsieur le Préfet, I am going with a battalion of my regiment and some Vincennes sharpshooters to release forty Municipal Guards who are surrounded and threatened at the Fabrique Lepage in the Bourg Abbé Street. You have placed a detachment of the National Guard at my service, but what am I to do with them if you give me no cartridges?"

Fortunately six months previously I had secured twenty thousand for Sebastiani. Formerly (after the year 1830) there had always been a large magazine at the Hôtel de Ville, but I had been obliged to remove this, whilst the public works were being carried out, to avoid all risk to the twelve hundred workmen. But I was then able to satisfy both the Colonel and Taillandier, who came in at the same moment. It was just then that we heard of the attack on the Mairie of the Seventh Ward as well as that

on the Place S. Jean, where the captain of the 7th Light
Infantry was killed. And still no assistance had reached
us. I had sent three letters without getting any reply.
When Ministers go out of office, they don't care to compromise themselves by any last measures; they leave their
successors to get out of the scrape as best they may! At
six o'clock they came to tell me that a delegation from the
deputies of the Seine wished to wait on me. MM. Carnot
and Vavin were among the delegates. I received them in
my library.

They told me they were sent by their colleagues to
entreat me to convene an assembly consisting of the
Municipal Council, the Mayor, the colonels of the National
Guard, and the fourteen deputies of the Department, to
discuss the dangers with which the city was threatened.
They declared that the confidence reposed in their Prefect,
both by the common people and the Council, had led them
to take this step, as well as their respect for the Opposition,
and that the aim of the conference would be to bring
about a reconciliation between the King and his people.

I answered: "Messieurs, on accepting my functions,
I swore fidelity to the King. I will never lend a hand to
the restoration of the Commune of Paris. I should no
more think of being the President of such a body than I
should think of being a Mayor of the Palace. I thank you
for the honour you do me, and I hope you will take my
refusal in good part. If you believe that my presence and
personal influence can stop bloodshed, I will accompany
you to the barricades—only give me time to put on my
uniform." They replied that such was not their mission,
that they respected my sentiments, that they had intended
to warn me against such imminent dangers, and that they
regretted the view I took with regard to my duty. Two
years afterwards I had a conversation on the subject with
M. de Lamartine at a dinner given by the Council-General
of the Seine-et-Loire. "You should have accepted the
offer," said he, "and the Revolution would have been *un
fait accompli*." "I knew it," I retorted; "but I preferred to

leave you to take the initiative and the responsibility of a calamity that will weigh heavily on France for a long time to come."

Great excitement prevailed during the whole evening. There was, however, good news from the Faubourg Saint-Antoine, which had, so far, remained quiet. The troops in the Place de la Bastille had no trouble in communicating with us, and we were every moment expecting a new Ministry and the appointment of a Commander-in-chief, who would, at last, take some definite steps. Suddenly, about ten o'clock, the news of the firing on the Boulevard des Capucines burst on us like a thunder-clap; then came the torchlight procession with the bodies of the slain, along with the rising of the more remote quarters and the descent of the Faubourg. At eleven, the tocsin rang out from Saint-Étienne-du-Mont and Notre-Dame: it meant a general insurrection, and for thirty-six hours we had been without a Ministry or a Commander-in-chief!

I had distributed to the troops all the provisions that were left. I had emptied the bakeries and butchers' shops as well as the grocers' and wine merchants' stores of the quarter. Colonel Boutarel and his one hundred and eighty men still remained with me; but, foreseeing that a serious attack would be made on the Hôtel de Ville, I decided, towards midnight, to put my wife and children in a place of safety. I sent them to M. Jacquemin, a judicial agent of the Hôtel de Ville, whose house in the Rue de la Truanderie was close at hand and protected from bullets. I did not allow them to carry away the smallest parcel with them, and took care that no disorder in my apartments should betray an intention of leaving, lest a panic should be created by any indication of a possible *sauve qui peut.*

After the departure of my family, I spent a melancholy hour pacing those salons, now lit up by flashes of fire, with the ringing of the tocsin and the whizzing of musketry in my ears, saying sadly to myself, "For fifteen years you have been a father to this people, and yet, perhaps, after the next few hours, you will leave behind you the reputation of a murderer, for you are bound to do your duty and defend this threshold to the end." At length, worn out by fatigue, I threw myself on a couch, having previously given directions that I was to be awakened on the first alarm.

I slept four hours. At five in the morning, everything was in the same condition. At six, Sebastiani arrived with General Garraube, whose hat had just been pierced by a bullet. He told me Thiers was at the Tuileries, having been sent for during the night; Bugeaud was appointed Commander-in-chief and was resolved to act vigorously—a column was already sweeping the boulevards; he himself had orders to protect the Hôtel de Ville, and would establish his communications with the forces of Bugeaud by the Rue Saint-Denis and the Rue Saint-Martin. I remarked that these two streets were fairly bristling with barricades, that fifteen of them would have to be carried by storm, and that this could not be accomplished without loss, for our soldiers would have to march in the open, raked by a cross-fire from the windows. I reminded him that we had only four pieces of artillery, and that it would be easier for him could he effect his coalition in the line of the quays and boulevards, because there were only two barricades between the Hôtel de Ville and the Bastille; both of them weak and not able to offer much resistance. In this way I maintained the city could be cut into three sections, which might be easily kept separate by cavalry and cannon.

We were discussing these tactics in the hall of the Council of the Prefecture, which served as our headquarters, pointing to the positions of the barricades on a plan of Paris, when in came Roger de Sérensai, an aide-de-camp of Sebastiani, who had left him with Marshal Bugeaud. He brought the Marshal's order, written at the King's desire and probably dictated by the new Ministry, to suspend hostilities everywhere, to withdraw the troops, and leave to the National Guard the task of restoring order and policing the city. But the National Guard had no longer any chief! In most of the legions no one knew who was their colonel or who were their officers: it was the abdication of authority in the presence of riot, to be followed in a few hours by the abdication of the Crown. Sebastiani was not deceived: he tore his sword from the scabbard and flung it on the table, crying, "I am no longer anybody; I shall not interfere with anything, my command has come to an end." Boutarel declared he could no longer restrain his men, and he also would retire. I entreated the Generals not to remove the troops, to mass them together, order them to ground arms, and keep them well in hand, so that if this conciliatory measure had not the anticipated success, they would, at least, be able to resume the offensive, in case they received fresh orders. They agreed to do as I asked, and the troops remained on the square and quays until two in the afternoon, when they returned to barracks.

After that our Generals turned all their attention to the subject of breakfast; Sebastiani was also anxious to make his toilet, so I conducted him to my apartment. I was rather surprised to see him lay a well-filled purse containing 10,000 francs in gold on the mantelpiece: he was evidently prepared for all emergencies, which proved to me that he had very little confidence in a successful resistance.

While they were breakfasting I noticed some disarmed Municipal Guards in my courtyard. I was told they were amongst those who had been rescued from the Lepage workshops by Colonel de Luzy, and that they had been only released on condition of laying down their arms. At the same moment I was also informed that the courts of the bureaus were being invaded by an insurgent column, bent on finding these Municipal Guards and massacring them. I implored Sebastiani to place them between two companies of Cuirassiers drawn up on the quay, and then to conduct them to the barrack of the Celestins, which was close at hand, where they would be in safety. He flatly refused. "I have received formal orders," said he, "to avoid every collision; I cannot risk taking any step which would provoke a discharge of fire-arms. I am grieved to the heart, but for all that I do not care to have to appear before a council of war."

And yet, how could I allow these poor people to be murdered? Thanks to the devotion of MM. Buffet, Hudry, and Mignes, who stripped themselves of all the garments they could spare, we disguised some of them, shaving off their beards and moustaches, and thus enabling them to escape in time. The others succeeded in hiding in different parts of the Hôtel de Ville, notably three who took refuge under my daughter (Mme. de Mesgrigny's) bed, where she discovered them on returning to her chamber on Friday. Two of the rioters were stretched on the same bed so dead drunk that she had no trouble in securing the escape of the fugitives. But, alas! all were not so fortunate, and many perished whose courage, fidelity, and devotion to duty I had so often had good reason to appreciate.

Still hoping to receive better news, I remained in my cabinet, surrounded by the Generals and seven or eight members of the Municipal Council, who had been urging me all the morning to convoke the Assembly. Among them were three or four evidently familiar with the progress of the insurrection; they were there, I have good reason to believe, to provide for my personal safety, although they never said a word to me on the subject. At one o'clock we heard of the King's abdication. Half-an-hour afterwards a deputation from the National Guard was announced. About fifteen officers entered, and their spokesman said : " Monsieur le Préfet, the Hôtel de Ville belongs to the people ; it is the people who will give orders in the future; we have come to inform you that your authority is at an end." " Very well," gentlemen, I answered ; " you see before you Generals who have assured me that the troops are powerless to protect or obey me ; you see before you members of the Municipal Council who can testify that I have done my whole duty, and yield only to force ; I retire, and surrender my cabinet to you." " No, no, Monsieur, we do not wish to banish you from

your apartments, and we intend to take up our quarters
elsewhere." "God forbid, gentlemen, that I should consent to remain in a place where I have no longer the right
to command. I shall be gone in a few minutes." They
passed out, but it was quite clear to me from their attitude that some of them were there to protect rather than
offend me.

The Generals had vanished at the first words spoken.
I was alone. I then summoned my faithful Buffet; I
threw all the papers I did not wish to leave behind me
into the fire; then, taking my cane and hat, I descended
the staircase of the bureaus, passed through several platoons
of insurgents, and made my way along the entire north
façade of the Hôtel de Ville, keeping inside the railing,
for I could not very well force a passage through the bands
of rioters that still thronged the square. I met Victor
Hugo and the Mayor of the 7th Arrondissement, who
asked me for news; I confirmed the tidings of the King's
abdication. They made at once for the Chamber, whilst
I hurried to rejoin my wife and children, whose anxiety
on my account may be easily conceived. After embracing
them, I went upstairs to find my secretary, Boullenois, who
was staying in the same house, for I wanted to send a
detailed report at once to M. Thiers.

At nightfall we had to separate. We had heard that
our apartments had been ransacked. But how could we
waste any thought for our personal misfortunes in presence
of those of the poor Royal Family? My daughter and her
husband sought an asylum in the home of M. Louveau,
Ile Saint-Louis; we found a safe shelter in the residence
of M. Buron, the optician of my worthy friend and business
agent, François Fabier, Rue des Trois-Pavillons. We were
obliged to cross several barricades. I was often recognised,
but never insulted or threatened. On the contrary, hands
were often stretched out to assist us; and I was even frequently invited to have a drink. I may also mention that
this feeling of sympathy and respect was still more strongly
manifested at the Hôtel de Ville. When the people, in-

toxicated with their victory, were hurrying from salon to salon, pushing and hustling one another, they stopped before my portrait.[1] Several voices cried out, "We must not hurt it; he was a father to the workmen." During the whole night well-disposed men mounted guard before it, relieving one another; then, at daybreak, they detached it from the frame, carried it in procession through every part of the Hôtel de Ville, as if bidding it take farewell of its home, and laid it gently on my bed, saying :—

> " Dors, papa Rambuteau,
> T' as bien mérité de faire dodo."
>
> (Sleep, Papa Rambuteau,
> Well hast thou earned thy lullaby.)

On the other hand, I regret to confess that our wardrobe was entirely plundered; but I am pretty nearly certain that the thieves were the women of Saint-Lazare, who came on that night, with other unfortunates, to ply their sordid trade at the Hôtel de Ville.

The next day, which was Friday, I traversed the whole of Paris, starting from the Ile Saint-Louis for the Faubourg Saint-Honoré. Here again I was repeatedly recognised, for I was on foot, with my daughter Amable on my arm, and her husband beside me. I was treated with the greatest courtesy. My wife also, who joined us in a cabriolet, under the protection of a student of the École Polytechnique, overcame every obstacle without experiencing the slightest annoyance. At length, we found ourselves all together in the Hôtel Sinet, where a suite of apartments had been offered to me, and I was urged to accept them by M. Rougier, a son of the owner, and an employee in my office. The same day, I wrote the following note to the Mayor of the 1st Arrondissement :—

"MONSIEUR LE MAIRE,—In 1830, I did not consider that my rank as deputy should prevent me from uniting

---

[1] The portrait reproduced in the frontispiece. The original is at Champgrenon.

with my fellow-citizens for the preservation of public order. To-day I desire to resume my place in the same legion, as I do not feel that my age should dispense me from again defending the rights of order and property."

I was soon afterwards enrolled in the company of Captain Marcotte, a druggist, and, as soon as I received my uniform, I joined the ranks. So, when a journal announced that I had left for England, I was able to assure the editor personally that this was not the case.

Some days later, I had taken a cab for the purpose of driving to the École Polytechnique, and thanking the young gentleman who had escorted Mme. Rambuteau. On alighting, the driver addressed me as, " *Monsieur le Préfet.*" "So you recognise me?" I said. "Yes, Monsieur, I suspected who you were when you got into my cab, and on the way some of my comrades assured me I was not mistaken. Ah, Monsieur le Préfet, you might drive through every street in Paris without paying a sou; for there is not a single one of us who would not gladly drive you for nothing! You have done so much good to us that it wouldn't be much of a return!" These simple words, this genuine gratitude on the morrow of a bloody revolution, I regarded as an ample reward for all my labours, and as an honour that would follow me into private life.

I took part in the seizures of arms that occurred on the 16th of March, 17th of April, and 15th of May. I belonged to one of the battalions which drove the mob from the Chamber of Deputies, with Laporte, Seguin, Generals de Ségur and de Saint-Yon, the Beauvaus, the two Bouillés, Vicomte d'Albuféra, Magnoncourt, Nadaillac, &c. These gentlemen had their servants with them to load their weapons. At night, we all met at the house of one of their wives, and, notwithstanding our differences of opinion, we were all perfectly united, which was a new state of things. This lasted until the end of May.

Before quitting Paris, I went to say good-bye to Marshal Gérard. He told me that he had seen the King twice during the three fatal days of February, the first time being on Wednesday morning. Knowing what dangers were impending, he went to the Tuileries for the purpose of conferring with his Majesty. He had much difficulty in getting himself even announced, because the King was in the Queen's cabinet. He found his Majesty highly excited, exclaiming the instant he saw him, "You have no idea what these business people are like! I have been arguing with them for actually three hours! They want me to pay a hundred and ten thousand francs above what I ought to pay for the expenses entailed in connection with the property I inherited from my sister, and in spite of all I can say they won't listen to reason!" Gérard was dumbfoundered, and, try as he might to make the King grasp the situation, the latter cut him short very sharply, protesting that everything was going on well. Perceiving that the Marshal was not convinced on this point, he dismissed him abruptly, saying, "Duchâtel is waiting for me; so I cannot keep you any longer; but believe me, my dear Marshal, there will be an end to all this soon, and a very good end too!"

The following Friday, the King sent for him in such haste that the aide-de-camp who carried the message would not give him time to put on his uniform, which had to be sent after him to the Tuileries. He had hardly entered when the King handed him his deed of abdication, commanding him to mount his horse immediately, and read it to the people; as the uproar could only be quelled by these means. Gérard took the King's own horse. He advanced as far as the Rue de Rohan, intending to ride into the Rue Saint-Honoré; but here his progress was checked by the mob, which was partly composed of detachments of the 3rd legion, who had forced their Lieutenant-colonel to march on the Tuileries at their head, to the cry of, "*Vive la Réforme!*" Driven back by the rabble, and deafened by their yells, he could make himself neither heard nor understood, and was forced to return to the Tuileries. Thereupon the King prepared for flight.

The Revolution was over.

And I also took my departure, but not till three months later, when the spring had returned with its clear sunshine and its gentle breezes. What had become of Champgrenon and Rambuteau, and of my dear trees which I had neglected for fifteen years in favour of other clients? I longed for their silence, their perfumes, and their verdure. Once more I sought my beloved Burgundy, feeling sure that, among my pines and larches, my oaks and elms, and beside my still waters, I should recover the peace which is born of a quiet conscience, and, in reviving my pleasant intercourse with nature, should likewise revive the sweet memories of the past forty years.

CHAPTER IX

BRIEF OUTLINE OF A FIFTEEN YEARS' ADMINISTRATION IN PARIS

I NOW come to the most laborious part of my career. I should have to disturb many piles of dust-covered documents which are at present reposing in the Archives, if I attempted to describe it fully. No one has any idea of the amount of figures, reports, inquiries, plans, &c., which the construction of the most insignificant aqueduct entails. This, however, has no bearing on the facts I am about to narrate. Moreover, various volumes of statistics were published by my direction during my term of office. May my successors find them useful, and may they serve as a contribution to our municipal history! I therefore propose to give a simple but comprehensive account of a work to which I devoted all my energies, without pause or respite—a work which I hoped would have had even larger results. May I not be permitted, in the closing years of my life, to cast a backward glance on my labours, like the wayfarer, who, at the end of his journey, sits down on the last kerbstone and measures with his eyes the distance he has travelled and the long road that winds behind him? There is no vanity, no ambition, in this review of my past. I am a landholder taking a survey of his property.

I. Hospitals

The day after I was installed as Prefect, I went to visit the Hôtel-Dieu. Although bound by the very nature of my functions to regard all Parisians as my children, I had a special predilection for the poor and for those whose poverty is an inheritance. They were the first-born of the family, and should have my first visit by right of prima-geniture. The impressions I received were sad enough: neither the food, hygiene, nor the attention paid to the inmates were what one had a right to expect in a city like Paris. I hoped to be able to change the situation; there is no condition that may not be improved by time and determination. Moreover, my plan lay plainly traced out before me; I must avail myself of the means at my disposal for the betterment of existing affairs; later on I could gradually improve these conditions and create new ones.

The first detail to be studied was that of the food. I had been struck by the difference between the creamy, savoury, appetising look of the soup when it was in the saucepans, and the insipid, colourless, almost repulsive, appearance which it presented in the tureens.

I soon saw the reason: round loaves, almost all in crumbs, were broken into it, and these absorbed the liquid and deprived it of its savour. I had the loaves made long, with more crust, to the great satisfaction of the patients. Then, as there was more demand for soup in the hospitals than for meat, and in consequence an undue proportion of water and vegetables was used in its making, I applied to the Compagnie Hollandaise for samples of its products. Every week samples of soups from the different hospitals were laid on the table of the Conseil des Hospices, and it did not take us long to recognise the superiority of those supplied by the Compagnie. I visited its establishments, and found that the secret of their success lay in the application of steam heat and in the great number of saucepans which they used, each containing fifty kilos[1] of meat at the most. I ordered an experiment to be made at the Salpétrière with thirty saucepans, which replaced the two enormous cauldrons in which two entire oxen had hitherto been boiled every day. Soon afterwards this plan was generally adopted.

---

[1] Kilo, about 2⅕ pounds avoirdupois.

The Comte de Rambuteau. 1862.

Heliog. Dujardin. Paris

I found the central bakery so useful that I established a corresponding butchery; these two institutions, combined with the general cellar of the hospitals and the pharmacy, amply secured the success of my alimentary system.

I also set up a vast piggery on the Saint Anne farm. I had noticed that the nuns in certain convents fattened a few pigs and fowl on odd scraps and remnants, greasy water, &c. It occurred to me that by following their example the revenues of the hospitals would be increased, and a little variety would likewise be introduced into the fare of the sick. So I started two huge carts to make the round of the hospitals three times a day, collecting all the fragments that had hitherto been destroyed or wasted, but which were now found sufficient for the fattening of three hundred head of stock, renewed four times a year. The hospitals were supplied with nearly three thousand kilos of meat a week from this source alone, and thus a saving of, at least, a hundred thousand francs was effected annually.

As for hygiene, it was absolutely necessary to enlarge the old buildings and construct new ones. This would require time, but there was no reason why the sanitary condition of the premises as they stood should not be improved without delay. I had wooden floors substituted for the rough brick and stone pavements; large windows were made for the purpose of airing the wards; the lavatories were isolated; all the bath-tubs that could possibly be introduced were set up; special operating wards were established; the supplies of linen were doubled; I issued the strictest orders in regard to everything that had the slightest bearing on cleanliness. I took care that those under me exercised a scrupulous vigilance in all matters, whilst the surprise visits which I paid now and then (followed occasionally by a dismissal) did not decrease their circumspection. In short, I was getting along at a rapid rate, and certain fortunate occurrences enabled me to go even faster. Thus, thanks to an opportune legacy of two hundred thousand francs, I erected a building at Necker containing one hundred and eighty beds for the sufferers from scurvy and scrofula, who had been previously lodged in low, unhealthy rooms.

One day when I was visiting this hospital, I expressed my surprise at the wretched quarters into which the poor children were crowded, when they ought to be breathing the fresh air; the answer I got was that there were no recreation grounds. I called for a map of the institution. Seeing there were more than four acres of unoccupied land, I asked what use was made of it; one part was appropriated by the cows, another by the ass, and another by the goats of the Lady Superior!

I had all these useless tenants promptly sold, and, after that the children had an ample playground.

There were many other abuses that required to be suppressed. For instance, it had become customary for the sick to pay two sous a week to the nurses, male or female, who attended them. Those who could not pay this imposition were, naturally, neglected; whilst, on the other hand, those who were better off than their neighbours would exceed the sum in order to insure corresponding advantages. I put a stop to this tax levied on misery by obtaining a supplementary grant of 40,000 francs for the hospital attendants, and insisting that the same care should be given to all the patients without distinction.

I insisted also on the nuns taking their share in the night watches, arranging that two, four, or six of them should spend the night in the wards, according to the number of patients, and thus prevent any negligence on the part of the nurses. I met with some opposition from the nuns, for they belonged to an Order whose rule imposed on them a sort of cloistral retreat during the night. Consequently, they retired at nine to what they called the "Convent," and did not appear in the wards until five the next morning. But I maintained that the hospitals were not founded either for the Government, or for the doctors, or for religious communities, but for the sick.

As Prefect, I was responsible for all the good that was left undone, and for the shortcomings of all my subordinates. Sometimes I was obliged to have recourse to the Sisters belonging to Orders whose rules were less strict, and I always found these holy women admirable exemplars of abnegation and self-sacrifice.

As for the medical staff, I arranged that my appointments should be renewable every five years, with an age limit of sixty years for surgeons and sixty-five for doctors, because I discovered that some of our medical officers never came near the hospitals, being either incapacitated from age or unwilling to lose the fees of their private patients. But the title of hospital doctor is not merely honorary, it involves obligations.

I also abolished the dissecting-rooms which were established in all the hospitals, where the absence of surveillance and the levity of the students were likely to lessen respect for the dead and endanger the health of the living. A vast building was erected at Clamart, with a hundred tables, an abundant water-supply, perfect ventilation, and complete isolation. All that remained in the hospitals was the indispensable room for the autopsies needed by science or exacted by judicial authority.

But relieving the needy is not everything. In addition to that we have to protect ourselves against the knaves and impostors who swarm among the poverty-stricken classes. To give alms to them is to thieve from the real poor, for these rascals frequently appear far more interesting than their honest competitors. I put a stop to a good many frauds, to one especially which was practised upon a benevolent scheme of M. Monthyon. This generous philanthropist, among his many other benefactions, had instituted a considerable fund, the interest of which was to be distributed among the sick on leaving the hospital. The amount given to each of them was twenty sous, in addition to ten francs paid into the charity bureau of their "*Arrondissement*." I found out that many came into a hospital five or six times every year, solely for the purpose

R

of receiving the spoils. These rogues would spend some three or four hundred thousand days in the hospitals, entailing an outlay of 400,000 francs on the part of the Committee for Public Charities; nor was this all, for they usurped the place of the genuine sick folk, who were often refused admission for want of room. The twenty sous pieces which were to be distributed were secretly marked, and were nearly all recovered in the low taverns of the neighbourhood.

I therefore modified the regulations, appointing agents who were to visit the homes of the sick poor, and bring back as accurate an account as possible of the nature of their illness and their circumstances. After that, a committee, over which I occasionally presided, discussed the applications that had been presented. These measures were also rendered necessary by the constantly increasing number of the afflicted. In 1832 there had been 32,000 patients in the hospitals; in 1837 there were 85,000, although there was no epidemic; still, the average duration of diseases fell from twenty-seven to twenty-two days, and the deaths were 7000 instead of 8000—a diminution of the death-rate from 13 per cent. to 9 per cent.

Naturally, a considerable enlargement of the premises became necessary. It was at the Hôtel-Dieu that the most important additions were made. The Saint-Charles wing, built on the left bank, and containing six hundred beds, completely intercepted the line of the quays. I had just finished the canal of the Bièvre as well as the lower wharves, and the public warehouse for wines; I had accomplished the widening of the Jardin des Plantes; and the Quai and Pont des Miramiones were nearing completion. But it was absolutely necessary to open the Quai Montebello and unite it with the Quai des Augustins, if the 12th Arrondissement was to be included in the boundaries of Paris. Nevertheless, I met with strong opposition in the Commission des Hospices, which was unwilling that one of its buildings should be sacrificed, even for the public good. With the help of the doctors, however, I convinced its members that wards containing two hundred beds in five rows were necessarily unhealthy, not having sufficient ventilation. I further pointed out that the buildings on the Rue de la Barillerie would accommodate some of the beds, whilst Necker and Beaujon would be enlarged to receive the others. I assured them, moreover, that I was planning an extensive establishment on the grounds of Saint-Lazare, and that, finally, the city would pay two-thirds of the expenses. I won my case. The opening of the Quai Montebello cost more than 1,800,000 francs; but was that too much to pay for the clearing and improvement of the left arm of the Seine and the line of the quays? I do not believe that Paris has regretted its money.

I introduced important reforms into the Hôpital du Midi. It was in a deplorable state. Although the object for which it was founded[1] should have insured it special attention, there was no distinction made between sexes, ages, and circumstances. The fallen woman sent thither by the police elbowed the respectable wife contaminated by her husband; young children, the victims of shameful outrage, came here to be cured, and when they left were the victims of a moral corruption far more difficult to heal than their physical disease. I separated the sexes, founding at Lourcine an establishment with three hundred beds, and an annexe at Saint-Lazare for repentant girls.

Lourcine had existed since 1829: it was the work of a charitable association which had intended it to be a home of refuge, a sort of almshouse. But at Paris benevolent impulses, however generous and ardent, are quickly chilled when the attraction of novelty is over, and the obligation of a yearly subscription becomes burdensome. Then an appeal is always made to the city to take the place of the founders. The work is offered to it as a free gift, or rather its obligations are; and no one objects to providing it with a treat, provided it pays for the entertainment. Hence many institutions have gone under which owed their origin to a sudden impulse born of temporary enthusiasm. This

---

[1] Intended for the treatment of venereal diseases.

was the case with Lourcine, hired by the city at the time
of the cholera, and purchased afterwards. I was very glad
to have it within my reach, and better pleased still at
finding a community willing to undertake duties of such
a repulsive character. Every person not belonging to the
staff was forbidden to enter, and I had an isolated dormitory
with thirty beds for patients under fifteen, victims for the
most part of violence, or of the abominable superstition
which teaches that the disease can be cured by communicating
it to a child.

I wrought a similar moral improvement by separating
the hospital from the neighbourhood of the prison. Crime
and misfortune were so closely connected in this institution
that its very name had become synonymous with every
scourge of humanity, moral and physical. The prison
belonged to the Department; it was acquired by the Commission des Hospices for a million, and the prisoners were
transferred to the block of buildings in the Rue de la
Roquette, which had been erected in eighteen months.

The next thing to be done was to improve the lot of
the insane. At Bicêtre, as well as at La Salpêtrière, their
condition had absolutely appalled me. Most of them were
shut up in vaulted dungeons paved with flagstones; their
bed was a big box filled with straw, and their only covering
was a counterpane. There were neither chairs nor tables,
because they might break them; there were grated windows
with no glass in them, with a wooden shutter fastened
outside to protect them from cold by depriving them of
all light; whilst the keepers might inflict the strait-jacket
whenever they felt disposed!

In La Salpêtrière these dungeons were built round five
large yards in which the milder cases were allowed to take
a few minutes' exercise daily. And these regulations applied
equally to 2800 unfortunates, of whom about 500 were
epileptics! Not a fourth part of those entering left cured;
douches on the head, falling from a height of ten or twelve
feet, were resorted to both by doctors and keepers, as the
best medical and disciplinary measure that could be adopted

for the patients; but there was no compassion shown them, no amusement provided, nothing done to alleviate the miseries of a captivity which would in time have deprived the sanest men of their reason.

For fifteen years I worked unceasingly to reform these practices, and I had the comfort of seeing the number of those restored to society and to their families doubled, and also that of improving the lot of the incurable. Because a man has had the misfortune of losing his reason, he should not be cut off from human sympathy.

One of my most successful methods was the employment of the insane in manual occupations, which supplied them with healthful exercise and relaxation. They cultivated the land belonging to Bicêtre and Sainte-Anne, washed the woollen bedcovers of the seventeen thousand beds of our hospitals, bleached the cloth woven for the linen goods, &c., experiencing a certain degree of satisfaction in their labours and enjoying their sleep after them. They were allowed, moreover, to have some agreeable additions to their fare, besides escaping for a time from some of the evil consequences of their isolation. The women were occupied in picking cotton, making lint, and sewing. Some of them were very skilful. They were paid from six sous to six francs for making a shirt, the material being furnished. Nine-tenths of the proceeds were given to the workwomen, and represented a hundred thousand francs a year; the remainder belonged to the institution.

I sought to combine amusement with business; so we had music, concerts, even theatrical representations; but the latter did not produce good results. On the other hand, there were idiot boys in whose case I discovered that sparks may be struck from minds apparently dead. A patient and intelligent professor taught them to weave straw mats and coarse list oversocks; then he tried to instruct them in reading and writing. You may imagine my surprise when, one fine day, a hundred copy-books were set before me, of which at least sixty would have done credit to a school. The success of the enterprise was proved by the fact that the class which at first numbered twenty-five pupils had more than a hundred and twenty at the date of my retirement.

Naturally, the buildings were enlarged to keep pace with the requirements. At La Salpêtrière, a new quarter was erected, with lodges and pavilions isolated in the middle of the gardens; at Bicêtre, the old prison was converted into dormitories. Everywhere I demolished the cells and dungeons, and replaced them by warm, healthy rooms; some were wainscoted, and even padded, for the use of the violently insane; and so the dreadful places that had been the scenes of so many horrors disappeared.

It was in the Gabriel pavilion at Saint-Louis that I made the first trial of *paying beds*. I had been struck by the well-bred manners and appearance of certain patients, and, on inquiry, I discovered that many of them were not only above want, but in easy circumstances; and had been sent by their relations who had been prompted by economical motives to usurp the privileges of the needy. Now, while it might be inhuman to reject them, it was but just that the committee should be reimbursed for the expense of receiving them. I had been cogitating my plan for a long time, and should have wished to extend it to all the hospitals, particularly to those in which there were surgical operations, as well as to those designed for a special purpose. It met with serious opposition from members of the Commission des Hospices, who saw no reason why the Assistance Publique (the Administration of Public Charities) should ask for money, save, no doubt, that which came from the city, for these gentlemen never declined accepting our annual six millions. But I maintained my opinion. There are people who, though far from rich, are not entirely without means; why should they be put on a par with those who have absolutely nothing, and why should not a fair assessment be levied on them for the benefit of the destitute? I therefore devoted all my energies to the task of establishing homes where persons of slender means would find an asylum without having recourse to charity. A candidate for the Incurables had to wait four or five years before obtaining admission. The price of board at the Rochefoucauld was nominally two hundred francs, but in reality it was four. It struck me that an institution where four hundred francs were charged would be probably well supported. But the chief thing was to find suitable premises.

The Commission solved the difficulty by sending the orphans of the Saint-Antoine to the Foundling Hospital in the Rue d'Enfer, and making over the building to me. Thereupon, my house was established: it took the name of Saint-Ferdinand, in memory of the Duc d'Orléans.

On the other hand, Sainte-Périne received persons who, because of their social position and because they had still some scant remnants of their fortune left them, did not feel inclined to enter the municipal asylums, but were in search of a retreat where they could combine economy with independence. The number of applications in such cases far exceeded that of admissions. I had new pavilions constructed to meet this demand, and never was a single apartment in one of them vacant. Who can tell how many lives which had opened with every hope of a brilliant future, some of which had been even famous, passed out of existence in these homes, making no sign and forgotten by the world.

On my first visit there, I saw Cléry, the brother of Louis XVI.'s *valet de chambre*, who had received a pension after the Restoration; there, too, I saw Lady Stainville, who, after having devoted thirty years to providing amusement to all Paris, had retired from her dreary trade to die in a home! And there were many others, too, whom I do not care to name.

I would rather record the names of generous benefactors, like M. Brézin, who left four millions to found on his estate at Guarches an establishment for two hundred skilled workmen over sixty, who had been the architects of his fortune; they had been respectively cutlers, carvers, foundrymen, locksmiths, &c. Or again there was M. Boulard, one of Napoleon's upholsterers, who bequeathed 1,800,000 francs for a similar house at Saint-Mandé, reserved for twelve aged workmen belonging to his party. Unfortunately, with the plan of the buildings he also left those for his tomb and a chapel; thus four-fifths of the legacy were absorbed in the construction of the two latter, so that it was necessary to modify the clause in his will, which directed that no less than fourteen attendants should be engaged to wait on the twelve inmates.

Devilla's legacy, equal in amount, but better employed, established a home for old people of both sexes; the Lambrecht legacy founded a similar institution at Courbevoie for Protestants. We obtained, in fact, several donations like the latter; among others, one from Pastor V——, and from certain Protestant congregations, to establish a home for penitent young women, under the management of deaconesses.

But none of my works was more successfully accomplished in all its details, I think, than the Hôpital Louis-Philippe,[1] so named because I wished to testify my respect for the King by associating him with a popular institution. In this case there was no question of simply effecting a transformation but of beginning at the beginning. The city owned a large piece of ground at Saint-Lazare, upon which the Church of St. Vincent de Paul had been already erected. The site was perfect, whether viewed from the standpoint of health or convenience. I appointed a commission, consisting of some of the ablest physicians, to determine the main outlines of the plan, but they discussed the subject for two years before they could arrive at any conclusion. Moreover, the Commission des Hospices and the Conseil Municipal, who considered the hospitals and colleges as belonging essentially to the left bank, dreaded any sort of rivalry with the Hôtel-Dieu, and accused me of sacrificing Paris to the suburbs. Eventually, the city consented to bear two-thirds of the expense, estimated at six millions, but the cost was actually ten. This fine structure consisted of ten buildings united by a two-storey gallery;

[1] At present the Hôpital Lariboisière.

it might have been made still finer from an architectural point of view for the same sum; my chief object being to insure the conditions that would best promote the preservation of health, all other considerations had to take a second place. Without entering into too many details, I have described what I did for the sick in the hospitals. I had now to deal with a class not less interesting, the sick in their own homes.

Here it seemed to me that external charity should supplement the care given to patients by their families. In the first place, I laid it down as a rule that, in all cases of urgency or accident, every sufferer should have the right to enter the hospital, and that the formalities of admission should not *precede* but *follow* the admission. A wound, or any serious accident, should at once command admission; an inquiry as to who the applicant was, and where he came from, could be made later. But, in ordinary cases, when the patient can find a bed, linen, warmth in his own home, why remove him from the care of his family, when all that is needed for his comfort is a little outside assistance? Why break up those domestic associations which form the noblest and most moral of all ties, and must contribute powerfully to the patient's recovery? By adding to the medical attendance and the medicines (both, of course, given gratuitously) about 1 fr. 35 c.—the average wages of a day labourer—a poor family could be kept together, provided care was exercised to prevent abuses. I commissioned M. Vée, Mayor of the 1st Arrondissement, and well known for his charitable zeal, to undertake the introduction of this new regulation. The results justified all my expectations, and I was about to extend it to the twelve arrondissements when the revolution of '48 burst out. I know that it has since become general.

FOUNDLING ASYLUMS

I now come to the branch of the public service responsible for the foundling hospitals. This is one of the heaviest burdens on the Assistance Publique; more than 4000 infants are confided to it every year, and it must not only provide for those of the capital, and of the entire Department, but also for those of the neighbouring Departments as well. Out of 1500 women who are confined in the Maternité, nearly two-thirds come from the suburbs or from the provinces. There are always 17,000 children in the Paris hospitals. Naturally, the administration tried to reduce the number, either by restricting the use of the "tour"[1] or by exercising a strict watch on the stealthy depositors who brought the children. I insisted that every woman at the Maternity should give the breast for three days to her baby before relinquishing it. Steps were taken, at the same time, to induce her to keep it; she was offered a supply of baby linen or a nurse's wages for the first month. Occasionally the maternal instinct came into play, and the number of foundling infants diminished by a quarter.

The "tour" may have its advantages, but it also presents serious objections; it smooths the way for moral irregularities, and sometimes results in the abandonment of even legitimate children. To have a child is a pleasure, to rear it is a burden. Hence the tendency in some women to rid themselves of the burden altogether, or to minimise it as much as possible. For this reason, a superioress advised me to have the children that were deposited in the "tour," removed at once to another hospital, in order to prevent their mothers from coming to recover them afterwards by offering themselves as wet nurses, and thus obtaining the remuneration which was given in such circumstances. The State should certainly do nothing to befriend misconduct, and it is against its own interests to promote the growth of a population without family ties, the majority of which are usually unhealthy.

In Paris the Conseil de Révision never had to go

---

[1] A box at foundling hospitals, working on a pivot, in which an infant could be secretly deposited. A bell rang automatically, and the infant was taken charge of by a nurse.

beyond the number 180 when recruiting 100 men for the service; but in the 12th Arrondissement, in which the children brought up in the hospitals were enrolled, it had to make its selection from 300; and when the choice was made exclusively from them, this figure was far surpassed.

In this department of my administration I was under many obligations to M. de Watteville; I succeeded in having the office of inspector created for his special benefit, so that he might not only co-operate with me, but take my place when necessary. I am ready to do full justice to the zeal and enlightenment of the Commission Administrative, but it had one great defect: *impersonal authority*, in other words, collective responsibility and the consequent absence of individual responsibility. Everything was done in the name of the Prefect, who was expected to sign measures at the discussion of which he was rarely present, save at the important sessions held three or four times a year. At first, I had not missed any of them; indeed I used to preside for four hours during the week, and I often refused my approval to motions voted by the dozen in my absence. I also suppressed the supernumerary employés, which resulted in saddling the bureaus with unnecessary officials; and at last I convinced the members of the Council (not without some unpleasant collisions in spite of my good temper) that I wished, not to diminish their authority, but to prevent it from being made—unknown to themselves—an excuse for acts of nepotism and useless expenses. One day M. Desportes, with evident self-satisfaction, informed me that he had caused some of the silver-ware in the Hôtel-Dieu to be sold, and two of the wards to be laid down in parquetry with the proceeds of the sale. " I am tempted to change places with you," I answered. " In order to be able to spend money without official sanction or authorisation, it is clearly better to be a councillor than a prefect."

BUREAUX DE BIENFAISANCE

The Bureaux de Bienfaisance received 1,800,000 francs from the city, and about the same amount from private charity. One of my first acts was to double the number of beds belonging to them in the hospitals, feeling sure I could not make a better use of them. I had excellent opportunities for appreciating the admirable qualities of many of the men at the head of this service in the several arrondissements. Thanks to them, the number of the indigent remained almost stationary, although there had been an increase in the population of 300,000. Thus, there were 63,000 on the lists of the bureaus in 1837, and 67,000 in 1847. I did everything in my power, therefore, to help the Bureaux de Bienfaisance; they had a right to a percentage on the receipts at the theatres and public *fêtes*, a percentage always hard to collect and sometimes disputed. The returns from it scarcely amounted to 400,000 francs; I managed to have this sum increased to 1,500,000 francs, and I hear that the increase continues to progress. I am glad to know that this is the case. It is but fair that the poor should derive advantage from the amusements of the rich.

Such was the organisation of the different charitable institutions; consequently, when the cholera threatened to break out on two separate occasions, I was prepared for it. In 1834 there were nearly 200 cases a day. I had taken all the necessary measures without incurring a dangerous publicity which would have provoked a panic and tripled the peril. It is easy, then, to conceive my feelings on being summoned before the Conseil des Ministres, and requested to have 20,000 huts constructed on the Champ de Mars for a possible 20,000 victims of the epidemic. I represented that it would be like ringing the tocsin, to put all the foreigners to flight; that it would be the death-blow to trade and industry, and spell starvation to the working classes by depriving them of work. It would, moreover, excite universal terror, and propagate the disease by working on people's imagination. I said that all the necessary preparations had been undertaken at night, so as not to attract attention by the lugubrious sights of 1832 ; in short I succeeded in reassuring the Council, and, thank God, my measures proved to be only preventive ones. It was the same in 1846 ; then I was equally prepared, and more than prepared. But Providence came to our aid and rendered our precautions superfluous. Heaven be praised !

Now, what was the cost to the city of the works mentioned in this summary, works which gave to the hospitals three thousand more beds?

Sixteen millions, with six additional millions for the Hôpital Louis-Philippe. To this must be added the quota of the hospitals levied on their ordinary resources, for which, however, a profitable transaction indemnified them to a certain extent. In fact, they owned lands in every direction of considerable value ; but as the property yielded an insignificant revenue, I prevailed on the governing body to dispose of them, with this reservation, that a fifth of the proceeds of the sale should be placed in the Government funds, the interest being capitalised, so as to replace the probable increase in their present value. The property in the Rue Neuve-des-Mathurins was sold for 640,000 francs ; the income derived from it used to be 1200 ; that in the Rue Bergère went for 700,000 francs (rented at 10,000 francs) ; the property in the Boule-Rouge fetched 340,000 francs (rented for 40 francs) ; that of the Rue du Mont-Blanc as well as that in the Rue de la Victoire were sold for 1,760,000 francs (rented for 12 francs) ; whilst the rest of the land realised equally high figures, and had been rented for equally low ones. This notable increase of revenue had the effect later on of diminishing the subsidies granted to the hospitals by the city, and so was a double advantage for both.

II. Children, Education, Crèches, Asylums, Schools, &c.

If it is well to relieve misfortune, it is still better to prevent it by helping the people to rear their children and enable the latter to earn a comfortable living. With this object in view, I accepted assistance on every side, encouraging every one to do what they could, for I was persuaded that the widow's mite should not be disdained, and that the material and moral improvement of the workman is a duty in which all society, without distinction, should co-operate. Now all that has any real worth is the work of time, which respects and consecrates only what it has contributed to establish. Therefore, if we are to hope for lasting progress, we must begin with children, and make them our starting-point for the regeneration of the family of mankind.

The first crèche (day-nursery) was founded in 1840 in the Rue de la Pépiniere, by Mme. de Castellane, aided by M. Marbeau, adjoined to the 1st Arrondisement. It contained twelve cradles. Others followed, more or less important, and also due to the efforts of charitable ladies. I was prompt in visiting them, but I soon came to the conclusion that it would be impossible to transform this generous experiment into a municipal institution. In fact, the expenses were considerable: 180 francs was the minimum cost of each child, a sum far beyond the resources of a workman's family; and, even admitting that the city could bear the expense, would not this sum—about 50 centimes a day—do more good if given to the mother?

I used to see these poor little creatures brought in the early morning in all weathers to the crèche, wrapped in wet swaddling-clothes and a rag of a blanket. There the nurses made their toilet, and laid them, dry and warm, in their little beds. But the very reverse of this happened in the evening: they were again clad in their livery of woe, were handed back to their mothers in the wretched tatters of the morning, and returned to their home, garret or cellar, as the case might be. Could this sort of treatment be beneficial to the babies? Then, as regarded their food : if the mother came during the day to give the breast to her child in the crèche, she had to abandon some of her earnings; if, on the other hand, the feeding-bottle was substituted, how many difficulties arose, and how many became victims to this change of nutriment! The Maternité had, in fact, been obliged to abandon it, and engaged nurses whenever possible. Moreover, might not the mother's exemption from what should be her chief occupation result in lessening her maternal love in a proportionate degree? Thus it seemed to me that the first thing to be done was to give pecuniary help to the mother, and afterwards to supplement this help by receiving the child into a home.

ASYLUMS

The asylum—or infant school as we should rather say in this case—is an institution with a different end in view : it takes children of from two to seven years, trains them in habits of cleanliness, obedience, and religion, and awakens their budding intelligence by means of games and the sort of teaching that may be derived from recreation rather than from education. It supplies, in short, the place of a careful mother for fourteen hours, allowing the real mother to devote her time to her occupations, either her work at home or abroad, and thus earn her daily wages. And this costs the city only 32 francs. At the Home, the child does not change its clothes, and brings its food in a basket; and the walk to and fro provides wholesome exercise. Moreover, the intercourse with its little comrades makes it more sociable and docile, and develops a spirit of emulation. To understand and appreciate the value of an institution which I regard as the greatest evidence of the progress of our age and of priceless service to the people, the two Homes at the Halle aux Draps, with their 900 children, should be visited and inspected. When the Princess Bariatinski, appointed by the Empress of Russia, head of the charitable establishments of St. Petersburg, examined one of the Paris houses, she was simply amazed. She made a study of its smallest details, and could easily believe that fewer tears were shed by this vast number of children within its walls than amongst a score of those kept entirely at home.

Paris is indebted for its first asylums to Mmes. Pastoret, Mallet, and other pious persons, under the direction of MM. de Liancourt, Cochin, and Delessert. With their own resources, they founded seven establishments, receiving about 700 children. As they had a rather precarious existence, I authorised the hospices to grant them subsidies; the latter soon undertook to defray all the expenses; the number of institutions increased from seven to twenty, and that of the children to 4000. The expenses had already reached 100,000 francs. The work was now sufficiently developed for the Municipal Council to recognise it as a legalised institution. It was acknowledged to be a work of public utility, and was incorporated into the budget of primary instruction.

It was a piece of good fortune for the Homes to pass into the hands of the city; they at once experienced the benefit of the change. Premises that were too cramped were enlarged; every directress received an assistant; the staff was recruited from those who had been mothers, rather than from the communities; a committee of lady patronesses were deputed to act as superintendents and overseers, whilst a general inspectress was appointed. In 1848 the number of homes was thirty-four, the number of their inmates about 8000, and the expense of maintaining them 250,000 francs.

Perhaps my only regret at leaving the Hôtel de Ville arose from the severance it involved from this work into which I had put my whole heart. For childhood has always specially appealed to me, and the sight of those baby scholars was very pathetic. I loved to think how day by day they carried home the seeds of the religious teaching

they received, and how fervently I hoped that the sound of
the lisping prayers they were taught to repeat would rekindle a spirit of devotion at their own firesides, and remind
their elders of the prayers which they, too, had offered in
other days.

SCHOOLS

After leaving the Home, the child naturally enters a
regular school. There were two classes of schools in 1830;
the _coles simultanées_, entrusted to the Brothers of the
Christian Doctrine or to the communities and the _Écoles
mutuelles_, in the charge of laymen. The first were specially
protected by the Government, the second by liberal opinion,
but all the schools were supported by the city. I was
careful not to espouse either side, allowing the parents to
choose freely, according to their opinions, or even prejudices. I took an equal interest in the two systems,
because elementary instruction is a debt owed by society
to those who depend entirely on their manual labour, and
it is a public duty to advance their welfare by education.
This impartiality had the double advantage of being just
in itself and promoting emulation.

Nevertheless, I noticed among the working classes a
marked preference for the schools of the Brothers. This
was the result of their modesty, their kindly discipline,
their devotion to the cause, and also of the competition
between the two systems. On one occasion I remarked to
Brother Philippe, the Superior-General (a man of high
principle, and actuated by the noblest motives) : " Before
1830, my dear Brother, an imprudent and ill-advised
favouritism had roused the suspicions of certain classes
with regard to you. But when that compromising protection was removed, you felt that you had henceforth to
rely solely on your own services, your undeniable capability,
and the goodwill which all the teachers of the young inspire equally. You have, by your efforts, opened the eyes
of those who wished to keep them closed—you have surpassed yourselves, and gained far more than you have lost."

S

In 1831, there were in Paris only seventy-one Brothers ;
in 1847 there were one hundred and twenty-two, with
thirteen thousand pupils of all ages, thanks to the addition of classes for adults, about which I intend speaking
later ; these courses were attended at night by young men
between twenty and thirty ; some pupils, indeed, were
over forty. One evening that I happened to be visiting the
École de la Rue Mongolfier, I said to some of them :
" How do you like the teaching and the teachers ? " " Very
much, Monsieur ; the teaching is first-class, and, above all,
we feel that the Brothers *don't look down upon us.*" This
was the secret of the preference shown for the Brothers.
As to the Sisters' schools (inferior to the lay schools so far
as the system, of teaching was concerned), they were also
much appreciated by the working classes, because they were
generally associated with charitable institutions, and were
managed by the nuns who were always ready to help the
families in times of trouble, moreover ; the children learned
more religion at these schools, and were taught domestic
economy and deference to their parents.

The *Écoles mutuelles* possessed several advantages above
those of their rivals ; each school had room for close on
three hundred, and the standard of instruction was higher ;
consequently they drew their pupils from the bourgeois
and manufacturing classes, and were especially encouraged
by the Municipal Council, which made great sacrifices in
order to multiply them. In short, more than forty-five
thousand pupils were being educated in two hundred schools
of all descriptions in 1847, and the budget of primary instruction reached eleven hundred thousand francs.

But what was the best means of stimulating these little
people, and rousing in them a spirit of generous emulation ?
For several years the Council had been granting to the most
deserving, free places in the Écoles des Arts et Métiers.
But the result was disappointing. Most of the graduates
were not sufficiently trained to make good foremen, and
had too much pretension to make good workmen. I
therefore instituted *apprenticeship prizes.* In every school,

for boys or girls, the best pupils, after selecting their
several trades, were apprenticed to trustworthy persons,
with an allowance from the city of three hundred francs
for the first year, two hundred for the second, and a
hundred for the third. One hundred and twenty-six prizes
were distributed annually, and seventy-five thousand francs,
an expenditure which we had no reason to regret.

I also gave savings-bank books as rewards, and this idea
was so pleasing to the Duc d'Orléans that, desiring on
the occasion of his marriage to show his interest in the
industrial population of Paris, he distributed seventeen
hundred bank-books among the most distinguished pupils,
each starting an account with thirty, forty, or fifty francs,
on condition that the interests on these sums, as well as on
the sums previously deposited, should be capitalised, and
that no money should be withdrawn before the depositors
reached their majority. Eight or ten years later, some
of these bank-books came under my eyes, and I saw deposits
for four, six, and eight hundred francs.

On the other hand, my visits to the schools became
more and more frequent, and the inducements I held out
increased in proportion : I arrived unexpectedly, examined
the children, inspected the premises, and wrote down my
observations on the register, always adding a word of
approval : it is so pleasant to be able to praise !

I presided at the distribution of prizes, taking each
district in its turn. The last time I did so, it was in the
12th Arrondissement, in 1847. All the schools were
gathered in the amphitheatre of the Jardin des Plantes.
There were more than three thousand children present,
with their families. I said to them : " For the last fifteen
years I have come here to praise the pupils of this district,
and to congratulate their masters on their success. To-day
I wish to express my obligations to your parents. Thanks
to their care, nay, to their self-denial, I do not see a single
child among you who is not decently clad. I know what
toil and sacrifices this must have cost them ; I admire them,
and tell them so in the name of the City of Paris ; the fact

that they belong to the poorest of the arrondissements increases our admiration and love. And you, too, my children, should love them more than ever. Never allow your hearts to forget what they have done for you ; your highest duty in the future will be to make some return to their old age for the care they have lavished on your childhood."

Courses for Adults

But in a city like Paris, besides elementary instruction, there is need of supplementary education. Drawing, especially, is essentially necessary. Now, there was only one single school, attended by 400 workmen, in which this branch was taught in the evening classes. Various attempts were made in this direction by private individuals and by the Brothers. The governing body proceeded immediately to develop these useful experiments. In the first place it furnished money for all the expenses, then it provided buildings, regulated their management, increased their number, and granted diplomas, while the Brothers on their side started practical courses in all their establishments. These efforts met with complete success. In 1847 Paris had thirty-four schools of art, frequented, from eight to ten in the evening, by 10,000 workmen, who were thus rendered more skilful, were consequently better paid, and, best of all, were kept out of the public-house with all its fatal temptations.

I also owe a debt of gratitude to the Association Polytechnique, directed by M. Perducet: it not only gave popular classes in drawing, but likewise in applied geometry, mechanics, chemistry, &c. It served as a preparation for following the courses of the Conservatoire des Arts et des Métiers; in fact, it rendered incalculable service. At the time of the English Exhibition of 1835, I heard that the commissioners attributed the superiority of Parisian industry to our art schools, which imparted a culture and taste to our artisans which were unequalled elsewhere.

Of course I encouraged lessons productive of such useful

and moral results by being frequently present at them. I often passed a whole evening at a class talking familiarly with the good fellows, who were wonderfully responsive to my least advances. I always impressed on them that labour, even when not compulsory, was honourable, and that the time had gone by when idleness was considered the privilege of the well-born: no one had a right to spend their days in sloth, not even those who had spent more or less time in amassing a large fortune. To give up work then, I declared, was like unyoking the horses from the plough in the middle of a furrow. For that was precisely the time when a man ought to profit by the experience he had acquired, by the credit and public esteem he had won, and to insure a wider and more bountiful harvest for his family and country. I showed them that the value of their manual labour could be doubled by knowledge and intelligence, and that by educating themselves they would certainly improve their condition. I also pointed out to them that it costs dearer to feed a single vice than to feed two children, and I quoted the names of many individuals who had begun as they were beginning, and were now managing important enterprises, like Denière, Cavé, Charrière, Cail, Biétry, &c.[1]

Every time the King visited the Exposition de l'Industrie, I made a point of bringing to his notice those who had started at the bottom of the ladder and were now at the top; and although the prizes were granted without distinction of persons, he did not conceal his sympathy for those winners who owed their success in life to their own merit. When the Princesse d'Orléans visited the Cail and Derosnes workshops, I drew the Comte de Paris aside into a dark corner. "Monseigneur," I said, "it was from this spot that M. Cail, then a simple fitter, started twenty-three years ago to become the head of this great manufactory, in which he now employs fifteen hundred workmen. In his

---

1 Denière, manufacturer of artistic bronzes ; Cavé, the great mechanist, whose business was purchased by the Cail factory ; Charrière, maker of surgical instruments ; Biétry, manufacturer of French cashmere.

case, his factory represents his Minister's portfolio. You are going to see twenty splendid locomotives, six large machines for cooking sugar by steam, and other machines, worth, at least, eighteen hundred thousand francs."

I also introduced the teaching of singing into the schools. Doubtless, music may not be of much practical utility, but it lightens labour, shortens the hours, draws men pleasantly together, and tends to make them forget the pernicious gratification derived from strong drink. I sought the co-operation of M. Wilhem, who was successful beyond my hopes. In the *Écoles mutuelles* the introduction of music was comparatively easy, but in the schools of the communities I met with some obstacles. I had too great a respect for Brother Philippe's superiority of mind and his progressive sympathies not to wish to have an explanation with him. He confessed frankly that he did not care to have outsiders introduced, as they might possibly interfere with the customs and rules of the Order. I perceived that in this he was not entirely wrong. But luckily M. Wilhem solved the difficulty: he offered to give a course at the mother-house in order to train the monitors from among the younger Brothers. Singing-classes soon became general, even in the schools for adults, where they were very popular. For several years I was present at masses and vespers, sung by societies numbering three or four hundred workmen, on festival days at Saint Nicolas-des-Champs or at Saint-Méry. I heard a high mass at Notre Dame sung at Christmas by eight hundred voices. The presence of the orphéons was soon considered indispensable to all school functions. I could never have believed that music would become popular to the extent of attracting thirteen hundred young people.

But in the schools for girls, and especially in those taught by the Sisters, things did not work so smoothly. The nuns (and in this they had the approval of many mothers) apprehended certain dangers for little girls possessing a fine voice. It was quite possible that some might consider their training as a preparation for the Conservatoire, and might renounce the modest careers that lay before them for the illusive temptations of the stage.' The matter required consideration. I surmounted the difficulty by deciding that there should be no soloists, that the solos should be executed by a minimum of from eight to ten voices, trusting that by this arrangement no single child would find an opportunity for displaying her own voice, and for cultivating her vanity in its possession.

WORKROOMS

As I have been speaking of girls' schools, I should add that, until 1830, they were connected with charitable institutions founded by the hospices and managed by the Sisters. In that year the Society of Elementary Instruction opened some alternative schools, which prospered rapidly. For both classes of schools I appointed inspectresses, whose supervision extended to the convent boarding-schools as well as to all private schools. But, notwithstanding the success of my efforts, I could not close my eyes to the fact that one serious defect still existed.

Primary education generally comes to an end when the pupil reaches twelve or thirteen years. At this age boys enter special schools or are apprenticed; but it is not so in the case of girls, who are not received as apprentices if they are under fifteen. What could be done for them during the two years they remained at home? How were their parents, away at their daily labours, to guard and protect them? There is no need to dwell on the dangers incurred in such cases during the absence of the father and mother.

Acting on the advice of M. Parent-Duchâtelet and of the Superioress of the Hôpital de Lourcine, I established workrooms for these young girls, in which they might be taught all branches of needlework. This plan would prepare them for life, and also be a moral protection. Thirty workrooms were opened, attended daily by 1800 children. Several others were founded by private charity; one of the most important of the latter was dedicated to Saint

Ann, and was placed under the patronage of Mme. de Rambuteau, who presided over it for fifteen years. Fourteen hundred young girls were trained in this school. It was so generously financed by gifts, lotteries, collections, and grants from the Municipal Government, that my wife, before resigning, was able to deposit 92,000 francs to the credit of the Society, which was henceforward placed under the protection of the law.

I have now described in general terms the improvements I effected in elementary instruction. As regards higher instruction, it is neither an obligation which is binding on the nation, nor a right to which the people have any claim—it is the business of those able to pay for it. At the same time, it is well to facilitate its achievement as far as possible for those who desire it. Persuaded that the chief source of fortune lies in commerce and industry —for which a ten years' study of dead languages is not necessary — the Municipal Council, at my suggestion, opened two great schools in which Latin and Greek were replaced by modern languages. They were afterwards known as the Collége Turgot and the Collége Chaptal. Their success testified to their usefulness, and my only regret was that they were not larger. Every year it made me sad to see 1600 young men applying for admission to the École Polytechnique, while only 160, or at the most 200, were received. Thus 1400 of them, disappointed in the hope of attaining the goal of their ambition, were vainly groping about in search of a career that would have been thrown open to them if their expectations had only been less ambitious. They would have started as excellent subordinates, then advanced to be foremen, then engineers, and, finally, masters. Why should men of education and energy shrink from devoting their talents to the true sources of wealth? Why should this prejudice in favour of the *liberal* professions exclude from our manufactures young men who are often without private means, and thus condemn them to a life of questionable expedients?

One day, when Louis-Philippe was expressing his uneasiness at the increase of the working population, I said to him, " No, Sire, that is not the danger; it is not the workmen we have to fear, not the men who can earn their living with their own hands, not the men whose wages are steadily increasing, and whose condition is constantly improving. Their labour is a guarantee for their peaceable behaviour. It is the *déclassés* you have to fear —the doctors without patients, the architects without buildings, the journalists without journals, the lawyers without cases, all the neglected, the unappreciated (as they consider themselves), all the hungry, who, finding no place for them vacant at the banquet, seek to upset the table, in the hope of picking up the fallen dishes. These are the people who make revolutions—the preachers of anarchy, the freebooters of education! Leave me, then, to provide the people with the amount of instruction which its requirements demand."

Out of the 1200 lawyers inscribed on the register in Paris, twenty become famous, eighty rich, 150 achieve a modest competence; the rest lead an idle, aimless life. God only knows how they live, and doubtless many of them bitterly regret not having turned their talents to account in the pursuit of commerce or industry. This state of things prompted me to persuade the Municipal Council to reduce the exhibitions in the colleges a full third. And there were still too many left. The half would have sufficed. Twelve or fifteen exhibitions annually would have amply sufficed for the free education of the children of those old city employees who deserve a reward for their fidelity; more than that number simply promotes a system of shameless intrigue on the part of those who have no right to enjoy the advantages of a liberal education without paying for it.

This does not mean, however, that the colleges were neglected : Rollin, founded and administered by the city, was considerably enlarged : Henri IV. was altogether transformed by the removal of the Bibliothèque Sainte-Geneviève; Saint-Louis had an entire new façade constructed on the

Rue la Harpe; Bourbon received an annex which allowed it to double its classes, and the isolation of Louis-le-Grand was in progress by the acquisition of the neighbouring houses and the transfer of the École Normale to the Rue d'Ulm. I was less fortunate in my attempt to found a college with a full curriculum, attended· by day students only, on the extensive grounds belonging to Saint-Lazare. It had struck me that the dense population of the Faubourgs Poissonnière, Montmartre, Saint-Denis, Saint-Martin, &c., required an educational institution, which, with the Church of St. Vincent de Paul and the Hôpital Louis-Philippe, would have completed the prosperity of this new quarter.[1] Time was not allowed me to overcome altogether the opposition of those who believed that the left bank ought to have a monopoly of the colleges and hospitals.

III.—PROVIDENT INSTITUTIONS

GOVERNMENT PAWNSHOPS, SAVINGS-BANKS, MUTUAL AID SOCIETIES, CONSEIL DES PRUD'HOMMES

MONT DE PIÉTÉ

The Mont-de-Piété is, in a certain sense, the *bank of the people:* it is, therefore, needless to state that I took particular interest in it. My first care was to obtain an absolutely competent director, who would help me in effecting useful reforms, especially in the way of economy, for we ought to be able to lend to the poor for nothing. M. Laffitte was at the head of this service, appointed after the Revolution of 1830 for political rather than administrative reasons. He resigned in 1834. The King insisted strongly on the nomination of an ex-deputy, M. B——. I had an audience with his Majesty, in which I told him that more

---

[1] The idea was acknowledged to be excellent, and it was realised soon afterwards by the foundation of the Lycée Condorcet, which is one of the largest colleges in Paris.

than 3000 employees were attached to the various departmental services, and that most of them were very poorly
paid, their acknowledged honesty being the more meri-
torious on that account. Bur how could such disinterested
integrity be expected of them if their career depended, not
on merit, but on nepotism and ministerial and parliamentary
influence. If we cannot afford to be generous, we should,
at least, be just. Now, the place should by rights be filled
by M. Laroche, chief of the branch office for the last ten
years, and his nomination should mean the advancement
of fifteen other employees. The King yielded to my
representations, and consoled M. B—— with a general
receivership.

The Mont-de-Piété lends every year about 44,000,000
francs on pledges amounting to 1,500,000. But it pos-
sesses neither capital nor endowments. It disposes only
of the municipal securities paid into its treasury, which
amount to about 1,800,000 francs. Now, it needs ten
times that amount. It might have realised a portion of
this sum from the capitalised profits, but the law requires
that the entire amount of the annual proceeds from all
pledges (*boni*) be paid to the hospitals. There was no
other resource than to borrow at 3 or 4 per cent. As
the rate of interest on loans is 8 per cent., the difference
served to cover the costs, which are far higher than is
supposed, for the half of these loans are less than 12
francs, and do not produce sufficient interest to balance
the expense. Yet 8 per cent. is a rather high figure.
Might it not be possible to reduce it?

The first thing I did, with the consent of the Council,
was to abolish the custom of paying the annual *boni* to the
hospitals. In fact, what could be more illogical than to
relieve the poor at the expense of the poor? Then we
adopted certain measures for the advantage of the borrowers.
Thus we reckoned the interest by the fortnight instead of
by the month, and this put 80,000 francs in their pockets.
The partial redemption of an article for the fraction of a
franc was authorised; an exceptional service was instituted

for Sunday mornings, but only for the redemption of single articles, because, as the workmen were paid between Saturday evening and Sunday morning, it was wise to protect them from the temptations resulting from the possession of ready money, by allowing them to pay off their debts at once. For, as a rule, how much of their wages survive till Monday morning! The number of pledges that were not redeemed and sold fell rapidly in consequence from 140,000 to 50,000. The expense of the valuation of small objects was shared by the administration.

The heaviest burden for the public was the intervention of the *commissionnaires particuliers*. In fact, the Mont-de-Piété, according to the terms of its institution, ought to have had four branch houses, and it had only one. The so-called commissionnaires supplied the place of the other three branches, without any authority to do so except a commission from the Prefect, which could be revoked at his pleasure. But the difficulties of a complicated liquidation at each change of office had established a sort of tolerance that worked out for their advantage. They were allowed to name their successors. The office was in great request, for it was not only lucrative, but had a sort of Ministerial character. Their commission on their operations was 2 per cent. for the loan, and 2 per cent. for the repayment, or 4 per cent. added to the 8 per cent. of the administration. It would seem that such conditions were calculated to induce intending borrowers to give them a wide berth ! Nothing of the sort. Nearly three-fourths of the loans were made through them, either on account of distances or from a desire for concealment. There were twenty-three of these commissionnaires, and they divided annually among themselves 450,000 francs.

I had, of course, the right to suppress them ; the Ministers even proposed twice that I should do so by means of a royal ordinance. But I did not like to adopt such a drastic measure : rigorous justice is not always equity. Capital had been invested in the enterprise in all good faith. I could not ruin honourable families at a day's notice. I therefore preferred adopting a system of gradual suppression, and for ten years I refused to sign a new nomination.

To supply the place of the three branches, I created auxiliary bureaus, which were managed inexpensively, and every day sent the articles in pawn to the central house. This innovation was very well received by the common people : it had less success with borrowers of a higher social status, who preferred to carry on their transactions through the commissionnaires and so insure secrecy. The poor were not the only persons who had recourse to the Mont-de-Piété. I have seen princes of reigning families there ; and have had caskets of jewels in my hands and silver plate of great value. It is no secret nowadays that individuals belonging to the most brilliant society are often obliged to resort to the most disagreeable expedients to raise money ! I imagine, however, I am hardly expected to give the names on the present occasion.

After all, the commissionnaires were not grateful for my moderation : they had, moreover, powerful supporters in the Council, and, as they could not very well quarrel with me (for I held their fate in my hands), they did their best to make life miserable for the directors, MM. Laroche and Sauvé, who died successively at their posts. I am glad to pay a passing tribute of respect to these upright and benevolent men.

SAVINGS-BANKS

I have referred incidentally to my interest in savings-banks. A thrifty workman is on the right road to become an employer. I never missed an opportunity of discharging my duties as an administrator with the zeal of a private individual engaged in a work that concerned him personally, for, as Prefect, I kept myself informed of all the details of the service through the chief of the bureaus. Furthermore, the Municipal Council never withheld their support from me. The twelve mairies of Paris and eighteen cantons were endowed with these useful institutions, to which the suppression of lotteries brought increased prosperity by substituting substantial benefactions for a deceptive illusion. In 1848 there were 82,000 bank-books belonging to workmen, and 75,000 to individuals in service, the total representing a capital of sixty-five millions. But the proportion varied considerably, according to the trade of the workmen. Thus, 13,000 carpenters and stone-cutters owned 10,000 bank-books, while 14,000 tailors and 17,000 shoemakers had less than 3000.

I had requested the magistrates of the Police Courts to put this question to every prisoner brought before them: " Have you a savings-bank book ? " The immense majority answered " No," naturally enough ; because those who are industrious and economical seldom trangress the law. Still, the savings-banks did not give satisfaction to everybody. Thus, M. François Delessert was defeated in his candidature for election to the Chamber in the 6th Arrondissement by a coalition of tavern-keepers, café-proprietors, &c., who accused him of his unduly influencing their customers and persuading them to lodge a good half of the money in savings-banks that rightfully belonged to them. Was not this his noblest title to the Presidency of the Caisse de Paris, a post which I succeeded in obtaining for him as a recompense ?

MUTUAL AID SOCIETIES

Another form of thrift was promoted by the Workmen's Mutual Aid Societies, which I likewise encouraged. At the time of the marriage of the Duc d'Orléans they numbered 176, with 20,000 members. At my suggestion, the Council voted them a grant of 100,000 francs, representing a year's assessment at two sous a week. Ten years later these societies had increased to 560, and, although I was unable to have them all scheduled, I got far enough to discover that 280 of them had 35,000 adherents, with a capital of 3,200,000 francs.

One day, after I had presided at one of their meetings in the Halle aux Draps and given them my customary advice, a little old man stopped me as I was leaving, and requested me to furnish him with a summary of my remarks in writing. "I am," said he, "*the little blue mantle*,[1] and your words are of more value than my money. I want to have them printed and wrapped round my little donations; every one will read them, and, long after the money is spent, they will retain them in their memory." I thanked M. Champion, with whose warm-hearted liberality I was well acquainted. He had 20,000 copies of my address struck off. Perhaps they were read by some of the men who mounted guard before my picture at the sack of the Hôtel de Ville.

Conseil des Prud'hommes

Another proof of forethought in the working-man was the institution of the Prud'hommes, a body of magistrates to act as arbitrators between masters and workmen. It had existed already in most of the industrial and manufacturing cities, and I have recorded elsewhere my appreciation of its services in 1814 at Saint-Chamond and Saint-Étienne both before and after the Invasion. I was therefore anxious for Paris to benefit by this institution. But the multiplicity of Parisian industries seemed an insurmountable obstacle, and the most clear-headed men in the Tribunal of Commerce and in the Municipal Council did not believe in its success. Nevertheless, I was encouraged in the effort by some great manufacturers. They thought that it would be possible to unite a reasonable proportion of employers and employees if certain industries, more or less similar, could be grouped together. These we divided into four sections : metals,

---

[1] Name given to a generous philanthropist, M. Champion, who was to be seen always on foot in every quarter of the city wearing a blue mantle, and distributing alms of all sorts. He was an orphan, picked up by a poor woman, became first an apprentice, then artisan, and finally a master goldsmith. He had made a considerable fortune in the jewellery business.

woven goods, chemical products and ceramics, and *articles de Paris*, as they are styled.

The members of these four chambers were to be elected by the common assembly of masters and workmen. This last point was warmly contested in the preliminary discussion of the Council of State, where no one had any faith in the possibility of a mutual understanding. I defended my plan with great persistency. I said that if the interests of either party were exclusively at stake, each party would naturally vote for their most influential members, but that as, on the contrary, it was a question of electing members for a court of arbitration, I felt convinced that the workmen would vote for the employers they liked best, the employers would vote for the most intelligent workmen, and that I, for one, had confidence in the good feeling of both employers and workmen. I won my case.

Of the 3160 disputes brought before the Tribunal of Conciliation, nearly 3000 were settled on the spot. Only a few were carried to the Tribunal of Commerce. The Section des Métaux was the first to act, and at the beginning the Chamber sat in the Palais de Justice. It had a home of its own in the Rue de la Douane as soon as the organisation was in full activity. Two years later the three other sections were inaugurated in their turn. In 1847 they arbitrated in the case of 6,000,000 industries and between 50,000 patentees and 200,000 workmen.

IV

[The very ample notes which Comte de Rambuteau has left on this part of his administration are full of figures and statistics which could not very well find a place in this sketch. These notes are instructive, but a little dry. We shall therefore confine ourselves to explaining his principles and the motives which actuated him. We may possibly fail in conveying a complete impression of all he did, but it would need a technical work to furnish an exhaustive account of his labours, which were the beginning of the transformation of Paris.]

"The three things I am especially bound to secure for the Parisians," I once said to the King, "are water, air, and shade"—I might have added: "And not to the inhabitants of Paris only, but to all those within my jurisdiction," for I have always considered that Paris should be the eldest sister of the suburbs, and should treat them the more generously in consideration of the fact that she is every day becoming more and more indebted to them. A considerable proportion of the artisans and workmen of all grades employed in her commerce and industries have their homes in those outlying districts, where living is cheaper, and have therefore strong claims to administrative protection.

The Municipal Council frequently demanded that the communes within the fortifications should be annexed to the city. I always refused my assent. I did not believe that the benefits derived from the octroi [1] supplied a sufficient reason for the change, and I never failed to recall the fact that, when a similar plan was brought before the Council of State in 1811, the Emperor had formally opposed it.

"In a great capital," he said, "the wages of the workmen are often insufficient to lodge and support them decently. It is absolutely necessary for them to get away from the city, and so escape the urban taxes and the high prices, unless we are prepared to imitate the English, who give parish relief to their workmen. It is right that the hard-worker should have a chance of finding health and recreation outside the walls."

I added that two-thirds of the 70,000 horses employed in Paris were stabled outside the barriers, by which a saving of 50 francs a head was effected; that, if the communes were annexed, their inhabitants would migrate beyond the boundaries in the same fashion; that an experiment had

---

[1] A duty on comestibles levied at the entrance of Paris.

been made in the case of Le Gros-Caillou ; [1] and that in the three districts on the left bank there was an immense extent of waste land, while Ivry, Montrouge, and Vaugirard were tripling their population. Indeed, new buildings were rapidly springing up in the outlying districts ; villages and hamlets were becoming important additions. There was every facility for erecting churches, schools, markets, fountains, &c., for the Arrondissement of Saint-Denis, where the population—34,000 in 1804—was to increase during 1848 to 185,000.

I worked, therefore, for the interests of the outlying districts. I completed two great lines of circumvallation, one a league, and another three leagues distant from the fortifications, in order to establish easy communication between the thirty-two roads leading to the capital, and to permit the rapid transmission of merchandise. Three millions were expended on this improvement, independently of what was spent on the new bridges over the Seine and Marne, and on the works for navigation.

The question of sanitation occupied me equally. The suburban population was abundantly supplied with water by companies, but little attention was paid to the removal of household slops; hence, pestilential sewers were the result of the lack of proper drainage. I had water-courses made in every direction, and thus the approaches to the city were cleansed from this nuisance. There was an enormous cesspool near Montfaucon, which served as a receptacle for the night soil of the whole capital; and whenever the wind was in the north, Belleville and La Villette were infected by the tainted air. This I succeeded in removing. I selected a spot in the forest of Bondy whither all this foul matter could be transported. But it was no slight matter to convey 600 cubic metres of detritus every night, and in all weathers, to a distance of fifteen kilometres. The difficulty was overcome by a distinguished

---

[1] There were, in fact, only 22,000 inhabitants in Le Gros-Caillou, while in the suburban quarters, each occupying a similar area, there were 200,000. Yet the expenses for police, lighting, paving, sewers, &c., were the same.

engineer, M. Mary, who suggested that a vast trench should be dug at La Villette, from whence a conduit 16,000 metres long should start, through which the refuse might be propelled by means of a forty horse-power steam engine. I also isolated the knackers' enclosure in the plain of Aubervilliers; whilst the Bièvre and the water-furrow of the Gobelins were embanked, paved, arched over in parts, and furnished with sluices.

Perhaps there is nothing of greater importance to Paris than its streets and highways; I was therefore a sort of road-inspector Prefect. The first point to be gained was to ascertain clearly what were the undisputed rights belonging to my jurisdiction. There is no doubt that, at the time of the Revolution, when the sales of the convents and of other national property took place, their rights were infringed as regards the extent of the frontage of their domiciles, either for the purpose of opening new roads or for the widening of those already existing. But these rights were for the most part forgotten, and become, as it were, a dead letter. So I had all the contracts which had been made at this epoch overhauled and a general analysis drawn up of the reservations stipulated, in order that all plans, present or future, should have as much light shed on them as possible.

During his reign the Emperor had ordered the undertaking of great works, almost exclusively at the expense of the State, and, consequently, on his own responsibility. Under the two Restorations, however, things were different. The Municipal Administration alone took the initiative in all such enterprises, subject to the laws of expropriation, to which it had to conform. Hence many embarrassing circumstances arose which involved many sacrifices. Thus, it could only appropriate ground that, in a certain sense, was really a part of a public thoroughfare; every other part remained under the absolute control of the proprietor, and so we had buildings, in our finest streets, without depth or breadth, wretched constructions, unworthy of a great city.

I had made an offer to the Government to extend the

Rue de Rivoli to the Hôtel de Ville and the Rue Saint-
Antoine, without any expense to the State, provided I were
allowed to take possession of a side strip of fifteen metres
on each side, the sale of which would have covered a good
deal of the cost.   It was the only way to insure fine houses
and to embellish the city, and yet it was not until 1850 that
a law ratified what I had been vainly demanding for fifteen
years.

I have often been reproached, as has also M. de
Chabrol, with not having prepared or followed one grand
uniform plan.   I could easily have done so; I had only to
make use of the numerous projects already produced, and
construct a vast programme from them, with which, perhaps, posterity would have associated my name.   But we
must not forget that the plans of yesterday are no longer
those of to-day—what will be those of to-morrow?   Since
1790 more than 1200 streets have been laid out on a
system which is now condemned as defective.   The increase
in population, the briskness of traffic, the use of vehicles in
industries formerly dependent on hand labour have trebled
the number of carts and waggons; moreover, the sidewalks, useful though they are, have lessened the width of
the streets, which no longer suffice for the increasing business.   Should all the streets be widened, then?   But if so,
would not the rights of all those house-owners be interfered
with who originally built their residences within the limit
prescribed by the authorities?   Was it not better to
facilitate traffic by the great branch roads, which were
successively opened and prolonged, such as the Rues de
Rivoli, Lafayette, Rambuteau, and the lines of the quays
and boulevards?

All these plans, executed with patience and perseverance,
cost considerable sums, but much less than they would
have done had all the schemes been published simultaneously.   In fact, when the city decides on either opening
new roads or widening others, all the real property affected
thereby is at its disposal.   Consequently the owners could
neither let it, nor raise a mortgage on it.   They have a

right to their land or to an indemnity.   Now, the city may
not, at the moment, have the necessary resources.   It must
have recourse to a loan, and we can easily conceive how
onerous such a system would become when applied to a
general plan.

Never could the Municipal Council, as a vigilant guardian of the finances, have consented to mortgage them in
this fashion.   A plan of alignment, on the other hand,
gives the owners time to rebuild, and they can be treated
with on the basis of the incoming revenue shown by the
Budget.   It is time enough to borrow when the estimates
are very high.

Another reason for not undertaking a great number of
important works at the same time is that, by so doing, a
certain risk is involved with regard to the workmen who
are employed.

About this I should like to say a few words.   Under
normal conditions, the opening of streets in Paris and the
construction of private dwellings (which is a natural result)
gives employment to about fifty thousand artisans.   Extraordinary works have the effect of disturbing the equilibrium,
because they increase the price of provisions, and they cause
a rise in wages and rent.   Added to this, they draw crowds
of workmen from the provinces, who are attracted by the
hope of higher wages and greater comfort, and who, having
once tasted the pleasures of city life, cannot make up their
minds to return home when the job is ended.   Being unemployed, they are a prey to all the temptations of want
and idleness, not to speak of the pernicious influences and
wrong-headed ambitions of the club orators.   Thus, in
1828 and 1829, the public works having declined for lack
of funds, less than the average number of workmen were
employed, consequently more than half the combatants
of July were recruited from the unemployed.   Eighteen
years later the same causes produced the same effects.   The
completion of the fortifications threw between thirty and
forty thousand workmen out of work ; the events of
February had suspended all activity.   The only resort the

Provisional Government could think of was to fall back on the National workshops, from which resulted the days of June, which cost France more blood than a glorious battle would have done.

I was always desirous of avoiding such perils by maintaining a just proportion between the works undertaken and the men needing employment. The Masons' and Navvies' Labour Exchange met every morning on the Place de l'Hôtel de Ville; that of the joiners and carpenters on the Place du Châtelet. When I saw that many of them were idle for several days in succession, I anticipated by some months the expropriation voted by the Municipal Council, and thus the one or two million francs granted to the Street Commission produced four or eight millions worth of immediate labour. When conditions were reversed I delayed the expropriations in the same proportion, and I believe, by maintaining this sort of counterbalance, I avoided those great panics so productive of that kind of speculation in which the contractors are ruined and the workmen not benefited.

But I do not care to give a detailed account of the streets I opened, levelled, and aligned, nor of all the works accomplished under my direction. I only wish to speak of the principle upon which I acted. For example, I was never anxious to open thoroughfares in places where the indemnity to be paid was three or four times greater than the value of the ground. That would have been imitating the scullions of the Duc de Richelieu, who burned the wood for the sake of selling the ashes. I gave up my scheme for widening the Rue Saint-Denis and the Rue Saint-Martin, because my plan of uniting the Place du Châtelet to the boulevard by a new street was less costly. I tried especially to open thoroughfares in places where fine buildings with magnificent façades were likely to be erected, such as the Rue de Rambuteau, for instance, which cost nine millions, while the buildings fronting it must have cost fifty. But I did not sacrifice "Vieux Paris" to any privileged quarters. On the contrary, as

I was myself a child of the Marais, brought up in the Place Royal, where my grandmother Laviefville had her hôtel, I was fond of sauntering through the little Rue Sainte-Avoye, where my father was born, and where his father and mother had died.

I made special efforts to improve the thoroughfares in this quarter, and certainly they needed it. As soon as it rained most of them were transformed into rivers, which had to be crossed on planks; there were no pavements, no gutters; so that the foot-passengers were drenched with the drippings from the roof. In summer there was no street-watering; the slops of the household could be seen stagnating in front of the houses, and diffusing that characteristic odour of rotten cabbage which always enabled the Parisian, on his return from abroad, to recognise his native city. Hence malaria, fever, and other diseases, all of which disappeared before cleanliness. The lighting was so insufficient that, after the shops were closed, the few lamps placed at long intervals only served to make the darkness more visible.

Every year I had from seven to eight thousand cemented sewers constructed, which not only disinfected the soil, but made it possible for convex causeways to take the place of the old cisterns, cleft in the middle by a gutter. I tried every sort of paving, all of which I could describe most technically, from the homeliest kind to the muddy, dusty, costly macadam, which, however, has the virtue of deadening the sound of traffic; I reserved it for the approaches to hospitals, courts, and theatres. In 1833, there were hardly 16,000 metres of pavements; in 1848, there were 195,000 for the streets alone—not to speak of the squares, quays, boulevards—all fully equipped with sewers, sidewalks, gutter-pipes, and making in all 1400 streets, that had been metamorphosed, covering an extent of about 260 kilometres. Still, with all my efforts, I never was able to have a law passed compelling proprietors to construct footpaths.

Naturally, in these circumstances, a good deal of soil had

to be carted away, and it was the fashion for some time, to call every hole, ditch, or obstruction a *Rambuteau*. People are like children ; they always forget that no lasting advantage can be obtained without a temporary sacrifice. This did not prevent me from pursuing my task, and I hope Paris will remember all I did for its boulevards, which I levelled, smoothed, and repaired, from the Bastille to the Madeleine, as well as for its quays, which were reconstructed from the Louvre to the Pont de Bercy, besides those which were newly built. I hope it will remember how I improved its squares and the Place de la Concorde, which cost the city two millions, and the Place du Trone, which occasioned a further outlay of two millions and a half, with its barrier and its columns surmounted by statues in bronze.

I tried to embellish them by planting trees, those good friends of man which gladden the eyes and purify the air. Was I not bound to make some compensation for the many gardens which had been destroyed to make room for public or private buildings ? I was so careful of my plantations that the people were in the habit of remarking, with good-natured sarcasm : " The Prefect would rather have a tooth pulled out than a tree pulled up." And to increase the convenience of the pedestrians, I had benches placed wherever I could find room. Is it credible that, until then, there had not been a single such bench in Paris, so strong was the opposition to any interference with the hiring of chairs ? So when, later on, I saw heavily laden men resting for a moment on those benches, or old people taking a sun-bath, with their canes between their knees, or looked at mothers indulging in a little gossip as they supervised their children at play, or when at eventide I watched whole families seated together in happy groups, I felt rewarded with my efforts, and satisfied with them and with myself.

WATER

It is by the management of the water supply that the administration of a city can be best judged. Now it is an actual fact that, not so very long ago, the Parisians were limited to less than *eight* litres of water a head. To-day, each of them may dispose of a hundred litres. In 1830, there were in Paris 146 street-fountains; after I abandoned my office, the number was 1840, with a discharge of 20,000 litres for each. I must admit, however, that I found this necessary work in a fair way towards execution. M. de Cabrol had pretty nearly completed the works on the canal of the Ourcq which were to give to the city 4000 water-inches.[1] The next thing was to distribute it, and this required 200,000 metres of cast-iron pipes and six great reservoirs, each 10,000 cubic metres. That of the Rue Racine, built on the moats of the Enceinte de Philippe-Auguste, those of the Panthéon and Vaugirard, fairly honey-combed with ancient quarries, involved the laying down of considerable foundations; it was necessary to dig wells from 50 to 60 feet deep and 10 feet in diameter, in which columns of concrete were sunk to support the arches. These reservoirs were filled during the night, and doubled the consumption in the daytime.

But this was not enough. I laid down pipes for the waters of the Clignon, and increased the resources by 25,000 cubic metres; the city bought back all the private concessions that lessened the water supply at Arcueil, and they were reserved for the upper quarters of the left bank, which those of the Ourcq could not reach. It was for the same purpose that I sank a well at Grenelle on the advice of a commission of engineers and scientists, for which M. Arago acted as reporter. But what trials, nay, what disappointments, fell to my share during eight years! Nevertheless, I was not left to myself; no sum that I asked for was refused to me, and my joy may be conceived when, one fine day, the water suddenly gushed forth, rising 35 metres high, with an unexpected volume of 2400 cubic metres!

Afterwards, I proposed to the Government to sink a similar well, 800 or 900 metres deep, in the Jardin des

[1] A water-inch is twenty cubic metres.

Plantes, to furnish warm water to the hot-houses, baths, lavatories, and different offices of a thickly-populated district. The Revolution of 1848 prevented the realisation of my project, which would have been set on foot at once if there had not been a division of opinion on the choice of a contractor. I supported M. Mulot, the contractor of Grenelle, who had already proved his capacity, and who, from being a simple workman, was now a man of mark— thanks to his industry and intelligence.

To these resources should be added the steam pumps of the Seine, which were costly and clumsy, particularly that of Notre Dame, which obstructed the great arm of ˌthe river. We conceived the idea of replacing them by tur- bines, erected at the fall of the Pont-Neuf : in this way, the great arm would be freed, and then trains and boats would require only three hours to go from the Pont d'Jéna to the Pont d'Austerlitz, while previously it took three days to make the passage, at great expense, and sometimes it entailed considerable risk. The sluice of the Pont-Neuf was furthermore to serve as a waterway for the little arm, into which fourteen sewers emptied themselves, and which, when dried up by excessive heat, became a regular hotbed of infection.

But to have water is not enough. It must be whole- some. The waters of the Arneuse and the Mory, which, in summer gave an unpleasant grassy taste to the Ourcq, were reserved for cleaning purposes, as were those of the Ménilmontant, the oldest water brought to Paris. As the number of vessels anchored in the basin of the Villette was a source of contamination, the canal water was carried back to the Pont de Flandre ; filters were connected with pumps on the Seine. Thus, in a sense, I exhumed street-fountains from the bowels of the earth, thus turning to account the supply of water which before my time had been allowed to run away under the footpath which was parallel with the street. I can still see the women, squatting on their heels in order to ladle this rare and precious water into their porrin- gers, and now that water flows abundantly ! It had always been my wish to enable every one to draw freely from fountains rising to the height of fifty centimetres from the ground. Private individuals, however, were forbidden to transport it in water-carts for the purpose of selling it. Every one has the right to drink at the river; but it is only fair that those who wish to have the river brought to their homes should pay for it.

Of course, this improvement was rather costly, but the city was amply compensated for its expenditure by the subscriptions. In 1848, 5300 householders were subscribers; the lowest price was 70 francs a year, and conferred the right to a daily supply of fifteen hectolitres. The lavatories, baths, and industrial establishments obtained notable reductions, and yet the yearly water-rate rose from 240,000 francs to a million and a half. So the undertaking was not unprofitable—indeed, it proved so lucrative, that an English company offered to supply the water to all the houses and to every story in them. The Municipal Council gave careful consideration to the proposal, but, after much deliberation, refused to alienate the rights from Paris, which, if the measure succeeded, would have lost the fruits of its sacrifices, and, if it failed, would have to confront a difficult liquidation.

Finally, wishing to blend the useful with the ornamental, in following the precept of our good friend Horace, I determined to embellish Paris with some ornamental fountains, most of which were designed by Visconti: among them, those of the Place Richelieu, the Place de la Concorde, and the Champs-Élysées, whose waters, after pleasing the eye, were restored to the canals, for I never sacrificed what was needed for practical purposes to the promotion of mere display. I wished in this way to perpetuate the memory of some great men. A beautiful fountain was erected at the gate of the Jardin des Plantes as a tribute to Cuvier; another, the work of Pradier, took the name of Molière, and rose in front of the house where he died. Another, on the Place Saint-Sulpice, was adorned with statues of Bossuet, Fénelon, Massillon, and Fléchier; whilst behind Notre Dame, in the midst of a garden which I had myself planted, a fountain was erected of a religious character, and with a statue of the Blessed Virgin.

GAS

Next after water came light. For a long time Paris had been demanding gas. Two private companies had made an attempt to supply it, one to the neighbourhood of the Luxembourg, the other to the Boulevard des Italiens and the adjacent quarters, but neither of them had succeeded. There were only sixty-three gas-lamps in the public streets. As it would have been rather difficult to embark on one general undertaking to include the whole capital, I divided the city into six sections, each section having its own company. All the companies, however, were bound to help each other in case of need. The chief point was to obtain a perfectly secure canalisation. For, out of six thousand cubic metres starting from the gas-works in the Faubourg Poissonnière for the Faubourg Saint-Germain, hardly three thousand crossed the Pont-Neuf. The rest was lost in the soil, not without contaminating it. This difficulty was disposed of by testing the pipes with boiling oil.

I was inclined to be generous with regard to the first prizes I offered for private as well as public lighting. It was only right to encourage the initial efforts of the companies, for they were devoting considerable capital to an enterprise that might, or might not, prove successful. I was not troubled, either, by the expenses incurred by the illumination of the Place de la Concorde and the Hôtel de Ville, for both furnished a practical proof to the Parisians of the advantages of gas. And the experiment was most convincing. Very soon afterwards the streets could boast of their nine thousand burners; only three thousand lanterns survived, and these were in out-of-the-way quarters. Result: the companies were able to multiply their capital sixfold. After that, the success of the enterprise was assured, and the city could then regulate its conditions according to its own interest.

I persuaded my colleague, the Prefect of Police, who directed the lighting department, to join me in appointing a committee to confer with the companies in order to fix the rates, get them to form a combination, and to insist on the construction of 150,000 metres of new causeways to the confines of the boundaries of Paris, &c. For two years the point remained under discussion. At length there was an agreement, which was submitted to the Municipal Council. But that body could not agree amongst themselves. Some members considered the commission too exacting; others, and they were the majority, preferred not to bind the city by a contract: they advocated an award, after competition, to the highest bidder. This I promptly combated. I declared it would be grossly unjust to despoil, as it were, those who had risked so much on a most hazardous enterprise, which they had undertaken quite as much for the good of the city as for their own. I pointed out that competition in the present circumstances did not offer any guarantee; that they must either repeal the concessions (an act of robbery to which I would never consent) or maintain the *status quo* until their expiration, even though these concessions might deprive Paris of incontestable and immediate advantages. After a fortnight's discussion the contract was accepted.

I have often congratulated myself on the fact that in this affair, as in every other, I was never tempted to engage in any speculation, and that I never dreamed of putting even the smallest portion of my capital into any of those enterprises. Consequently, I was always able to speak as Prefect, and not as an interested party. I was always able to give an energetic support to the causes I believed good, and thus the reproaches of neither my opponents nor my conscience interfered with the absolute independence of my actions.

V.—BUILDINGS

Prisons

I did for the prisons what I had done for the hospitals. Besides that of the Rue de la Roquette, which preserved the unfortunate inmates of Bicêtre from the odious contact with criminals condemned to death, I hastened to finish the construction of the new penitentiary in the same street intended for young prisoners. Until then, little attention had been paid to them. Now, however, philanthropy had founded the colony of Mettray, and generous men like MM. Demetz, Bérenger, Charles Lucas, Moreau, Delessert were devoting all their energies to the task of saving the young. The Courts were more inclined to retain such prisoners in their guardianship, the more such chances of moral improvement increased. There are now six or seven thousand of these juvenile criminals in France, and surely they have special claims on our assistance, for the door of repentance is never shut in the face of the young, who are always either the victims of passion or of bad example, and who are generally guilty of a " first offence." How many would have escaped from further crime if they had been set on the right road in their early years !

The same feeling prompted my reformation of the Correction Paternelle, which I transferred to a section of the prison for young offenders. There, unknown to one another, bearing a number instead of a name, visited only by the director, chaplain, or persons deputed by their families, they would have an opportunity of coming to their senses and preparing for a new life in which there would be nothing to connect them with their past. Important improvements were undertaken at Saint-Lazare, the Conciergerie, and the Madélonnettes, as also at the almshouses of Saint-Denis and Villers-Cotterets. I purchased a piece of ground in the Rue de Clichy, upon which I erected the Debtors' Prison, and I converted Sainte-Pélagie into a prison for political offenders. But my great experiment was made at Mazas, where I introduced the system of cells. I hesitated for a long time before embarking on an undertaking involving an expenditure of five or six millions. Nevertheless, inasmuch as my daily relations with the courts, magistrates, and prison directors convinced me that the prisons were schools of crime, that robberies and murders were planned among the prisoners, and that most of the worst crimes were arranged to take place on the very first day of their discharge; when I reflected that those merely under arrest, and who were perhaps innocent, were thrown into this horrible promiscuous crowd, and then, even if they were acquitted, were soiled with an indelible stain, it seemed to me that hesitation was no longer possible, and that I had a social duty to fulfil. I planned a vast building, with all the improvements lately realised in Europe and America; I even visited the English prisons, and I consider Mazas is an unique establishment, with its numerous parlours, its hundred enclosed walks, its fourteen hundred cells, furnished with gas, ventilators, water-taps, &c., and all in sight of the altar which occupies the centre of the building. Here all are able to gaze on the promise of divine compassion and forgiveness, for it is written : " *There is more joy in Heaven for a sinner who repents than for ninety- nine just persons who need no repentance.*"

Mairies, Markets, &c.

The town-halls[1] also date from this period, and cost about three millions. Until then, the only buildings devoted exclusively to the official business of a district were those of the 8th and 9th Arrondissements. In the other districts the officials had their offices in a hired house, and these were sometimes scattered in different buildings, thus rendering the performance of their duties very difficult. I did my best to provide each arrondissement with a municipal building, with offices for the registration of births, deaths, and marriages, and for the use of the Justice of the Peace, the

[1] Mairies—public-halls for the official business of the arrondissements.

staff of the National Guard, and the Bureau de Bien-faisance.

I was not less liberal in expending money in the interests of commerce : the bonded warehouses, the foreign shipping buildings, the salt emporium, and the toll-house were erected on the banks of the Canal Saint-Martin. This district began to assume the appearance of a Dutch city, and its population rose in a few years to 30,000. Numerous markets were either built or enlarged, and others contracted for.

As to the Halles Centrales, although I was not allowed to complete them, I had, at any rate, the honour of seeing my plans adopted, of obtaining twenty-two millions from the Municipal Council, and of removing every obstacle to their construction. Nothing was omitted in the preliminary draughts. I sent a Commission to visit the finest markets in Germany, England, Belgium, and Holland, so that we might profit by the experience of our neighbours. They were to cover fifty-four thousand metres of ground, and be handed over to the public in 1850. They have since been extended, and the total expenditure has risen to forty millions. I do not regret it : " The Halles," so Napoleon used to say, " should be regarded as *the Louvre of the people*."

Another building which I had not time to erect, but whose plans I had studied and drawn up, in concert with the Municipal Council and the Government, was the Opéra. It was intended to rebuild it on the Place du Palais-Royal, which was to be extended as far as the Rue de Rivoli and the Rue Saint-Honoré. The principal façade would have fronted the square ; the lateral façades, the Rue de Rivoli and the Rue de Saint-Honoré. This project would have corresponded admirably with the clear spaces in front of the Louvre, and with the extension of the Rue de Rivoli to the Rue Saint-Antoine, while going straight to the Tour Saint-Jacque, recently acquired by the city with the object of restoring it and enclosing it with a square. The Opéra would have then stood on a magnificent thoroughfare, two leagues in length, joining the Barrière du Trône to the Barrière de l'Étoile. It would have imparted life and charm to the centre of Paris, which foreigners were beginning to abandon for the boulevards. With reference to this I remarked to the King : " If your Majesty does not look out, in twenty years, old clothes, brought from the Temple, will be sold under the arcades of the Palais-Royal ! " And there was some foundation for this statement. In 1812, each arcade was rented for 3000 francs. In 1848 they brought in only two thousand, although rents had then been doubled. The Revolution, however, put a stop to my plan.

Place de la Concorde

I was more successful with the restoration of the Place de la Concorde. Disturbed by the scheme of M. Humann to alienate the whole line of the Cours-la-Reine for building purposes, I at once demanded the cession, already stipulated, of the Champs-Élysées to the city, and I next proceeded to prohibit the erection of any structure between the square and the Avenue de Marigny, in order to preserve the view of the gardens and hôtels. To carry out my plan, four squares would be needed, with four handsome fountains, so as to unite the Tuileries to the Champs-Élysées without interfering with the beautiful view. But the King was not at all satisfied. " When completing a work," he said to me, " we should always conform to the main idea of the artist who originally conceived it. Now Gabriel designed the square with the buildings of the Garde-Meuble to limit its extent, with towers to indicate the corners, and with two fountains and a central monument. As it is the city that defrays the cost, I cannot enforce my wishes, but I can withhold my approval. Besides, I have another reason for placing the obelisk [1] in the middle—as it commemorates no political event it is sure to remain there ; whereas, if the space were left vacant, you might, some day or other, see

---

[1] The Obelisk of Luxor (Thebes), presented in 1831 to Louis-Philippe by Mohammed Ali.

an expiatory monument or a statue of Liberty instead of the obelisk."

Seeing that there was some force in the King's reasoning, I yielded. Indeed, I had no wish for a repetition of those huge snow-mounds of 1828, which were nicknamed, "les Alpes Mangines," after the then Prefect of Police, nor the temporary buildings erected for the Exhibition of 1834. But I regretted that the King refused his consent to the demolition of the moat which ran in front of the Tuileries, for I should have greatly liked to erect a handsome flight of steps at each end with a plantation of lime trees. These latter would have afforded a grateful shade to those foot passengers who were obliged to cross the square, where the heat in the summer was quite tropical. The King presided at the inauguration of the obelisk. There were more than 900,000 spectators at this curious function. Throughout the ceremony, the Queen persisted in placing herself in front of the King. I besought her to allow the crowd to catch a glimpse of his Majesty.

"Do you undertake to be responsible for his life?" was her answer. And the poor woman, haunted by the recollection of Fieschi, could only think of exposing her own person in order to protect her husband.

PALAIS DE JUSTICE—CHURCHES

But there was perhaps no public edifice that required enlargement and restoration so much as the Palais de Justice. I appointed a Commission, consisting of representatives from the different judicial bodies, to report to me on the defects and mistakes of this building, and the best methods of correcting them. Then I entrusted M. Huyot with the task of making an estimate of the necessary expenses: 22,000,000 francs would be needed for carrying out the repairs, which were not to involve any disrespect to the works of the past, or to the artistic souvenirs of eight centuries. The Cour des Comptes, transferred to the Quai d'Orsay, was acquired, and the Prefect of Police installed in it. In the great hall of the Cour Royale I placed the famous picture of Jean de Bruges,[1] I restored the kitchens of Saint-Louis, and, above all, I rescued the Sainte-Chapelle from the neglected condition in which this pure Gothic jewel had lain so long. But M. Huyot died, and the Revolution of '48 arrested all these works. Thank God, they have been resumed and completed.

Naturally, I did not sacrifice the other churches of Paris to the Sainte-Chapelle. Each one of them was embellished and improved in some way or another, which it would take too long to describe.

Everybody is familiar with the vast works at Notre Dame, of which the State bore the chief expense. Saint-Severin was extricated from the mass of houses which surrounded it, and its front was rebuilt. Saint-Philippe du Roule was greatly extended; Saint-Paul, Saint-Louis, were restored, as likewise was the Chapel of the Virgin at Saint-Gervais, one of our most charming specimens of the Gothic style. I made Saint-Germain l'Auxerrois into a place of worship, and with the help of the 900,000 francs voted to me by the Municipal Council, I was able to remove all traces of the onslaught which the blind fury of the mob had made on the building. I completed both Saint-Denis du Saint-Sacrament and Notre Dame de Lorette by having the marble pillars and arches in the interior of each highly polished, so that these might harmonise with the other details of their brilliant Italian decorations. But I made one great mistake, namely, that of having a magnificent Piétà executed in gilded bronze at a cost of 700,000 francs, and which would have been far more beautiful if it had been carried out in marble. As to the frescoes for the walls, these were so successful that they suggested to me the idea of substituting similar frescoes for the pictures which the city had ordered to be painted for the other churches, notably at Saint-Thomas d'Aquin

---

[1] It is the triptych generally attributed to Memling rather than to Van Eyck. We know that in consequence of the circular of May 1, 1904, forbidding religious symbols in all the Courts, this masterpiece of early art has just been removed. It is now in the Louvre.

and Saint-Germain-des-Prés : the latter was our only church in the Byzantine style, and this I wanted to serve as a sort of souvenir of Saint-Marc at Venice.

The Government had left the task of restoring all the interior of the Madeleine to the city, except the works of art which were not universally popular. I can still recall the holy indignation of the Princesse de Craon as she stood before the Pècheresse of Marochetti, and I well remember the letter she wrote to me protesting against "that *colossal Juno*" with her opulent charms, less likely to inspire repentance than sin.

Saint-Eustache was scraped, swept, scrubbed, and these proceedings brought to light some old frescoes which served as models for the complete restoration of all the chapels. It was also decided that the clumsy portal of Soufflot, so different from the Renaissance style of the building, should be removed and replaced by an arched doorway in harmony with the general architecture of the building. This task was entrusted to M. Lesueur. One of the most agonising hours of my life was that which I passed in this church when the grand organ, which had just been put up, caught fire. I was there, alone with the curé, watching the progress of the flames, which the engines were unable to control. Suddenly, the captain, pointing to a trap-door overhead, exclaimed : " If the fire finds an outlet yonder, the roof timbers will be involved, and the church is lost, for our pumps cannot reach such a height, and then I am afraid that this forest of flames will destroy the whole district." Fortunately, his fears were not realised. The damage to the church amounted to 200,000 francs, not including the loss of the organ.

I finished the seminary of Saint-Sulpice, as well as the square and the fountain. I had hoped to reconstruct the Archbishop's Palace in front of the Hôtel de Ville, the plans having been ready and accepted in 1848. However, I had the good fortune to be able to build two fine new churches, Saint-Vincent-de-Paul and Sainte-Clotilde. I wished the latter to be, in some sort, a monument to the

Héliog Dujardin Paris

L'Hôtel de Ville. Paris.

as completed by The Comte de Rambuteau.

virtues of the Queen, and therefore would have liked to dedicate it to her patron saint, just as I had built a hospital bearing the King's name. The Queen, in her modesty, refused me permission. "You must yield to her," said the King; "but on the day of the consecration, *Sainte Clotilae* shall become *Sainte Amélie!*" As many of the churches I had built or repaired were Greek or Roman, I intended that the new church should be Gothic, a style which is more in harmony with our traditions and religious customs. So I took Saint-Ouen of Rouen as my model. The Municipal Council approved, but I had to struggle for five years with the Conseil des Bâtiments Civils, which was supported by the Institut. This delay and the events of '48 prevented the execution of the plan. But, at least, I had the gratification of seeing it completed after me.

Hôtel de Ville

I have kept the reconstruction of the Hôtel de Ville for the close of this long narrative. It was my house, my home, and was the scene of the last days of my life, which ended there; for, though since my retirement my days have been calm and restful, I do not reckon them amongst those which belong to my life—they have been too idle. Certainly, I do not claim the entire credit of having initiated this superb edifice: another would have done as much; but its reconstruction had become necessary and had long been expected. Napoleon had dreamed of it already. My merit is to have overcome the resistance of the Municipal Council, and, in a new structure, to have preserved for Paris her old monument. Besides urging the advantage of centralising all the municipal services in the heart of Paris under one roof, and the beauty of this district, which (with its new thoroughfares radiating in every direction) was quite transformed, I turned to account the great saving that was effected in the public fêtes given to the people and to royalty. Till now they had been held in temporary structures, and had cost more than six millions, from 1810 to

1830, without leaving any visible result behind them. On this point I addressed myself to two men who differed very much from each other in the nature of their talents, M. Godde, the city architect for twenty-five years, and M. Lesueur, Grand Prix of Rome, and well versed in Renaissance architecture. The programme I proposed obliged them not only to preserve the ancient Hôtel with a religious respect for the past, but also to stamp the new parts with its characteristic style, just as if the monument, begun in 1535 by Boccador, had been completed in accordance with his plans three centuries later.

The estimates, *for the buildings alone*, were fixed at seven millions. The Municipal Council made a protracted resistance; there was only a majority of one in favour of the project, and, after the vote, MM. Aubé and Ganneron came to me and said, "We voted for you against our conscience and because of our personal attachment to you, for we are persuaded that the expenses will be much greater than you think." Now, on the 1st of January 1848 I had expended altogether thirteen millions; all that was left for decorative purposes was about 120,000 francs. And there were other things I had not foreseen.

In the first place, I realised that the inner court between the old and new building, which was sixty feet high, would resemble a well. Why should it not be covered with a dome of iron and glass, in the interior of which the finest staircase in Paris could be built capable of being transformed on grand fête days into a living Veronese? My idea was adopted. It cost 1,300,000 francs. Then, we found the old Hôtel in such a state of decay that all that remained of it was the façade on the square and three walls on the court. The rest had to be rebuilt, including the roofs.[1] But the

---

[1] This renovation stirred up the author of *Notre-Dame de Paris*, who wrote the following letter to Comte de Rambuteau :—

"I am overwhelmed with work, Monsieur le Préfet, at the present moment ; nevertheless, it is impossible for me not to abandon it for the moment and write to you. You have started work on the roofing of the ancient façade of the Hôtel de Ville. This operation, Monsieur le Préfet, alarms all the friends of art in the highest degree. Is it possible that any

expenses went on increasing, although I was always waging war with my architects on this subject, with M. Lesueur especially, who, carried away by his artistic impetuosity, gave orders without counting the cost.

Nevertheless, I exceeded by forty-two thousand francs the sums voted by the Council for the decoration of the Grand Staircase, and, after 1848, it was suggested that I should have to pay the money. I replied that it was the only case in fifteen years where I had pledged my personal responsibility, and that I was ready to make good the amount, provided I were allowed to have inscribed on the pedestals of the sculptures that, after having paid for them out of my own pocket, and acquired the right of doing what I wished with them, I had made a gift of them to the city. I heard nothing more about the matter. Although the fittings of the interior were very costly, all that was spent on the private apartments of the Prefect and his family was *forty thousand francs*.

The King thought the structure very beautiful. He was a delicate judge in matters of art and taste. He deigned to remark that I had collected many memorials of royalty in a municipal palace. He admired the woodwork, carved by Jean Cousin, placed in the Salon du Zodiaque, in which the Duchesse de Longueville gave birth to a child; and the statue of Henry IV. over the door, and that of Louis XIV. in the court. He promised that I should have his, and said, on leaving: "I thank you, my dear Prefect, you have given me a fortress hidden beneath roses." The defensive arrangements had not escaped his notice.

I may be permitted to add the testimony of Marshal

---

one should dream of lowering this roof and modifying its angle in any fashion whatsoever? I cannot believe it. However, an attempt of some sort has been made. In the case of a building which is so complete, so graceful, so perfect in every way, as the Hôtel de Ville of Paris, the lowering of the roof (a proceeding which is always barbarous) would be an act of the utmost gravity, an outrage on a masterpiece. I appeal to your enlightened and noble intelligence. Do not, Monsieur le Préfet, allow this distressing undertaking to be carried any further.—Receive, &c.

"VICTO HUGO.

" 15th of August 1839."

Bugeaud to that of the King. In 1845, on his return from Algiers, he spent a whole morning inspecting the Hôtel in its smallest details, from the great stable—which could accommodate two hundred horses—to the roofs, so arranged that a battalion could manœuvre on them, and he said to me : " My dear friend, I pledge you my word I could defend the Hôtel de Ville, in case of an attack, with three thousand men against thirty thousand."

Why didn't he, then ?

The fêtes of the Hôtel de Ville have been much talked of.[1] The finest was the one given at the marriage of the Duc d'Orléans in the old building, at which six thousand persons were present. M. Visconti had surpassed himself. He had erected in the court a salon, cooled by playing fountains, and perfumed by thirty-two thousand pots of flowers. Two thousand four hundred bouquets were prepared for the ladies. Dinner and supper were both got ready in the Hôtel itself ; all passed off in an orderly fashion not often seen on such occasions. And, as the Ministers had previously made me responsible for the safety of the King, from the moment he crossed my threshold, twelve colonels of the National Guard acted as his bodyguard during the seven hours.

The balls and receptions I gave in the old rooms in winter, at which the Princes were always present before their marriage, were very successful, especially those from 1835 to 1841, in spite of the magnificence of the new apartments. One of the reasons probably was that not

---

[1] It was after one of these fêtes that Louis-Philippe, on his return to the Tuileries, wrote the following note to Comte de Rambuteau ; it was accompanied by the toast he had pronounced :

" *Monday night,* 19*th of June.*
One o'clock in the morning.

" MY DEAR PREFECT,—You know that I had no stenographer to-day ; but as you desire it, I have tried to remember what I said to you, and I send it to you enclosed. I am not at all sure that I have recalled the exact expressions which I used, but I am quite sure that my heart beats now as then, and that my sentiments do not vary.

" Good-night, my dear Prefect. I thank you once more for the beautiful fête the city has given me, and for the manner in which it has been conducted. " L. P."

more than a thousand persons could be accommodated in the old apartments ; consequently the company, to a great extent, was very select.   Later, the standard was lowered by the increase in number, although Mme. de Rambuteau always took care to do the honours of the house herself, and never received any lady who had not been presented to her.   Our duties, our relations, compelled us to give a larger and larger place to the municipal element.   But I would never consent to allow the city to defray the expenses of my receptions, because I wished Mme. de Rambuteau should be the mistress and not the housekeeper of the Prefectoral salons, free to open or close their doors at her pleasure.   I paid out every year forty thousand francs more than my salary.   Although my personal resources suffered, the dignity of my office was enhanced, and I did not think that less was due, on my part, to the first magistracy of Paris.

And yet it is not of these fêtes, adorned by the presence of the most distinguished men of France and of foreign lands, that I sometimes recall the memory ; it is not to gilded figures and decorated wainscots that my mind most frequently turns : it is to the garden of the Hôtel de Ville, where, whenever I felt harassed and fatigued, I found a refuge among my flowers, where I re-created my patience and courage, where, away from men, I took my rest and threw crumbs to the birds.

And to-day, as I look back on this long administration, it seems to me that I did not fail in my task.   Grander and finer things have been achieved since, bolder things have been done ; money, too, has been spent more lavishly.

Well, I left the city without debts ; I made no heavy demands on the taxpayer ; I was sparing of the people's money, and I always remembered Sully's encomium in praise on Henry IV. : " *The late King was a good economist.*"

INDEX

A

Achon, Comte d', victim of revolution, 9
—— Marquis and Marquise d', victims of revolution, 9
—— Mlle. d', her marriage and death, 10
Adélaïde, Madame, the King's sister, 181, 182; her friendship with Rambuteau, 207, 208; discusses affairs with him, 223, 224; only person to whom the King would listen, 223; her death, 225
Alexander, Emperor, his answer to M. de Narbonne, who had brought him Napoleon's final proposals, 67
Allier, the, Rambuteau appointed Prefect of, 133
Angoulême, Duchesse d', Rambuteau's interview with, 118–120; her interview with the Duchesse d'Orléans, 121, 122; Mme. de Rambuteau introduced to, 122; her pleasure at Rambuteau's reception of her, 122
Army of Italy, its dilapidated condition after Leipzig, 93; loss of soldiers while crossing the Simplon, on account of storm and avalanche, 94; difficulties of making a passage for it through the snow, and hardships endured by, 96, 97
Artois, Comte d', Lieutenant-General of the Kingdom, 114, 123; his interviews with Rambuteau, 124, 125; at St. Étienne, 125, 126, 127; his reception in the Loire, 127, 128; his behaviour on the occasion of Napoleon's landing, 131
Augereau, Marshal, in command at Lyons, 103; his despair at his small number of troops, 103, 104; Rambuteau procures horses for him, 106, 107; sends latter the Cross of the Legion of Honour, 109; retreats from Lyons, 110; his movement on Franche-

Comté, 111; retires behind Isère and burns the bridge, 112; he is under suspicion, 123; is recalled, 128

B

Balbi, Mme. de, 142, 143, 154, 159
Ballet *des échecs*, the Emperor and the author take part in, 36, 37
Barrot, Odilon, 185
Barthelot, family of, 1 *seq.*
—— Sire Claude de, 2
—— Claude de, grandson of above, 3, 4
—— Claude, father of the author of the Memoirs, 4; marries Mlle. de Laviefville-Vignacourt, 5; refuses to emigrate, 7; his blindness, 7; his arrest, 8; his deliverance, 9; partly recovers his sight, 11; his advice and generosity to his son, 15, 16; his death, 49
—— Philibert, de, 2, 3
—— Philibert de, son of above, tragedy of his life, 5, 6
Bassano, Duc de, 35, 41, 44, 50, 66; appointed Minister of Foreign Affairs, 135; his return from exile, 159, 163, 183
Berry, Duc de, assassination of, 159
Berthier, Marshal, dinner given by, on occasion of the Comte de Rambuteau's marriage, 34; his answer to Mme. de Souza's request, 34
Bertins, rendezvous of Ministers at, 170, 171
Beugnot, his answer to Rambuteau about titles, 187, 188
" Black Cabinet," the, account of, 203, 204
Black Cardinals, 37
Bohemia, separatist movement in, 31
Bordeaux, Duc de, proposal to place, on the throne, 183, 184

315

X

Printed by BALLANTYNE, HANSON & Co.
Edinburgh & London

www.ingramcontent.com/pod-product-compliance
Lightning Source LLC
Chambersburg PA
CBHW021214090426
42740CB00006B/211